D1649125

INTO THE UNKNOWN

INTO THE

Unknown

By BRUCE PRICE

Introduction by Dr. Maynard M. Miller

Professor of Geology, Michigan State University,
Chairman of the World Center for Exploration Foundation
of the Explorers Club

Illustrated by Mort Künstler

PLATT & MUNK

PUBLISHERS

NEW YORK

Contents

Author's Introduction

I would like the reader to know two things about *Into the Unknown*. First, this book is based on interviews. Each explorer was kind enough to grant me several hours of his time, and the interviews were essential in giving me a close personal understanding of these men and their objectives. Second, this book attempts to present a comprehensive picture of contemporary exploration. The various sections do not overlap, as would have happened if I had chosen the explorers at random. What I did, in fact, was to select 10 men who, it seemed to me, represented the full spectrum of true, non-laboratory exploration. So there is a section on land exploring, another on cave (or geological) exploring, still another on outer space, one on the exploration of the wild animal kingdom and so on. I venture to say that no major type of exploration has been left uncovered. This comprehensiveness will, I hope, make *Into the Unknown* more valuable to the reader.

The explorers in this book are all members of The Explorers Club in New York City. I wish to thank them and the Club for their cooperation and assistance.

New York, New York   BRUCE PRICE
May 20, 1968

Introduction —

The Explorer's Way

"To strive, to seek, to find and not to yield" . . .

This famous phrase from Tennyson's immortal poem "Ulysses" was carved on a wooden cross erected in 1912 on a bluff overlooking Ross Island in the Antarctic. There it stands today to commemorate the courageous efforts of Captain Robert Falcon Scott and his four companions who reached the South Pole that year, only to perish in a relentless blizzard only eleven miles from their base and after 900 torturous miles of man-sledging on their return journey from the unknown. The great explorations of man have often combined tragedy with triumph, and even the lesser explorations of history have been characterized by obstacles and frustrations which have tested the nobler qualities in men.

Future explorations in the new frontiers of space and in the remote depths of the sea will have their hardships too, and will require their share of sacrifices. Answers to the questions, what is exploration; what defines an explorer; what are the capabilities and limitations of the machines needed to explore; and indeed why explore at all, are more important than ever.

Exploration, simply defined, is the search and study of the

unknown—the unearthing of new information in any of a number of different ways, and for any of a number of different purposes. For the true explorer, the purpose is sometimes less obvious than his motivation or the reward he might receive. Whatever the immediate reason, vigorous exploration of our physical world has always been important to human progress, even when the benefits are not immediately apparent.

In 1845, the eminent British explorer, Sir John Franklin, attempted to find the Northwest Passage—a shorter trade route from Europe to Asia's treasures. Franklin undertook his expedition mainly for the profit these treasures would bring but also for political and national prestige. After two years of heroic forging into the unknown, his ships were beset and crushed in the most hostile pack ice the polar regions had experienced in 100 years. As a result, Franklin failed and 129 men lost their lives. But time was to prove that this defeat, like Scott's, was a victory for mankind. From the 70 some expeditions which followed, many searching to discover Franklin's fate, a whole new world was charted in the Canadian and Alaskan North. Now this land is a region of vast commercial significance comparable to that once dreamed of in the Orient.

Today's explorer has an even more challenging task. The time of easy exploration on earth has passed. Before us is a new startling age of exploration—more exacting, yet more rewarding than ever. The explorer must have a high degree of professional training and a special kind of scientific know-how, in addition to the courage and philosophic motivation which exploration has always demanded. The essential integration of mind and heart with professional excellence requires greater self-discipline and moral fabric. The barrier of the unknown remains uncompromising. It can often be breached only by concerted team effort, by combining the skill, dedication and selflessness of a number of men. In this vast scope there is the need for the team-conscious investigator.

An expedition is a microcosm of society. Adventure becomes challenge and encourages men to look beyond themselves to gain that perception which stimulates vigor and leadership in other facets of life. This spirit of adventure is to be cherished for other reasons. It teaches men patience which outwits despair, and allows them to adapt to swift and difficult change. It rejects that mediocrity that comes from too much concern for security, and it builds faith in oneself and one's fellow men. The way of the explorer symbolizes those qualities so desperately needed for the sanity and health of our free society.

The challenges and accomplishments described in *Into the Unknown* are significant beyond the fascination of the stories themselves. Each explorer in this book is a member of the world-famous Explorer Club, and the adventures of each reach into the still unknown realms of our physical world. Also, these men portray a variety of scientific expertise which opens special windows into the unknown. Thus we travel with these explorers into space, above and below the ionosphere, in search of illusive cosmic rays; and by sailplane we fly our planet's atmosphere below the jet stream to chart and understand the mystery of clear air turbulence which holds some dangers for supersonic flight. We pass into the hydrosphere, using scuba equipment for underwater treasure-hunting on a continental shelf; and in a bathyscaphe we penetrate and explore the ocean floor at an unprecedented depth of seven miles in an ocean trench. On land we go to the frigid interior of the south polar continent, learning scientific secrets of the ice, and to the humid jungles of the Amazon basin and Southeast Asia in search of disappearing tribes of men who still cling to the Stone Age. We study the territoriality traits of the gibbon, found to be not unlike those of modern man. We experience a unique exploration as we peer through the window of anthropological archaeology at Hebron, in the heat of the Holy Land desert. Lastly, with a speleological expedition we find unusual scientific adventure while descending half a thousand feet into unexplored limestone caves far below the surface of the Guatamalan plateau.

These accounts bridge the gap between the ways of the explorer of today and the explorer of not long ago who thrilled at getting a first look at regions never before walked by man. They tell the story of modern scientific field projects, performed by the new breed of explorer.

These are questing men who still require and thrive on challenge, and for whom the unknown holds high fascination. They represent the field scientist who has learned to assess his chances and knows the necessary measures to thwart danger, who understands nature, the greatest teacher of all, and learns his own place in it.

Implicit in all this is the concept that if man hopes to direct his evolution toward a higher destiny, he might well look to the spirit of the explorer for inspiration and for method. Sensing this, we should not only encourage explorations into the unknown, but continue to seek ways to understand progress and to put it to work in the service of humanity.

Desmond Morris, the zoologist, has given this concept a broader base by pointing out that man, "the naked ape, is essentially an exploratory species and any society that has failed to advance has in some sense failed, or 'gone wrong.' Something has happened to hold it back, something that is working against the natural tendencies of the species to explore and investigate the world around it."

To dare and do the impossible is the essence of exploration. But man has far more at stake than mere progress. In pitting his strength against high challenge and in succeeding, man mitigates some of those crumbling influences in society which too often abrade his more worthy aims. This basic theme may be applied to all of man's pursuits. Man's very survival may depend on it. Beyond survival, he can derive immeasurable benefits from this concept which enriches particularly those inner values that define him as a uniquely searching and significant creature in the long process of unfolding time.

For all of these reasons we must ceaselessly foster and nourish man's imagination and its expression through continuing and vigorous explorations into the unknown. It is to this very purpose that the World Center for Exploration, the action arm of The Explorers Club, is dedicated.

MAYNARD M. MILLER
Chairman, World Center for Exploration Foundation
The Explorers Club, New York City

June, 1968

one
Riding the Wind

THE AIR at 15,000 feet was clear, the sky a shining blue, the ground a vague patchwork seen far below through scudding clouds. Lofted by warm, rising currents, Captain Kimball J. "Kim" Scribner guided his sailplane, the *Explorer*, in the serene atmosphere. Bright sunshine gleamed on the bubble canopy of the *Explorer* as it soared like a huge, graceful white bird with tapered, flexing wings, its sleek lines marking it an aristocrat among sailplanes. Except for the slight hissing of the wind in the cockpit, the world three miles up was cozily still, peaceful and beautiful. Far off, 170 miles away, Scribner could see the New England horizon.

A large, well-knit man, Scribner banked the *Explorer* in a long, graceful curve. He maneuvered to stay within the thermal, a column of warm, rising air, which was carrying him up a thousand feet each minute. Watching his variometer, a sensitive rate-of-climb indicator, Scribner could tell where in his circle of flight he had gained altitude at the greatest rate. Gliding back around, he flew deeper into the thermal. The variometer's needle indicated that he was centered in the thermal and climbing fast. Hunting these airy elevators is part of the thrill of soaring. "The great satisfaction," Scribner says, "is outsmarting the elements and playing with the cloud formations. But these movements have to be performed with real precision, and in a smooth, coordinated manner, otherwise you're going to alter the performance of the sailplane and destroy its cleanliness of flight."

Scribner doesn't make that sort of mistake. He has been a pilot for 34 of his 50 years and has flown all kinds of airplanes. As a Captain with Pan American World Airways, he is likely 15 days of every month to be flying a Boeing 707 to Buenos Aires or Europe and the Far East. Between flights, he has often flown in air shows and competed in national contests, flying both propeller-driven planes and gliders. His skill at handling sailplanes has earned him several national and international acrobatics titles. He has been called a "precision glider ace," a man who can make a sailplane "dance."

Captain Scribner was not flying the *Explorer* high over the wind-swept Mount Washington area for his own pleasure, however. He was engaged in a unique scientific research project to study a phenomenon of the upper atmosphere called Clear Air Turbulence (CAT). This invisible, cloudless air movement, usually vertical, occurs most frequently at altitudes above 10,000 feet and can be very violent. Such fierce turbulence can bounce a huge airliner around like a toy balloon, and conceivably could injure passengers and cause structural damage to the airplane. CAT has become a matter of great concern to the aviation industry in recent years because planes are flying higher and faster. The problem, of course, is that the pilots cannot see this turbulence. The average thunderstorm, which announces itself with black clouds and lightning, is easily avoided. But a plane will fly into CAT without its pilot having any advance warning. Some authorities, both military and civilian, suspect that CAT might have caused some otherwise inexplicable jet plane crashes. There are many known reasons why CAT occurs, but how to detect this clear turbulence remains a major problem. This ignorance leaves pilots and their passengers very much at the mercy of the elements, and the search for a method of detection has been given even greater urgency by the advent of the supersonic jet.

In 1966, Scribner decided that he would try to solve the CAT mystery. Using a super-glider as a research platform, he would seek out CAT, enter the turbulence, study it and try to discover what telltale signs might give advance warning of it. Scribner believed that the sailplane, which has no engine and thus creates no electrical disturbance, would make an ideal laboratory for atmospheric research.

He proceeded to convince The Explorers Club in New York City that his plan was sound, and for the first time in its history, the club decided to sponsor an exploratory project of its own. The Explorers Research Corporation was formed, with George R. Wallace (a director of The Explorers Club) as its president and Captain Kim Scribner as a vice president and director of aviation research. Though simple in concept, the enterprise, by late 1966, involved scores of people and dozens of companies. A high-performance sailplane had to be built and it had to be fitted with some very advanced electronic devices. Despite the growing number of participants, however, Scribner was clearly the guiding spirit and the one who would actually fly the *Explorer*.

Built especially for the CAT project, the *Explorer* has very unique specifications. It is all metal; able to land on water; sturdy enough to enter very rough turbulence; capable of flying higher than 50,000 feet and of being flown at 300 miles an hour. It was designed to carry 500 pounds of equipment, including a 15-hour oxygen supply; a power source for instruments; smoke-trailing gear; radio and navigation equipment; tape recorders and movie cameras to record both the instrument readings and the panorama outside the plane, both in front and behind. Scribner unhesitatingly says that the *Explorer* is the best-equipped sailplane in the world.

The sailplane has several advantages over powered aircraft for research on CAT. It can almost become part of the atmosphere: since it glides at relatively slow speeds, it can easily remain within any turbulence it encounters. Its weight and speed remain constant, while an airplane loses weight and gains speed as its fuel is used. And the absence of an engine and propeller eliminates vibration, static and electrical interference.

At the present stage of the CAT project, however, the *Explorer's* most important component is a small 30-pound gray instrument box mounted in its nose which reads temperatures by infrared radiation at a distance in the atmosphere ahead of the sailplane. This instrument is central to Scribner's research. It is owned by the Air Force Cambridge Research Laboratories at Bedford, Massachusetts, and is on loan under a nonprofit contract to the Explorers Research Corporation.

His own experience with CAT has suggested to Scribner that it is always accompanied by sudden changes in the temperature of the air. The temperature may change in either direction, hot or cold, by at least two or three degrees. If this temperature change does, in fact, indicate CAT, then Scribner needs only to perfect the instruments and techniques which would enable a pilot to detect the changes in time to alter his course. But Scribner says, "We're not selling anything," meaning that neither he nor any of the other people in the project is trying to prove any particular theory. Scribner's concern is air safety. He intends to investigate all possible explanations and test any instruments that might be able to detect CAT.

Eventually Scribner will use equipment that indicates the air temperature about 25 miles ahead of a plane, since the pilot of a fast jet would need that much warning to alter his course. For his research with the *Explorer,* however, Scribner has beamed his temperature detector at distances ranging from 500 to 1,100 feet ahead of the sailplane. Considering the sailplane's slow speed, these distances are equivalent to the longer distance which would be appropriate for a jet.

Scribner became involved in the Clear Air Turbulence project almost by chance. He was scheduled to speak at The Explorers Club on November 9, 1965, the night of the famous northeastern "blackout." But, without electricity, Scribner could not show the film he had brought along. He improvised a speech by candlelight, telling his fellow explorers of the problems of the jet age and specifically of the supersonic age soon to be encountered. In the audience, a distinguished gentleman stood up and asked a question: "Are you the Captain Kim Scribner who was towed upside down into the ground at the Miami Air Races in January of 1952?"

When the speaker answered, "Yes. Did you see it?" the gentleman replied, "See it? I came to visit you in the hospital!"

At this point, he made his way into the center aisle and came to the speaker's stand, and an old friendship between Scribner and George R. Wallace was renewed.

At lunch the following day, Scribner and Wallace, president of Wallace Industries, discussed Scribner's speech. Scribner felt The Explorers Club would benefit greatly by becoming a direct and active participant in current explorations. He suggested one possibility: research into Clear Air Turbulence, using a sailplane (glider) as a flying laboratory, and studying all aspects of the atmosphere related to CAT. The goal of the research would be to develop some means by which a jet pilot could detect CAT.

Wallace invited Scribner to put his thoughts in writing and present them for consideration to a special committee of the board of directors of The Explorers Club. When this special committee met, Wallace announced that he would personally finance the project if the club decided to initiate it. The committee recommended that the idea be presented to the club's board of directors, and when Scribner made this presentation, the board decided that, for the first time in its history, The Explorers Club would participate in an exploration project which the club itself would control, operate and finance.

Out of this decision was born the Explorers Research Corporation. Not surprisingly, the ERC's first action was sending Scribner himself out to do some original exploration into finding the people, experts of various kinds, who would staff the project.

Next, after many consultations with the Schweizer Aircraft Corporation in Elmira, New York, the ERC purchased the *Explorer*, a high-performance sailplane capable of carrying three passengers. For the purposes of the project, it would carry equipment in place of two passengers but allow for the occasional substitution of one observer for some equipment.

Scribner made the first test flight in the *Explorer* on August 17, 1966, after the glider was towed from Elmira, New York, where it was built, to Springfield, Massachusetts. There were, it turned out, many technical problems, especially involving the installation of an infrared temperature detector provided by the Air Force. Scribner and the ERC's board of directors held many meetings and consulted with electronic firms, government agencies and university research groups. Though numerous refinements in the instruments still had to be made, Scribner decided to go ahead anyway, and in June, 1967, he began making regular flights.

The project was based in Fryeburg, Massachusetts, 20 miles from Mount Washington, for several reasons. Most of the companies and research groups involved had headquarters in the New England area. The Air Force was eager to help, since they would obviously benefit from anything Scribner might discover.

In addition, high-altitude CAT is often difficult to find. New Hampshire and Maine are noted for a similar kind of turbulence called "mountain waves" or "standing waves." Standing waves are strong vertical drafts that rise on the lee side of mountains. The wind flows over and down the mountain and then bounces off the plain, sometimes rising to many times the height of the mountain itself. These waves often produce a type of Clear Air Turbulence, especially on the lee side of the mountain. This turbulence is particularly common near Mount Washington, the highest mountain in the East, with an elevation of 6,288 feet.

Flying near Mount Washington, Scribner could test his instruments in these mountain waves and also learn the general characteristics of CAT. Standing waves are known to be a major cause of CAT at high altitudes, although there are other causes also, since CAT often occurs far from mountains, even over oceans. Whatever their relationship to CAT might be, Scribner decided that the mountain waves of northern New England would provide him with a convenient testing laboratory.

During the fall of 1967, Scribner made dozens of flights in

the *Explorer*. There were no dramatic breakthroughs. But each flight brought improvements in the sailplane's instruments, in the means of tracking the *Explorer* from the ground and in the techniques for finding and experimenting with Clear Air Turbulence. And, most important, Scribner was gathering more data about the possible relationship between changing temperatures and CAT.

When Scribner took the *Explorer* up to search for CAT, he spent hours aloft. Most of the *Explorer's* instruments—the temperature detectors, the smoke-releasing unit, the accelerometers, the sealed barographs and recording camera—had been prepared on the ground and, once turned on, functioned automatically. Scribner's primary task was to put his airborne laboratory inside the turbulence, so that the instruments could do their work. This task required two special skills, both of which Scribner possessed. He first had to find CAT. Then he had to fly the sailplane precisely into it.

One day in the summer of 1967, Scribner climbed into the *Explorer's* cockpit at Fryeburg. A propeller-driven plane towed the *Explorer* up to 5,000 feet. Scribner directed the tow plane pilot into position, via radio, east of the Mount Washington peak. He then released the tow line from the nose of the sailplane. Now he was on his own. To get on with the job, Scribner wanted to climb up to about 14,000 feet where he would penetrate an area of CAT, and for this he needed thermals. These often form over clear, light-colored fields as the hot air rises into a giant cone several miles high. Since the air cools and its water vapor condenses, cumulus clouds often form on top of thermals, marking their whereabouts. Now Scribner circled beneath a blossoming cloud and saw his variometer indicate he was in rising air. With luck he would soon be spiraling up faster than an express elevator. "A glider," he

explains, "is an airplane without an engine, that's all. So it's always coming down, in a glide. But if the air current is rising faster than you are descending, then you will rise. To the air, however, you are still descending." A well-designed sailplane like the *Explorer* has a glide-ratio of 30 to 1. In still air, from an altitude of approximately one mile, Scribner could fly more than 30 miles before he reached zero altitude, even if he never found a thermal.

But Scribner did. In 30 minutes he reached an altitude of 14,000 feet and found himself looking at a "roll cloud" on the lee side of Mount Washington. He knew that extreme turbulence is to be found inside of this boiling cloud, which is formed by the high-velocity winds coming over the mountain. Scribner knew he might find a violent turbulence near the roll cloud and that he had to be ready. He started his smoke-making unit by electrically opening a valve which, under pressure, released acid into the air behind the sailplane. The infrared temperature detector and the temperature probe at the side of the sailplane were on and the camera was automatically taking pictures ahead of the sailplane and behind it. Scribner began to fly in straight-line patterns directly into the area of the roll cloud that was curling and boiling from the turbulence inside it.

The *Explorer's* instruments automatically recorded the temperature and appearance of the atmosphere. The smoke spewed out behind the sailplane like a puffy white rope as the camera recorded its appearance. A curve in the smoke trail would indicate that the sailplane had entered CAT. At the same time the infrared temperature detector and the temperature probe gave the temperature of the air about 1,000 feet ahead of the *Explorer* and at the plane itself, while a tape recorder registered these readings.

Future analysis would prove whether these photographs and temperature readings supported the theory that temperature variation recorded in the line of flight could be used as a means of identifying CAT. Basically the question was: did the sailplane's entry into turbulence—as recorded by the photographs of the smoke trail—coincide with a change in the temperature of the air ahead of the sailplane—as recorded in the difference between the infrared detector's reading and the reading at the plane itself? The recorded data taken from this flight showed this definite relationship—as they did from many other flights.

To collect meaningful data, Scribner had to fly with great precision, in true straight-line patterns. If the reading taken ahead of the *Explorer* was to be useful, the plane had to pass through the air whose temperature was being recorded. Otherwise the photographs and the recorded temperatures would have no connection.

Scribner had no difficulty in flying the *Explorer* precisely where he pleased. He is more at home in the pilot's seat than many people are in a car. Scribner feels that the sailplane is easy to fly; he estimates that he could teach a person to fly one, landings and all, in 10 hours. But Scribner's own exceptional ability cannot be taught. It is the result of a lifelong love for all kinds of planes; a love, in fact, for all aspects of aviation. Whether he does it as a job, for prizes or for research, Scribner simply enjoys flying. He likes the feeling of freedom he can find only in a plane. And a sailplane, particularly, offers its pilot incomparable peace and serenity.

Scribner may enjoy the serenity of flying a sailplane today, but in the past his life included a wild assortment of exploits. Scribner can perhaps be called a serious daredevil. He has often displayed a casual indifference to dangers which more prudent men would call foolhardy. He has barely lived through many exploits which he himself calls "a search for great adventures." Though not one to let himself be shot from cannons, he did enjoy dangerous aerial hobbies. Somewhat battered by the fun, however, he gradually turned his attention to solving aviation problems. As a result, Scribner has contributed significantly to man's attempt to master the problems of the air.

Scribner's passion for planes and for aerial adventures is a long-standing one. He has been in the forefront of aviation's spectacular developments over the past 30 years, and his feats and achievements span the days from airborne Tin Lizzies to jets. His life is, in a way, a chronicle of the air age. Even when he has not actually been flying or exploring the air, he has worked to perfect the equipment needed for man's reach into the sky.

Ironically, Scribner's life as an explorer started underground. As a 12-year-old in the Chevy Chase section of Washington, D.C., he and four young friends explored in the drain pipes under their streets. Gas seeping out from a broken main nearly killed them. Luckily, another boy heard them calling for help beneath a manhole cover and sounded the alarm. Firemen came to the rescue. "Five Boys Overcome Exploring Sewer," the newspaper said. Young "Kim," typically, learned something from the experience, for he did not go back to exploring the pipe again after a week in the hospital—perhaps because bars had been placed over the entrance of the pipes.

A few years later Scribner's sights were raised to the skies. At 15 he began to find airplanes irresistible. He and his close friend, Raymond Morders (now a TWA Captain), started hitchhiking 20 miles out to the Congressional Airport near Rockville, Maryland. There they gawked at single-engine biplanes and monoplanes—antiques today. The pilots, sporting goggles and scarf, sat proudly in their open cockpits. From

some of these rickety craft a "professional jumper" made parachute jumps, after passing the hat to hundreds of people
parked in their cars on Sunday afternoons. The two boys liked
what they saw, the flying and the jumping. As long as planes
were involved, they were for it. After the first trips to that
small airport, they knew what they wanted to be.

Soon Scribner and Morders had their first jobs—as all-
around assistants to one of the local daredevils, a parachute
jumper. They took megaphones out to the main road and
advertised the death-defying deeds performed by their boss.
After a crowd had gathered and the jumper had gone up for his
jump, they passed the hat. When the parachutist landed in a
tree, the boys drove his car over to pick him up. As a reward
for loyal service, the old pro took them up to show them how
parachuting was done.

Kim Scribner and his friend, Ray Morders, decided that this
was the life. They were eager to jump themselves. But the
professional, who had also been a deep-sea diver, a high diver
in a circus and, as Scribner says, "other weird and wonderful
things," insisted that the boys obtain their parents' permission.
Knowing this was impossible, the two 16-year-olds solved the
impasse in a classic fashion. "I wrote my friend's letter," Scribner recalls, "and he wrote my letter and we signed each other's
letters and naturally we said, 'My father can't wait for me to
jump out of an airplane.' So we became jumpers." They were
soon doing the stunt work while the old-timer was collecting
the money—"which was great for us," Scribner says. "We
didn't want the money. We pursued this more from a spirit of
adventure than anything else."

Scribner and Morders were parachute jumpers for four
years. During this period, Kim was, at any given time, either
jumping or recovering from a jumping accident. Parachuting

is, of course, an increasingly popular sport in the 1960s, but in Scribner's day it was in the nature of a pastime for madmen. The early-model parachutes gave the jumper a stiff jolt when they opened and they allowed such a fast rate of descent that landing was hazardous. Still, Scribner never missed a chance to jump.

Scribner and Morders became licensed parachute riggers and Morders was nicknamed "Rigor Morders." They were soon jumping at air shows in Lynchburg and Winchester, Virginia, and at small towns near Washington, D.C. They sold spectators pictures of themselves to augment their take. The boys were guaranteed $20 for a day's work but they often made as much as $50. "We earned enough money to turn some back into flying lessons," Scribner says. "Soon we were renting airplanes and flying them around ourselves."

At 16, Scribner and Morders went to jump at the Cleveland Air Races, then the world's biggest air show. They took along their own parachutes, but, with characteristic casualness, jumped in street shoes. Receiving $20 for each leap, they competed in the spot-landing contests and the mass jumps, in which 30 chutists floated down together. Nearly 100,000 shirt-sleeved, flag-waving fans came to these shows. Overflowing the grandstands, the people stood in great clusters staring up at the racing planes or falling men. Adrift at 4,000 feet, Scribner did not think much about the spectators. He was too busy having a good time.

His father and mother, meanwhile, regarded their son with a suspicious yet hopeful silence. They knew, of course, that he spent a lot of time at the airport. He said he was just helping the pilots. But their strapping boy kept coming home with a variety of sprains, bruises and breaks. Scribner had landed on just about every part of his body, sometimes even his head, when he caught his feet in the shroud lines and hit upside down.

Scribner knows that his parents finally deduced the truth about his secret life in the sky. But even then neither parent would mention the subject. An open discussion might have required rules which the Scribners must have known their son would break. Bourdon F. Scribner, Kim's father, was a chemist and a paper technologist at the Bureau of Standards. He and his wife decided to play a waiting game. Their hope was that Kim's next injury would ground him. "Each time I was injured jumping out of an airplane," Scribner says, laughing, "they would naturally think, 'This is his last jump, he won't do that again.' My friend Ray Morders would carry me home and leave me at the door, ring the doorbell and run. And then my father would come to the door and say, 'Well, come in. Get the crutches.' Things like that. Each time I managed to survive, they said, 'He won't do that again.'" But he did. He even suspects that his mother, whom he calls a "courageous woman," was secretly proud of his daring.

His injuries, though not enough to stop him from jumping, did cramp his style as an athlete. At Washington's Western High School, Scribner was "mediocre" at his studies. But he did like sports, especially football. He refrained from drinking and smoking for the sake of his athletic career and he finally made the varsity, as both an end and fullback. But after a year of parachuting, he was no longer in shape for football. His many injuries had taken their toll, and his knee, in particular, had been badly banged up. When his feet had caught in the shroud lines, his knee had been yanked violently out of joint. Even today Scribner can produce loud clicks just by swinging his leg.

While still a junior in high school, Scribner had already

achieved notoriety. The *Parade of Youth*, a supplement of the *Washington Post*, featured Scribner and Morders on March 3, 1935: "Boys Start Air Career as Parachute Jumpers, 'Not As Dangerous As Folks Think,' Is Their Modest Claim, Landing in Trees Is an Old Story to Kim and Ray, Now They Seek New Thrills by Trying 'Delayed Jumps,' They See Nothing Unusual in Their Hobby."

The pace kept up throughout Scribner's high-school years. He averaged about a jump a week, although he sometimes made four in an afternoon. The handbill from one of the many air shows in which they starred evokes the spirit of the era:

Enjoy a Flight with the World's Most Renowned Pilot
Baron Von Schultz

Walter Brown
The Famous Stunt Pilot
and
Kim Scribner & Ray Morders
World Famous & Youngest Licensed Parachute Jumpers in U.S.
Will Fall 2,000 Ft. Before Opening Parachute
A Thrill That Will Live with You for A Life Time
Leonardtown, Md.
Sunday

Two weeks later, in June, 1936, Kim Scribner graduated from high school.

By now, Kim and Ray had learned some caution. They had seen a few men die and several times had saved their own lives with reserve chutes when their main parachutes failed. Still they always seemed to be taking chances, which they called "improvising." Scribner and Morders used chutes that had been rejected by the United States Navy and were supposed to be cut up. But they "knew" the man who did the cutting. "We slipped him ten dollars and he gave them to us. They had little things wrong with them. But to us they were beautiful," Scribner says.

Scribner went off to the University of Maryland where he studied engineering for two years, although most of his energy was spent parachuting and flying. These were Depression times but Scribner's father had a secure government job and paid all the bills, so money was certainly not Scribner's goal. What he made he spent on girl friends. On occasion he and Ray even "dropped in" by parachute for a visit at Sweet Briar or Randolph Macon; "Things that were fun to do," Scribner says.

The high point of Scribner's college career was his requested stunt in honor of Homecoming Game, September, 1937. Before the startled gaze of 30,000 cheering students, Scribner bailed out 5,000 feet over the gridiron, fell without opening his chute to about 2,000 feet from the ground, then popped his chute. Unfortunately, the wind was too strong. He drifted helplessly over the stadium, over a parking lot, across Route 1, where there were four lanes of traffic, over the cars, became tangled in some telephone wires, swung down between parked cars and came to rest six inches off the ground, suspended from the wires. "You know what I got for that? Free entrance to the game. They haven't forgotten that," Scribner exclaims with the interesting blend of pride and irony that characterizes his speech.

Meanwhile his extracurricular pursuits continued, with a number of calamities. When not traveling with a flying group titled "The Angels from Hell," Scribner was working his way from one air show to another. Back at the Cleveland Air Races as a college sophomore, Scribner again missed the landing point, this time with a less happy conclusion. Following a long delayed opening, or free fall, he had opened his chute on the wrong side of the grandstands and found himself heading straight into an "ocean of cars." He picked out a Ford sedan and slammed into the hood at a steep angle, sliding right into the windshield. He was stuck half in and half out of the car. A man in a motorcycle with a sidecar raced to his aid. More people gathered to help extract him. Scribner kept saying, "Watch the ribs, watch the ribs," some of which were broken. They finally pulled him back out the way he had come in.

Fifteen years later, flying a special VIP group from Washington to Bermuda, Captain Scribner asked his first officer, a stranger to him, where he came from.

"Cleveland," he answered.

"Really, what'd you do out there?" Scribner asked.

"I drove a motorcycle at the air shows and picked up the jumpers."

"Did you ever see anybody get hurt?"

"Did I ever see anybody get hurt?" the first officer said excitedly. "I saw a guy go right through the windshield of a car."

"What ever happened to him?" Scribner inquired.

"Oh, he must be dead a long time, that dumbbell. Went right through the windshield. Kept saying, 'Watch the ribs, watch the ribs.'"

Scribner started to lift his shirt, saying, "Do you want to see my ribs?"

"Captain, you were that crazy guy?" the first officer asked, looking at Scribner as if he were a ghost.

A few months after the Cleveland show, Scribner was jumping at night in Baltimore. While the pilot flew toward the grandstand, spotlights illuminating the sky, Scribner climbed out on the wing. He was only waiting for the right moment to jump. But the night was cold and wet and he had trouble keeping his grip. The pilot put on the power suddenly and Scribner tumbled off. Floating down through the darkness, after his chute had opened, he had no idea where he would land and thought he might end up in Chesapeake Bay. Instead he landed in a tree. In the darkness, he lowered himself down until he could almost touch the ground, or so he thought. Actually he was still in the top branches of the tree. Then he unbuckled himself. Down he fell, landing on his back and losing consciousness. Many hours later a troop of Boy Scouts found him lying there, still out cold.

Scribner's scariest moment and closest scrape with death—if one can be singled out—did not come until his last month at the University of Maryland. Scribner was never content with any past achievement. He and Morders, still partners in many of the shows, used to "sit around dreaming up thrilling new jumps." Free falls, where the jumper opens his chute only a few hundred yards from the ground, had become old hat. They had even tired of a more dangerous act involving a parachute with a swing instead of a harness: the jumper sat in the swing, then fell off to scare his audience, which would think that he had somehow lost his parachute; finally, near the ground, the jumper opened his regular chute. To top this daredeviltry, Scribner and friend decided that they would jump together, something which had never been done before. So they doubled their swing to make room for both of them, one sitting on the top rung and the other on the bottom rung three feet below. Their parachute was stuffed into a laundry bag which was tied to the plane. When, carefully positioned in the swing, they moved out of the plane backward, the bag was supposed to stay behind while the parachute came out of the bag and blossomed over their heads. They planned to descend together for several thousand feet, then dive away from the swing, free fall for a few more thousand feet and finally open their own chutes. In other words, they would do together the same stunt they had done separately many times before. When the organizers of the show at Lynchburg, Virginia, heard the idea, they said, "Absolutely not. You'll kill yourselves." Not accustomed to taking orders, the two college boys hid the bag in the back of the plane, determined to try their brave new formula for thrills. Down below the bands played and the Governor of Virginia himself presided.

They arranged themselves in their individual swings and together shoved out the door of the plane backward. Unhappily, instead of the bag opening, the rope broke. Scribner's recollection of what happened is still vivid:

"We were left holding the bag with no way to get the parachute out of it. Then we began to tumble. We were caught in the harness, the rope and the bag, all wrapped up together, falling from 5,000 feet. Instinctively we knew that we must not open our own parachutes or we'd wrap up in them and kill ourselves. We knew we had to get separated. I got hold of Ray and pushed him, I hoped, out to the side. But instead, as I tumbled around, I saw him right above me. He was all tangled up in the harness, struggling with it. The bag was flopping around him, the rope was whipping around and I thought he was finished.

"I had only one chance and that was to flatten out, turn myself so that I was looking at the ground, and fall as close to the ground as I had ever fallen in my life. Meantime I could only hope that Ray could get open above me. I couldn't see him. I wasn't over the airport, I was over houses. I picked out a house, and the roof grew larger and larger. As I fell toward the house I also fell below the line of sight of the people at the airport, below their horizon. I fell as close to the house as I dared. I knew in my mind when I had reached about 200 feet. I pulled the rip cord and out popped my chute and opened— boom! I slipped the parachute so that I didn't land on the roof and I landed right in the front yard.

"As soon as I hit I slid over on my back and opened my eyes and looked straight up in the sky. The sky was absolutely clear. I knew then I had been a part of the death of my friend. There was a woman in the yard with a rake, frightened and trembling. The first thing I said was, 'Did the other boy open his parachute?' And she told me he had landed in the back yard and his parachute had not opened. Feeling a great terror, I threw off my harness and ran around to the side of the house. I saw the bushes where he had landed; the bushes were torn. I walked up to the harness, which was in the bushes. I was just about to look at his body when Ray came over the fence.

"He was coming from the neighbor's yard. He had kicked himself free of the bag and the harness, and just as I opened, he opened right above me. He landed in the side yard, I landed in the front yard and the bag itself landed in the bushes in the back yard. The lady thought there were three of us because she had seen three objects. She thought the other boy meant the one in her back yard. So 'Rigor Morders' and I sat down on the lawn and talked about what had happened. We couldn't move, we were so scared. Then we heard sirens in the distance. The spectators thought we had killed ourselves, they hadn't seen us open our parachutes. People fainted. Great rejoicing when they knew we were alive. Then nasty comments in the papers that we had deliberately done it. I had to write a letter to the paper, my first letter to an editor, to put the record straight."

This episode had a second half which tells more about Scribner than the first:

"A week went by. We were to make a jump at College Park, Maryland, from 8,000 feet. We hadn't even talked about our first jump. But we finally got around to it. I said, 'If you aren't too scared, we could do that again.' And Ray said, 'Aaah, you'd be too scared.' So we challenged each other and dared each other. We knew better than to tell the pilot. We knew what the trouble was on the first jump—I had pinched the bag too tightly in my fingers—and it snapped the rope instead of the cord holding the chute in the bag. We went up to 5,000 feet, brought the bag out of hiding, tied it to the pilot's seat over his protests, got in the harness, same position, same everything, and we moved out backwards. The bag held and out came the parachute, beautifully. But what do you think happened? The parachute canopy blew into a million pieces, completely disintegrated. Left us sitting out in the air just as we were a week before. Looking into blue sky. All tangled up, tumbling. Our combined weight was too much for that old parachute. We fell awfully close to the ground but we both got our chutes open. That was the last time we tried that."

The summer after his sophomore year, Kim turned to more serious matters. The past year at school he and Ray had invented the first steerable parachute. With high hopes of making a killing in the business world, they and several technicians set up a small factory in Lancaster, Pennsylvania. The federal government granted the parachute a certificate of approval, and the group began to manufacture the Eagle Parachute.

Their design was fairly simple. In place of the usual hole in the top, they added two rear vents. With these open, and the air jetting out the back, the parachutist descended along an inclined plane. But the chutist could close either vent with shroud lines that controlled the vent flaps. When the left vent was shut, the jet of air shooting from the right vent turned the parachute to the left and vice versa. The chutist could turn himself in any direction, and, of course, he would fall forward in the direction he faced. So this parachute could produce very precise landings.

Scribner made many jumps for newsreels and for various prospective buyers. The government of Peru wanted a demonstration, and Scribner and Morders chose an abandoned airfield for this test. Scribner flew over, dropped Ray, and headed back to the airport where they had rented the airplane. On the ground, the Peruvians were talking excitedly in Spanish. The neighbors, unfortunately, saw Morders floating down and called the police. The people from the Peruvian government thought the police had arrived as an escort for the gentlemen from the Eagle Parachute Company, which of course was not the case, since they carted Morders off to jail. Morders claimed that he had fallen out of the plane. The police thought that unlikely but soon realized that the most serious charge they could muster was trespassing. Scribner came to the police station to embellish Morder's story, and ultimately Morders was released. That was small comfort, however, as the Peruvians did not submit an order for the new parachute.

Scribner and Morders did achieve some success. The Forestry Service gave them a research and development contract. Kim and Ray were convinced that the Eagle Parachute could help fight forest fires; with it airborne fire fighters could land at strategic points.

Then one day a lawyer quietly notified them that unless they desisted from manufacturing the chute they would be taken into court on several counts of patent infringement. They had not thought very deeply about patents. Designing the Eagle, they had borrowed one company's harness and another's clasp, blithely assuming that all relevant patents had expired. Since the patents were still in force, they had no choice but to go out of business, having made no profit from their invention and hard work.

One reason for Scribner's quick retreat was that he had reached the end of his jumping career. After 200 jumps, spread over four years, Scribner finally suffered the injury that convinced him he should retire from parachuting. On a long, delayed jump he was hit in the head with the D-ring, which holds the emergency chute. He landed safely, but the blow caused a concussion which resulted in slight loss of memory. "I didn't make much sense for a while," Scribner recalls, "and that scared me."

Deprived of parachuting, Scribner returned to one of his old haunts, the Congressional School of Aeronautics in Rockville, Maryland, where he had often rented planes. He became a flight instructor and then chief pilot. He had already acquired a wallet full of licenses, including a commercial pilot's license, a flight instructor's rating and six ground instructor ratings, which meant that he could teach everything from engines to flight theory. He was soon empowered by the Civil Aeronautics Authority as a flight examiner to give students their flight tests for their private pilot's license. The school prospered because the government financed instruction for many civilians and college students, under contracts with the University of Maryland, National University and George Washington University. With more students than he could handle, Scribner was working overtime and earning excellent pay.

Life brightened still more. Since these colleges had no ground instructors, they hired the most personable and experienced one around—Scribner. And so, at the age of 22, Scribner became a full faculty member of both George Washington University and National University teaching navigation, flight theory and other courses at night. Needless to say, Scribner was unusual among the faculty in several respects: he was young, he had no degree, and he had a somewhat unscholarly background—swinging beneath parachutes.

Scribner thoroughly enjoyed the academic world. For one thing, an experimental contract turned up, almost at his arrival, which required that he personally select 30 girls from the two schools and teach them ground-school subjects, training 10 for their pilot's license. Upon seeing Scribner's choices, the dean commented, "I have never in my life seen 30 such beautiful girls." Scribner acknowledges that "it was a unique experience."

The pressure from all his duties soon began to take the fun out of life. When a friend in Miami offered him the same money for fewer students, Scribner left Washington at the end of the school year. In Miami, Scribner had only four students, lots of time and plenty of money.

But Scribner wanted something more challenging. Late in 1940, he applied for a job with Pan American Airways. Astounded at Scribner's experience, the airline hired him as sort of a "guinea pig"—they had hired only ex-military pilots before. At 23, with 1,500 hours of flying time logged, Scribner became Pan Am's first civilian pilot.

Scribner was soon flying DC-3's from Florida through the West Indies to South America. When not in the cockpit, he took courses and very quickly worked up from fourth officer to second officer, flying the big flying boat *Clippers* out of New York as navigator. He was made first officer, becoming a full captain at 25 after only 18 months on the job. In 1943, Scribner was flying Boeing 314's across the Atlantic to Ireland, then to Africa and back to the United States. Scribner's passengers were usually military and diplomatic people. "Every one of these flights," he says, "was a unique experience. We flew under black-out conditions. No radio contact. The ocean was ours. We didn't have the equipment of today. We often had to drop down close to the water to see which way the wind was blowing the waves; then we would fly back above the clouds to take sightings on the stars. Sometimes we encountered such strong winds that we ran low on fuel and had to turn back."

In addition to his piloting duties, Scribner made a further contribution to the war effort. During his work upon the Eagle parachute, he had perfected a device to collapse a parachute after it was fully opened so that the chutist could fall quickly and then reopen only a few hundred feet from the ground. Using this device, an undercover agent or saboteur could jump into a dangerous area more swiftly and accurately than with the normal parachute. The Air Force was impressed and told Scribner not to tell anyone about it. Amused at the cloak-and-dagger secrecy, Scribner told the Air Force that he had demonstrated his invention for the newsreels before the war. "People forget," said the Air Force. They never would reveal to Scribner whether they used his device and told him he would have to sue the government for patent infringement if he wanted any money. Scribner said, "Let this be my small contribution to the war."

Early in 1944, Scribner was appointed Pan American's Master of Flying Boats, which put him in command of the airline's biggest planes. Under a contract between the Navy and Pan American, he was sent to New York to fly the Navy's huge Coronado (PB2Y3), the largest of the flying boats. To handle a Navy plane, the Navy decided, Scribner had to join the Navy. So he went for an interview and tests where he put "round things in square holes." The examiners wanted to know if Scribner had any military experience. "Yes," he said, "I was in the ROTC at the University of Maryland for two years. Went in as a private and came out as a private. I was the worst soldier they ever saw." Nevertheless, the Navy made him a lieutenant commander, which sounded very impressive to Scribner. But another department vetoed that rank because he was only 28, and Scribner became a lieutenant, senior grade. Scribner was sworn in by a commodore who noticed Scribner's unorthodox three-fingered salute and barked, "This is not the Boy Scouts." For the remainder of the war, Scribner flew soldiers and equipment to Casablanca and brought wounded men home. After flying Navy flying boats as a Pan American captain, he flew C-54's for the Air Force—with a Navy commission—paid as a civilian.

After the war, his career with Pan Am advanced quickly. Another year of flying DC-3's, DC-4's and DC-6's, and he was appointed a check pilot in 1947, with the responsibility of supervising 10 pilots. He would fly with an entire crew to observe the captain and the way the captain conducted his flight. Then he became a senior check pilot, checking the check pilots, in the airline's program to maintain flying standards.

Apart from his Pan Am flying, Scribner had discovered the joys of soaring. Shortly after the war he bought his first sailplane for $600, a war-surplus model that he and a friend put together. They hooked their new toy to a car and towed it at 40 miles an hour, but it wouldn't leave the ground. So they bought a Stearman open bi-plane to tow the glider into the air. Scribner had read about gliders but he had never even seen one fly before. He had his friend, another Pan Am pilot, tow him to 5,000 feet and learned how to fly it on the way down. Then he put it through a series of tests to explore its capabilities not only for soaring and flying on instruments inside of clouds but also for acrobatic exhibition flights.

Soon Scribner was putting on such acrobatic flights for the Miami Annual Air Show. In his first air show with the glider, on June 4, 1946, Scribner flew his all-white sailplane from a release altitude of 3,000 feet. His most spectacular maneuver was an outside loop, and he ended his exhibition by landing and stopping the sailplane on a newspaper. Later in the year he showed his form with a racing twin-engine P-38 fighter he purchased with money earned flying the sailplane in air shows. He flew the P-38 upside down and performed high-speed acrobatics, "feathered," or stopped, both engines, then landed and stopped the P-38 on the same newspaper he had stopped his sailplane on. For a show in November he signed a $4,500 contract to perform acrobatics in both the P-38 and the glider. He made $100 a minute for his flying. On the first day of the three-day show, however, his P-38 burst into flames on the take-off. A coolant fluid line had broken and the fluid caught on fire. He returned to the airport and landed with fire engines following him down the runway putting out the flames. Scribner borrowed another plane to fulfill the contract, but he was most unhappy because he couldn't "feather" both engines of the borrowed plane at the same time, as he could with his own plane.

During the years after the war, Scribner owned many different sailplanes and airplanes. He had a two-place all-metal single-engine SN-J, a Navy surplus trainer that he had modified to be a "skywriter." On his days off he would fly over Miami at 10,000 feet, spelling out such words as "Cobb's Orange," a soft drink. He continued to perform at air shows and then started to compete in the National Soaring Competitions in Florida, Washington, D.C., and, principally, Elmira, New York—the center of soaring activities.

Scribner scored his greatest air show and soaring contest triumphs during the next few years. In the first week of July, 1948, he won the National Aerobatics Championship at Elmira, New York. He flew a sailplane he had designed specifically for unusual acrobatics. Its wings were equipped with tanks which were filled with water. The extra weight allowed him to gain greater speed during the diving part of the loop. On the way up out of the loop he released the water in a rainbow stream, a Scribner Special which never failed to draw a gasp from the crowd. The loss of weight also let Scribner soar higher on the second half of the loop. In September, 1948, at the Cleveland Air Races, Scribner beat a Frenchman for the world championship, which made him officially the best sailplane acrobatic pilot in the world. The next year, at Elmira again, he won both the acrobatics and speed events, confirming his supremacy. The world championship sailplane title, which Scribner had won in Cleveland in 1948, was retired the following year, so Scribner still holds that title.

After three years as sector chief pilot of the Latin American Division, Captain Scribner moved up to senior operations representative at Pan Am. During these years, though still in his early thirties, Scribner was an administrator as well as a pilot. He flew all of Pan Am's land planes as they were purchased— the DC-3, DC-4, DC-6, DC-7, Constellation and Boeing Stratocruiser. On January 29, 1950, Scribner was chosen to fly the first Stratocruiser flight. This was then the world's largest airplane. The passengers were all VIP's. Scribner's next promotion carried him to the top of the pilot's ladder—chief pilot, Atlantic Division, also an administrative post. In this position, he had responsibility for all the Pan American pilots based in New York, Germany and England. He was in charge of all the assistant chief pilots who controlled the flight training department and their professional flight instructors; the meteorological department with personnel based in various parts of the world; the dispatch department; operations engineering which includes the "route section" responsible for pilots' manuals; and the navigation training department. In this position as chief pilot, Captain Scribner also represented Pan American with such organizations as the Federal Aviation Agency and the Air Transport Association.

Captain Scribner reported to his new assignment in a wheel chair. On January 6, 1951, five days after his promotion had been announced, Scribner smashed up his sailplane at the Miami Air Show. Scribner customarily turned upside down immediately after lifting from the runway—anything to thrill the customers. But the tow pilot climbed steeply, dropping Scribner's sailplane down so that it slammed into the ground. Scribner went headfirst through the instrument panel and ended up unconscious. "Kim Scribner, internationally known sailplane pilot," the Miami paper said, "crashed and was seriously injured Saturday night before 10,000 horrified spectators at the Miami Air Show." Scribner broke his right leg in three places and fractured his left hip. He needed bolts in his legs and plastic surgery on his face. But Scribner never lost his quiet good humor. Lying in the hospital, he told reporters that he was "waiting for my right ankle and left hip to make a labor agreement to go back to work for me." As a result of this, he stopped flying sailplanes—for a while.

Back on the job as Atlantic Division chief pilot, he put his mind to other things. He devised a system of flying directly from New York to San Juan without a navigator. He demonstrated that the commercial radio stations along the East Coast of the United States and in Bermuda could provide radio navigation bearings for the flight. The idea was "unheard of," and it took a good deal of persuasion by Scribner before the Civil Aeronautics Authority finally approved this type of navigation and permitted it to be used on the New York–San Juan flight, making it the longest flight in the world on which pilots themselves did the navigating. Scribner's navigation technique saved 116 miles of flying on every flight between New York and San Juan and eliminated one cockpit crew member—the navigator.

In the early 1950s, Scribner wrote a paper which discussed a simplified method of diagnosing aircraft engine wear. Scribner suggested that dismantling an engine at regular intervals might not be necessary. Spectroscopic analysis of the engine oil would better illustrate where the engine needed attention. By detecting concentrations of elements dissolved in the oil, this analysis would reveal which parts were deteriorating. Today Scribner's recommendation is becoming standard procedure in the maintenance of small jet engines.

In 1954 Scribner produced a training film for pilots, flight engineers and stewardesses. Then he formed the Aeronautic Visual Training Aid Corporation (one of several small consulting companies he has set up) to make more films on such subjects as safety, ditching, evacuation of passengers and aborted take-offs. Scribner's efforts have made films a permanent part of pilot training. He also persuaded the CAB that a pilot could be better familiarized with an airport new to him by film than by flying to and circling it. Here again he single-handedly brought about a change in the regulations, saving all the airlines money previously spent on qualification flights for their pilots—savings that amounted to millions of dollars. All airlines now use this system of qualification.

After seven years behind the desk, Scribner asked to be put back in a pilot's seat as a regular captain. He saw jets on the horizon and he wanted to fly them. In 1956 he began to pilot Constellations and Stratocruisers. On January 30, 1957, he flew a DC-7 to Paris from New York in eight hours and fifty minutes, a record time which has since been beaten only by jets. By the late 1950s he was flying the first jets. His flying career has continued uninterrupted to the present time and he expects to be among the first to fly supersonic jets in a few years. He calculates that so far he has covered at least 5,000,-000 miles in the air.

Between flights, Scribner moved from films to vocational guidance, a subject that has always interested him. With his own unparalleled background as proof, Scribner could state convincingly that anyone can fly and that aviation is an ideal career. During the early 1960s Scribner began to popularize these two ideas, especially in high schools. He formed the Air Industry Youth Development Association to interest teen-agers in aviation. He helped organize numerous trips for high school students to plane factories and airfields. He also established aviation career guidance courses for public schools in Washington, D.C., and wrote several papers on the subject. One, advocating glider flying for high school students in the Civil Air Patrol, was read into the *Congressional Record* by the then Senator Hubert Humphrey. As a result, the CAP now includes a National Glider Program. Scribner has also written a book directed at young people, extolling aviation as a career: *Your Future as a Pilot.*

Most recently, Scribner has become interested in runway barriers, which are, in effect, nets to catch out-of-control aircraft. He wrote and produced a film called *Utilization of Runway Barriers for Jet Aircraft,* and now is trying to convince

American airports to use the barriers. Essentially he wants the airports to install huge nylon nets at the end of major runways. These nets would not be visible. They would remain flat on the ground until the pilot pushed a "panic button." They then would snap up and catch the damaged aircraft before it could run off the airfield. The nets would be attached to cables whose tension would depend on the speed and weight of the airplane, and this information would be transmitted to the barrier in the pilot's emergency signal. Aborted take-offs are rare, but some of the worst accidents have befallen planes that never left the ground. Scribner insists that an aircraft barrier could have prevented them.

Though he has continued to work on projects such as the barrier net, Scribner is currently most involved in the CAT research, which is scheduled to continue through 1968, and perhaps longer. Scribner has concentrated on his temperature theory, but he has kept an open mind about all the other explanations he has heard to account for CAT. Some authorities have suggested that concentrations of ozone in the atmosphere may indicate the presence of CAT, while at least one famous rainmaker thinks that a change in star scintillation could be the telltale sign. Scribner himself has recently come to suspect that there may be some electrical phenomenon associated with the turbulence. To test each theory, Scribner would have to use new instruments and new glider techniques, so the CAT investigation might require an extended period of time.

The Explorers Research Corporation is prepared for a long and complicated project. They want Scribner to follow up any line of experimentation that looks promising. The ERC decided to send Scribner and his associates to Boulder, Colorado, in February, 1968. At Boulder, he worked with the United States Air Force, which is doing its own mountain wave research.

There are particularly strong standing waves in the Rockies, and the Air Force wanted to fly the *Explorer* in this turbulence.

Scribner had an ulterior motive for wanting to take the *Explorer* West. When the CAT project is finished, he hopes to glide back East across the United States and possibly break the world's record for distance flown in a sailplane. The *Explorer* was originally designed with this idea in mind. Scribner feels that with the assist of a jet stream—high westerly winds with a velocity of up to 200 miles an hour—he can reach an altitude of about 40,000 feet in a mountain wave, then glide from there. He may have to be protected from the cold and low pressure by an astronaut's suit and he plans to use liquid oxygen for his pressure suit and for breathing at high altitudes. The scheme, needless to say, is risky. But Scribner wants to break all glider records for height and distance. This accomplishment, he feels, would further the cause of exploration, as well as bring these world records to the United States.

Above all, Kim Scribner enjoys his activities. He seems to approach life with the same casualness he brought to jumping out of planes as a teen-ager.

His wife, Gloria, responds to Scribner's gliding plans with reservations. "The airline business is great," she says, "but I'm not absolutely mad about gliders. But it's a dream of his so I help him as much as I can. After twenty years of marriage, I should be used to his projects, but each one is a surprise, to put it mildly. He hasn't slowed down since I've known him. His enthusiasm is a joy to behold—even if it's sometimes hard to keep up with."

two

Coordinates of Ice

COMMANDER Finn Ronne (USNR), a compactly built man of middle height, looked across the white Antarctic terrain to where the *Port of Beaumont* lay at anchor. The date was May 2, 1947, the place, Stonington Island, off Antarctica's Palmer Peninsula. Until this day, turning before the chill wind, the ship had strained freely against her lines. But now, at the beginning of May in the Southern Hemisphere, winter was coming, and the slushy water was freezing, quickly and irrevocably. Ronne's ship, small enough to be described as an oversized tugboat, would soon be imprisoned by the ice. The Ronne Research Expedition was still busy setting up camp, seven weeks after its arrival, and its 23 members knew that the freeze-in marked the point of no return. The *Beaumont* and her crew would remain at their icebound station inside the Antarctic Circle until the next February, when the ice would thaw again.

Ronne (pronounced Ronny) hailed the few men working near the *Beaumont*. When he spoke, he smiled often and easily and his mellifluous Norwegian accent had a reassuring, almost tranquilizing effect. Ronne had already been on two previous expeditions to the Antarctic and seemed very much at ease in his heavy boots and bulky parka. He was, basically, calm and deliberate. But he could not totally contain his impatience when he thought of the work still to be done in preparation for the fast-coming Antarctic winter.

Ronne had kept half the men on the *Beaumont* to unload the supplies of food, coal and scientific gear. The rest had moved two-thirds of a mile inland to set up the expedition's living quarters. Snow tractors hauled loaded sleds from the ship to the camp, a cluster of squat, sturdy buildings. Ronne was pleased to see that the unloading job was nearly done. In a few weeks everybody could move to the camp, where they would live for the winter, four months of darkness. Not until September, when the sun again climbed above the horizon, would Ronne's expedition begin its geographical exploration.

The expedition had come to the Antarctic with challenging objectives. One: To map as much of the Palmer Peninsula and the unknown area to the south as time and resources permitted. In particular, Ronne wanted to pinpoint the configuration of the Palmer Peninsula's eastern coast, also called the Weddell Sea Coast. This 500-mile stretch was the last unexplored coastline in the world. Two: To conduct research in this part of the Antarctic continent on climate, tides, atmospheric phenomena, radiation, and glaciological and geological makeup.

Ronne and his men could well have been astronauts settling on a far-off planet. With its thousands of miles of desolate whiteness, the Antarctic makes intruders feel small and out of place. Man was not made to live in this harsh world, and he can survive only by following all the rules. Bundled up against the vicious cold, the men of the Ronne expedition looked like black spots about to be blotted out by the snow-laden wind, and the 183-foot *Beaumont* like a toy against the high ice cliffs which rimmed much of Back Bay Cove.

But Ronne felt elated to be there. Watching the bay water freeze around the *Beaumont,* he knew that now there was no possibility of turning back. For Ronne it was an altogether beautiful autumn day. In the clear air he could see far out into the Bellingshausen Sea, where towering icebergs slowly drifted. Nowhere, he thought, does the sun shine so brightly as in the Antarctic. Even distant mountains seemed to edge closer in this cold, clear world where man has left few traces. The 48-year-old explorer loved the bleakness and the almost tangible solitude.

Ronne also loved the continent's mystery. Man has seen such a small portion of this huge, ice-covered land mass which is, surprisingly, nearly twice the size of the continental United States. Most of this area of 5,100,000 square miles was still unexplored territory in 1947, as, in fact, a quarter still is today. And Ronne loved nothing so much as getting into the unknown.

Ronne is a perfect specimen of the traditional explorer. His fascination with the unknown is the mainspring of his character. And no part of the earth could satisfy his yearning so well as the polar regions.

I asked Ronne why he did not explore such places as the Amazon jungle, which in the 1930s and 1940s were still largely unknown to western map-makers, if not to miners, missionaries and natives.

He replied scornfully, "Somebody's been there."

Ronne has spent a quarter of his life going on, or preparing to go on, expeditions to the polar regions. He has made eight trips to the Antarctic and four to the Arctic. Evidently the south polar region can best satisfy his particular obsession. The

Antarctic, after all, is generally unknown to man, while Eskimos have long lived near the North Pole.

Ronne's passion for these remote worlds is as much a part of him as his hazel eyes. His father, Martin Ronne, was also a polar explorer, what Ronne nostalgically calls the "old hardy type." In December, 1911, when Ronne was a boy of 11, his father was a member of the party led by the famous Roald Amundsen that first reached the South Pole. This historic feat captured young Ronne's imagination, and he has studied and participated in polar expeditions ever since. His father made sure that his son's interest did not wane; from 1918 to 1921, while Finn Ronne was in college, Martin Ronne explored the Arctic, and in 1928 the elder Ronne returned to the Antarctic with the First Byrd Expedition. Finn Ronne justly remarks, "I grew up in exploration."

Ronne lived his first 23 years in Norway. As a youth he won medals for his skill at track, soccer, gymnastics and skiing. He took a degree in mechanical engineering at Horten College. Shortly after his graduation a school friend wrote that life in the United States was "very good." Taking this advice, Ronne came to America and settled down in an engineering job with Westinghouse in Pittsburgh. In 1929, while his father was back in the Antarctic, Ronne became a United States citizen. Far from losing his own youthful enthusiasm for exploring, Finn Ronne was merely biding his time. The exploration of unknown, faraway lands could not be carried out on weekends.

Ronne's chance to go to the Antarctic came in 1933. When Commander Richard Byrd, a close friend of Martin Ronne, was organizing his Second Expedition, he asked Ronne, then 34, to join it as a "ski expert." Ronne's first contact with the Antarctic confirmed what he had suspected all along: he loved it. But he did not care much for expedition protocol. Byrd kept close control over the expedition's programs. Ronne wanted to strike out on his own, but free-lance exploration was not on the agenda. Ronne's dissatisfaction made him resolve that he would someday bring his own expedition to the Antarctic.

Ronne made this resolution as he stood on top of an Antarctic mountain in December, 1934. He and another man had taken spare parts to a group whose tractor had broken down. On the return to Byrd's camp, "Little America," traveling by dog sled, they went out of the way to climb Mount Nilsen in the Rockefeller Group. Looking east across the white vista, Ronne thought, "If only I had my own expedition, I could explore that unknown land." Thirteen years later, Ronne would do just that when he brought the Ronne Research Expedition to Stonington Island.

Ronne's progress toward launching an expedition to the Antarctic was slow. His ambitious plans ran into some surprising obstacles—chiefly the dignity of the United States Government. In the years following the Second Byrd Expedition (1933), Ronne had carefully worked out the details of his planned expedition. A trip to the Antarctic, of course, requires a great deal of advance planning; the expedition leader should know exactly what supplies he will take, how much food and fuel, even how many needles and spools of thread. Ronne decided that he would take four other men for a stay of four months. He arranged for a Norwegian whaling ship to transport the group and prepared for a September, 1938, departure.

Then one of his own men publicized Ronne's intention. An American expedition would be using a foreign whaling ship for transportation, and to certain groups in the United States Government this was not ideal. Then, too, the feeling was that a five-man expedition would hardly add to the nation's prestige. Before he knew exactly what was happening, Ronne had lost control of the expedition. From what he calls the "bureaucratic whirlwind," the United States Antarctic Service Expedition emerged, fully planned, fully financed and ready to move. This lavish government undertaking, whose purpose would be to explore unknown territory and conduct scientific research, established two bases 1,500 miles apart, and lasted from 1939 to 1941. Ronne found himself at East Base, second in command to the man who had publicized Ronne's projected trip. He did not enjoy the turn of events, but he resigned himself to learning more about the Antarctic, in preparation for the day when he would have his own expedition.

Ronne also soothed the pain he felt at losing control of the expedition by doing a great amount of genuine exploration. He traveled a total of 1,284 miles by dog sled, mostly into uncharted regions—one of the longest sled trips on record. Ronne went most of this distance with just one other man, Carl Eklund. The 84-day trip spanned the summer months of November, December and January (1940–1941), when the sun never sets in the Antarctic. The two men headed south from Stonington Island and circled around Alexander Island, which Ronne proved was an island by finding George VI Sound. Like most bodies of water in the Antarctic, this sound stays frozen and covered over by snow, so that it resembles the surrounding land. Turning north, Ronne and Eklund sledged back to Stonington by a different route.

Life on the trail brought the men both suffering and satisfaction. More ineradicably, it gave them an intimate knowledge of a monumentally different part of the world. To appreciate the Antarctic, Ronne says, you must live in it. Senators and other VIP's, he notes sardonically, often go to the Antarctic for the weekend, primarily so they can say they have been there.

Ronne suggests that if a man really wants to know the Antarctic he must get out on the trail with a dog team.

Each morning Ronne and Eklund found themselves inside their small tent, camped on a windswept glacier or ice field, more than 600 miles from the nearest human being. Before sliding out of their warm sleeping bags, they started the cooking stove. Over the radio came music from far-off, irrelevant places like London and Calcutta. Outside, the vast and stately emptiness stretched, seemingly forever.

After a quick breakfast in the sleeping bags, the men broke camp. While Eklund went out to feed the dogs, Ronne rolled up the sleeping bags and packed the gear. Through the tent's drawstring he passed the bags out to Eklund who strapped them onto the two sledges. After hitching the dogs, they collapsed the snow-streaked tent, tied it on top of the load and started off.

Usually one man went ahead to break trail. Noisy and unruly, the dogs bounded off through the snow. The sled looked the same from front or back and was made of flexible wood so that it could glide over the uneven Antarctic terrain. Ronne skied along at the sled's front end and steered by pushing or yanking on a pole bolted upright on the sled's front corner.

Each day was officially dedicated to exploring new land and plotting the location of new mountains and glaciers. When the men returned, they would be expected to produce accurate maps—the tangible results of their exploration.

Beyond this, each day was a struggle for survival. The sub-zero gales and blizzards seemed determined to destroy anything alive. Only hard work and long experience kept them from freezing to death. A man cannot simply put on a parka and set out for a few months of sledging. He must first learn how to take care of himself. For example, the perspiration inside clothes and boots will freeze if a man is inactive for long. The explorer must be able to judge the danger and know what remedies to take. Frostbite is a constant threat and the effect of the wind can easily be misjudged. The United States Army has a 30-30-30 wind-chill rule: at −30 degrees Fahrenheit in a 30-mile-an-hour wind, human flesh freezes in 30 seconds. Ronne says that his skin takes a little longer. Even when the sun was high and the wind quiet, Ronne and Eklund still had to worry about falling through the sea ice, skiing off a cliff or getting smothered by an avalanche. They could not afford the smallest mistake or accident. Not all explorers come back: Robert F. Scott, famous for reaching the South Pole one heartbreaking month after Amundsen, perished with four companions in 1912. Trapped by a blizzard, they were only 11 miles from food and shelter at a base.

The greatest and most constant danger was crevasses—cracks in the ice or glacier which can be hundreds of feet deep. These small canyons were usually covered over by snow bridges, and, since the wind smoothed the surface, the crevasses were invisible until the two men were on top of them. Sometimes the dogs would break through, which was lucky, for then Ronne and Eklund simply pulled them out. But the dogs and the driver might pass over a strong snow bridge and the heavier sled would then crash through. If this happened, the dogs instinctively dug in and the nearest man quickly hammered "dead men" (wooden poles) into the ice. The sled usually ended up at a 45-degree angle, teetering on the edge of the crevasse. After a few curses, the men would spend the next hour or so working to put the sled back on the trail. Pulling the sled up was impossible, since it was loaded down with some 1,200 pounds of supplies. One man, secured by a safety rope,

had to climb down on the sled, unpack the canvas bags and hand them up one by one. Ronne, who is given to understatement, calls it "dangerous work, like working on skyscrapers." More than one explorer has lost his life by being swallowed up in a crevasse. Ronne claims that he has been around crevasses so much that he can sense them. On many occasions he has poked his ski pole into ordinary-looking snow and a black hole has opened up.

Another danger was the "white-out," one of the Antarctic's weirdest tricks, an atmospheric illusion created chiefly by glare. Caught in a white-out, a man thinks his eyes have gone blank. Everything looks white and fuzzy. Ronne says, "It's like walking around in cotton." In a white-out, Ronne could recognize familiar objects, but he learned not to trust his vision of strange ones. A matchbox 20 feet away might look like a village down in a distant valley, until you stepped on it. When this rare effect occurs, the explorer is wise to sit and wait until normal vision returns.

In a 10-hour day on the trail, Ronne and Eklund normally covered about 25 miles. (On their best day they traveled 49 miles.) With the sun low on the horizon and the temperature dropping, sometimes to —50 degrees Fahrenheit, the explorers hurried through their routine for pitching camp. Together they put up their tent, then turned to separate tasks. Having lit the stove and left some snow melting in a pot, one man unloaded the sleds. The other man unhitched the dogs and staked them so they could not fight. Ronne considers this daily struggle with the huskies the worst part of the trip. With his fingers numbing, the sweat in his boots turning to ice and the wind cutting his face, Ronne had to muster all of his self-control to undo the stubborn, frozen chains. When that ordeal was past, he could duck into the tent and find hot water on the stove.

One man made tea or coffee while the other pulled out biscuits and pemmican, the concentrated polar food made from beef grits, bacon grits, liver powder, beef fat, bacon fat, milk powder, green pea meal, oatmeal, soy bean grits, dehydrated celery, potatoes, carrots, lemon powder, ascorbic acid, paprika and seasonings, all mixed carefully together and frozen into 12-ounce bricks. Ronne and Eklund usually shaved their pemmican into water to make a porridge-like soup. But it can be eaten raw as well. To Ronne, it tasted like "greasy hamburger."

While eating dinner, they turned on the radio or swapped stories. Later, lying in his sleeping bag, Ronne wrote in his diary and brought his other paper work up-to-date. Some evenings Ronne clipped his beard, which he kept down to stubble. He had found during the winter before that a beard itched and that on the trail, icicles formed on it, making him look "like a walrus." When the explorers wanted to sleep, they had to cope with yet another Antarctic nuisance. The sun was still shining outside and the light came through the tent. Ronne and Eklund usually wore eye-shades.

Despite the hardships, Ronne thoroughly enjoyed this sledge trip and his many others, and, in fact, he has probably traveled more miles by dog sledge than any other explorer—a total of 3,600 miles. "Every mile you make is interesting," he said, speaking of his trip around Alexander Island. "You see mountains coming up over the horizon, find glaciers and shelf-ice. You know that no other man has seen them. I wanted to explore into the unknown. That had been my ambition for years, to get into the unknown. And I succeeded on that long sled trip for the first time. I was pleased by how well I reacted to the strain. The physical effort of going from sea level to an elevation of 7,200 feet is severe. But I came back in better condition than when I left. And I felt that I had accomplished something." What Ronne accomplished, specifically, was to map the territory, collect information about it and claim it for the United States.

When Ronne and Eklund finished their record sledge trip in 1941, Ronne knew that the job would not really be complete until he had flown over the same region and photographed it. A sledge party on the surface can provide the coordinates of the major terrain features and the heights of mountains. But only aerial photographs can indicate the terrain's exact contours, and this information is, of course, vital for map-making. Because he saw the need to photograph the area, Ronne's sledge trip of 1940–1941, which he counts among his proudest achievements, can be considered a part of, as well as a preparation for, his own expedition of 1947.

Upon his return from the Antarctic, Ronne obtained a commission in the United States Navy in May, 1941, and served on active duty in various capacities during World War II.

Taking leave from the Navy in 1946, Ronne again began to plan his own private expedition. This time he worked on a more ambitious scale. The scope of his plans and the memory of past misadventures led him to seek the government's help from the start. He had to obtain a ship and several airplanes, as well as funds for his supplies. Ronne somehow financed his expedition on less than $50,000. The money came from several sources. The Office for Naval Research granted him $26,000, in return for which Ronne would carry out a host of experiments. The Congress agreed to loan him a Navy ship. The United States Weather Bureau, the Franklin Institute, the North American Newspaper Alliance and numerous individuals who believed in the value of Ronne's project added the rest. He spent much time and energy rounding up the support he needed. He was practical, ready to work hard to realize a dream.

When the Ronne Antarctic Research Expedition at last departed from Beaumont, Texas, on January 26, 1947, Ronne could only think: "I am a fortunate man." Few men have the vision to imagine leading their own expedition to any place. Fewer still could beat the odds against transforming such a plan into actuality. But Finn Ronne had done that. He had knocked on doors and pleaded for support and material assistance. Now he was on his way. When he could forget for a few minutes the problems ahead, he felt pleased with himself.

Sad to say, however, Ronne was closing out history as well as making it. As he steamed triumphantly south, he ended an era. The Ronne Expedition was the last private American expedition ever to sail for the Antarctic. Though he was assisted by the government, Ronne was still the sole leader and highest authority on his expedition. All expeditions since Ronne's have been carried out by branches of the Federal Government, with the support of the Navy.

Ronne's 23 men belonged also to a vanishing era. A Navy expedition to the Antarctic today might consist of a thousand ordinary sailors. But the men on the Ronne Research Expedition were not ordinary. They were men bold and adventurous enough to volunteer to live for a year in the Antarctic, a place most had never been. They were not paid. Whether airplane mechanic, radio operator, doctor, physicist, cook, ship's captain or dog handler, the men shared the same desire to turn their backs on the familiar and safe and face the dangerous and unknown. Many of the men had just returned from military duty in World War II and did not like the idea of settling down. Most were young and single—all but five were under 30 and two-thirds were unmarried. Most—but certainly not

Ronne—regarded themselves as amateur explorers. Accordingly they felt free to enjoy themselves and let their leader agonize over the details. Ronne personally selected the men for their skills and experience. Many of them also had colorful histories and highly unique personalities. Ike Schlossbach, the rugged, one-eyed and ornery skipper of the *Beaumont,* graduated from the Naval Academy in 1915, led the first squad of Navy dive-bombers in 1925, and was navigator of the submarine *Nautilus* on its famous voyage under the polar ice cap under Sir Hubert Wilkins in 1931. Schlossbach had been to both the Antarctic and the Arctic several times. Dr. Robert L. Nichols, head of the Geology Department at Tufts College, was one of the expedition's oldest and most reserved members. A health enthusiast, he did daily exercises. Tall, handsome Andrew Thompson, only 24, the expedition's geophysicist, was a Yale graduate, noted for his quick intelligence, boxing ability and independent spirit.

Having weighed anchor at Beaumont, Ronne and his diverse crew headed south toward the Pacific coast of South America. With several stops along the way, the trip to Antarctica would take more than six weeks. On the *Beaumont,* a renovated Navy repair ship, the explorers competed for space with the expedition's supplies, which included three airplanes, tractors and 64 sledge dogs. But the crowded quarters could not lessen the group's high spirits. With the scent of the future sharp in their heads, they had one driving thought—"to get down there."

Halfway to the Antarctic, a minor tragedy occurred. A distemper epidemic hit the expedition's huskies. These tough animals can sleep covered by snow at —50 degrees Fahrenheit. But the tropical heat ruined their resistance. (All the dogs except the puppies had been inoculated.) Listless and without appetite, the huskies languished in their kennel on the ship's stern. The doctors at Valparaiso, Chile, where the *Beaumont* docked on February 21, had no vaccine. Ronne moved on, leaving instructions for an emergency shipment of vaccine to be sent to Punta Arenas, Chile, the world's southernmost city, where the *Beaumont* would put in. But help never caught up with them. As the ship neared the Antarctic, however, the gathering cold finally brought the surviving dogs back to yelping good health. But nearly half of the 64 huskies had died. The epidemic taught Ronne an old lesson: it's the things you forget to prepare for that defeat you.

In Valparaiso Ronne made a decision that would mark his expedition as different from any other polar trip. Up to then, the expedition included two temporary members, both women: Mrs. Finn Ronne and Mrs. Harry Darlington, the wife of one of the pilots. Mrs. Ronne handled the expedition's paper work, though the other woman had really come along for the ride. At first, they were supposed to leave the expedition ship in Panama, then in Valparaiso. But at Valparaiso, Ronne decided that his wife's background knowledge of the expedition and her reporting skills were indispensable. After much debate over the idea, the women officially became permanent members of the expedition. They would be the first women ever to winter in the Antarctic.

On the four-day crossing from South America to the Antarctic, the expedition encountered unusually quiet seas. The temperature dropped steadily and they were soon avoiding chunks of ice. The men had organized a betting pool, with a can of sardines for the one who guessed when the first iceberg would be sighted. The cook won, choosing the morning of March 12.

In the winter the sea around the Antarctic continent freezes in a ring dozens of miles wide, and in the summer this ice breaks up and floats north. The ship was in no great danger yet, for the ice chunks were not large, but the expedition would soon see enormous ones. The Antarctic iceberg, which makes the Arctic variety look puny, comes in sizes from the gigantic— the size of a city block of office buildings—to the unbelievable —measuring as much as 100 miles across, enough to cover the entire state of Connecticut. These huge ice masses break off from the Antarctic ice shelves or from glaciers that run into the sea. The sight of them impressed on the expedition members the fact that the Antarctic does nothing in moderation.

The *Beaumont* was approaching the west side of Palmer Peninsula (now referred to as the Antarctic Peninsula), a long finger land which points up toward South America. Ominously beautiful mountains, streaked with white and ruling over a kingdom of white, climbed into view as the ship drew closer. Robert Scott had written in his diary, "Could anything be more terrible than this silent, windswept immensity?" But Ronne, who was realizing a 13-year-old dream, felt only thankful excitement.

The *Beaumont* headed straight across Marguerite Bay. Ronne knew all the landmarks, for he had wintered here six years earlier on the United States Antarctic Service Expedition. When the expedition ended in 1941, Ronne and the others had to fly out because the bay was frozen over. Now the big oval bay contained only loose ice, and the ship could move through.

The Antarctic coastline is not friendly to explorers. Nearly all the way around, for 15,000 miles, the continent's edge is a sheer ice cliff. Most of the Antarctic is covered by a layer of ice, more than a mile thick at its center, which breaks off vertically where it meets the sea. These magnificent cliffs make awesome scenery. But ships need a beach for unloading. Stonington Island, in Marguerite Bay, is one of the few places in the Antarctic where the land slopes gradually into the sea.

Stonington Island is named after Stonington, Connecticut, the home port of Nathaniel Brown Palmer, the man who first saw the Antarctic mainland. Palmer, whose name has been given to the entire peninsula, made his discovery in 1820. The 21-year-old skipper was not very interested in his find, since he was there chasing seals, like scores of other captains who went that far south in the same decade. The discovery of the Antarctic did not, in fact, spark any great enthusiasm anywhere. Nobody even set foot there until 1895, when a Norwegian explorer name Borchrevink climbed ashore for a quick look around.

Through his binoculars Ronne sighted the British Base "E" of the Falkland Island Dependencies. Ronne could make out some men feeding dogs staked out in the snow. The British claimed Palmer Peninsula as their territory, and called it Graham Land. When the British Ambassador in Washington had first learned about Ronne's expedition, he had tried to make the United States Government stop it. Now that Ronne had arrived, protocol demanded that he meet the Base "E" magistrate, Major Kenneth Pierce-Butler, and so Ronne, his wife and two members of the expedition rowed ashore. Pierce-Butler immediately stressed his government's position: that England owned the land Ronne was about to explore. Several days after their first meeting, Pierce-Butler sent Ronne a formal protest over the United States flag being flown at the American base. "I assume," he wrote, "that the United States Government has made no claims to this territory and that the flying of this flag is merely the indication of the presence of a United States expedition."

The situation was even more involved, however. Chile and Argentina also insisted that they owned Palmer Peninsula. Ronne had one answer to such claims, which he patiently delivered to all parties. The United States did not recognize anybody's claim, but insisted that all territory be open for exploration and study. (Too late to help Ronne, the contending governments agreed, in December, 1959, to freeze all claims for 30 years.)

At their first meeting Pierce-Butler had also informed Ronne that the American base was in bad shape. Chilean and Argentinian Navy ships had anchored there for a few weeks, and the sailors had amused themselves by tearing up the base. Pierce-Butler escorted Ronne to the American base, half a mile away, and Ronne saw that the visitors had indeed done considerable damage. They had taken or broken about 80 percent of the property left behind when the United States Service Expedition of 1941 had been flown out. It would take weeks of work to clean the base up again, and repair the damage.

The American base consisted of five buildings, all sturdily built, with four inches of rock wool insulation. The main bunkhouse measured 60 feet in length and 24 feet in width. The science building and one machinery building, set parallel to the bunkhouse, were 32 feet long and 24 feet wide. Ronne and his wife would live in the fourth building, a 12-by-12-foot hut. The supply shack was even smaller than this. All of these buildings were connected by tunnels, for, during the winter, drifting snow completely covered the base. (Very little new snow falls in the Antarctic—about an inch a year. But there is little melting and the winds move the snow about in seeming blizzards.)

The expedition members quickly went to work. The shore party cleaned and swept, setting fires in damp stoves, nailing canvas on the buildings and generally trying to make the camp homelike. The men quickly learned not to leave tools around, since the drifting snow buried them. Fire extinguishers were set up and fire drills held, since a fire could easily wreck the expedition.

The pilots, meanwhile, readied the smallest of the three planes for flying—an orange-and-red, single-engine scout plane. The airplanes would be a vital part of Ronne's expedition. First used by Sir Hubert Wilkins in 1928 to discover new land in the Antarctic, the airplane allowed great leaps into the unknown. With aerial cameras that clicked off pictures at precise intervals, the explorer could easily record a region's appearance. But these pictures would be useless unless tied in with ground fixes, and the explorers had to use dog sleds to obtain those. So Ronne planned to use the modern airplane in perfect coordination with the Eskimo's ancient methods. This combination marks Ronne's as a transitional expedition. Before 1947, dog sleds had been the principal means of transportation. After this date, snow tractors were perfected and expeditions stopped using dog teams. Ronne's expedition was the last to discover new land using dog teams. And Ronne, who has been on both types of expeditions, is the only explorer who is still active to live through this transition.

Ronne has made a nostalgic truce with the new ways. He can not help noticing that airplanes whisk him over terrain in a few hours which, years before, he spent days struggling to cross. And modern expeditions feature gas heat and starched table-cloths, while he nearly froze to death many times when he was with Byrd. Ronne accepts the new as he accepted the old, with emotionless practicality. "I can adjust myself to almost any conditions," Ronne says. "Whatever comes is for the better."

Certainly the new brought its own problems. The men who looked after the airplanes, in fact, had one of the expedition's most demanding jobs. The planes had no hangar. All the tuning and repairing had to be done out in the cold. Fingers stuck tenaciously to the cold metal, and since the mechanics could not do delicate work with thick gloves on, they ended up with an assortment of blisters. Starting the engines was a major operation, too. The oil was heated on the galley stove, while the engine itself was warmed up for an hour by a special engine heater or, sometimes, a blowtorch. With this prodding, the engine might kick over and roar just as if it were back in the States.

The smallest airplane was quickly sent up to scout. Ronne planned to sail south to George VI Sound, where he would cache a food supply for the sleds to be sent out next spring. The photographer, Bill Latady, a tall, rangy man with black-rimmed glasses, who was also a mountain climber, went up to reconnoiter with Darlington, the tall wartime Navy pilot and veteran of the United States Antarctic Service Expedition. They reported clear seas but "a whole lot of bergs."

The *Beaumont* sailed cautiously south on March 23 from Stonington Island, and the explorers quickly discovered three large islands, not included on any maps. The islands must have looked like icebergs to earlier fliers, and their discovery reminded the explorers that they must view their maps with some suspicion. Most of the maps were largely incomplete guesswork, which was the reason Ronne had come back again. Before the expedition was over, Ronne would find that one mountain was a full 50 miles from where it had been located by a previous expedition.

The *Beaumont* reached 69 degrees 20 minutes, farther south than any ship had been before. But the icebergs prevented Skipper Ike Schlossbach from reaching a landing spot. The men enjoyed watching the sun dance and glitter on these enormous ice islands, but Ronne knew that if the wind changed, these majestic bergs might trap them 100 miles from the base. Ronne decided to turn around and go back. The trail food, aviation gasoline and other supplies would have to be hauled overland.

As March and April passed, the expedition readied itself for the winter. The buildings were repaired. The loading party brought ashore the 35 tons of coal, the wings for the two large airplanes, the heavy radio equipment, assorted food and equipment and the two snow tractors, one of which was stored away for an emergency. Every day a few of the men went out to hunt seals, a ready supply of dog food. The hunters needed no special skill, since the hefty, 600-pound seals had no natural enemies. They stretched in the sun and awaited the execution with wide, brown eyes.

The expedition's scientists set up their research equipment. To get the money he needed, Ronne had contracted with several scientific organizations to conduct experiments in many fields and to keep year-long records of such conditions as weather, cosmic rays, magnetic fields, earthquakes, tides, solar radiation, atmospheric changes, geologic formations. Andrew Thompson, the geophysicist, built a tidal shack to keep a record of the tides in Back Bay Cove, a non-magnetic shack to measure changes in the earth's magnetic field and a seismograph room which would house instruments designed to measure tremors in the earth's crust. Unfortunately the young scientist was not a carpenter. The floor of the seismograph room turned out to be slanted at a perceptible angle. Ronne asked one of the ship's officers to lend a hand, and a presentable building soon appeared. But Thompson neglected to anchor the hut. A 60-mile-an-hour gale came up—the Antarctic is the windiest place in the world—and scattered Thompson's handiwork over 250 feet of snow. Showing great perseverance, Thompson built it again, this time with professional results, except for a sign reading: "Lemonade at Five Cents a Glass."

Thompson then moved in the sensitive seismographs which would record earth tremors. Tied in with readings from stations around the world, Thompson's data would tell scientists new facts about the contour and thickness of the planet's crust.

While Thompson was putting up his shacks, Harries-Clichy Peterson, physicist, Harvard graduate and ex-Marine, built a weather station. He also began launching two orange weather balloons each day. The direction of their ascent and their horizontal speed told Peterson the speed and direction of the air currents at various altitudes. Robert Dodson, the assistant geologist, was the official tester of the United States Army's newest designs in clothing, tents and equipment. He was actually a human guinea pig. While the other men were snug in the bunkhouse, Dodson and others who helped him passed many uncomfortable nights discovering that some of the Army's tents and sleeping bags needed redesigning. In short, the half-dozen scientists were busy men, trying to keep track of dozens of separate projects.

A novel threat momentarily disrupted the hectic pace. Ronne noticed that a crevasse near the camp had widened over night. The iceberg, about 100 by 300 feet, would soon split off from the land and float into Back Bay. Ronne feared that it would drift into the *Beaumont*. The men stopped everything and conferred on what to do. If they could split the iceberg themselves they could move the *Beaumont* out of the way. Three men volunteered to try to speed up the splitting process with dynamite. But aside from shaking all the buildings, the explosion did nothing. The next day two men lowered 32 sticks down into the crevasse, again with no results. The ice was not going to move until it was ready—which turned out to be very shortly. The next morning, the iceberg split off from the ice shelf and drifted harmlessly out to sea.

Toward the end of April, when the expedition had been in the Antarctic for six weeks, the sea became a mass of jagged ice chunks. The men could no longer row supplies from the ship. The freeze-in had begun. On the night of May 2, 1947, the ice turned solid. After that, the *Beaumont* moved only up and down with the tide. Ronne was pleased with how much his men had accomplished and he watched the days shorten with anticipation. Already the sun came up for only a few hours. He knew the expedition would be ready for the winter and, more important, ready for the exploration in the spring.

The next week Ronne declared a holiday to celebrate the expedition's progress. Sig Gutenko, the cook, who had run the galley on expeditions to the Antarctic and to Greenland, prepared a chicken dinner fit for the occasion and the explorers toasted themselves with Chilean champagne.

The chicken came as a welcome change from the endless meals of filet mignon. Surprisingly, in fact, the men had even gotten to the point where hamburger struck them as being tastier than steak. Their disenchantment with first-class fare showed that the Antarctic has a strange effect on a man's tastes. As a result of the hard work and the constant cold, most men burned up twice the calories they did at home. As a result they craved—in gargantuan portions—foods with a high fat or sugar content, foods for which they had little enthusiasm before coming to the Antarctic. Candy, especially chocolate, had a strong new appeal. Some of Ronne's men were gobbling up a pound every day. Ronne had, of course, expected this; he had brought along several thousand pounds. The demand for pastry also jumped. The cook could hardly bake enough. On the night of the party, the men had a chance to satisfy fully their new appetites.

Ronne sat back that night and watched his men with satisfaction. With few exceptions, they measured up to Ronne's ideal explorer: intelligent, strong, helpful, cheerful and hard-working. He had gotten more than he had a right to expect and he would always remember his own expedition as the most pleasant of his career.

Some expeditions offer large bonuses and attract men who are not emotionally suited to the confinement and unrelieved work. Ronne much preferred volunteers. There was some risk, however. Antarctic exploration would naturally attract independent, even eccentric individuals. Thrown together in the small base for a year, they could not reasonably be expected to live in complete harmony. For one thing, the niceties and good manners expected in civilization are worn very thin by the harsh existence. Men are likely to show their worst traits. For another, an Antarctic expedition needs physically strong men and these are likely to be young men, perhaps lacking in maturity and self-control. Finding men with the proper balance of bodily strength and mental poise is difficult. Ronne had his problem cases: a few prima donnas, an occasional brooder, the "brain" who knew all the answers and so on. But he did not complain. He had been on expeditions which made this one seem like "one big happy family." For the most part, he found that his men measured up very well to his requirements. Having watched them for eight weeks, Ronne felt that the expedition would run smoothly, and he could relax and enjoy the party along with the others.

The last big job before winter came was putting up the radio antenna, which had to be carefully beamed on both New York and New Orleans. The men had to raise four poles so that their tops would be a level 60 feet above the snow. Though buffeted by snow and wind, they stuck at the exhausting work for two days. Two of the poles collapsed on the way up. Then Nelson McClary, an ex-Navy officer with three years of war duty on a destroyer in the Pacific behind him, almost killed himself. McClary was stretching out one of the guy wires, walking backward. The other men yelled when they saw how close he was moving to a 60-foot glacier cliff. But McClary didn't hear them. His ears were covered by a cap and the fur hood of his parka, and besides, he was concentrating on his job.

"Mac!" many voices shouted.

Then McClary disappeared. The other men raced to the cliff's edge. McClary had crashed through the ice 60 feet below and was bobbing out of sight beneath the cold, dark water. He desperately clawed at the two-inch sheet of ice, which crumbled in his hands. James B. Robertson, a quick-witted airplane mechanic, found some climbing rope and threw it down to McClary, whose limbs had already gone numb. Robertson ordered the snow tractor brought up. When the line had been attached, Larry Fiske, the climatologist and an ex-Navy pilot, revved up the engine and started off. McClary, spinning on the line which he had tied around his chest, was pulled straight up from the water. Ronne and Robertson dragged him over the top—eight minutes after he had fallen off.

McClary mumbled, "Get these things off me. Hurry—"

They wrapped the shivering, half-conscious man in blankets and carried him back to the bunkhouse on a small sled. Dr. Don McLean cut off his clothes and an arm cast he had acquired from an accident on the trip down from Texas. The doctor put hot-water bottles on McClary's body and assigned a man to massage each limb. They were warned, however, not to touch his fingers and toes, for they would be very delicate. During the next few days, McClary's fingertips turned white and peeled, and the newly exposed skin was even more vulnerable than the old. Still, Ronne concluded, McClary was lucky. If the ice had been thicker, he would have died from a concussion. As it was, he broke no bones, and after a few weeks in bed he went back to work.

With the ice around the *Beaumont* nearly four feet thick, Schlossbach and the crew literally packed her away for the winter. The ship's diesels and all exposed metal parts got a protective coating of graphite or tallow to prevent rusting. The men taped the radios up, putting silica gel inside to absorb moisture, and sealed all the hatches and ventilating ducts. The *Beaumont* had, in effect, been put into a cocoon. This care guaranteed that the ship would be ready to take them home the next summer.

By May the explorers had settled down to face the slow passage of winter. The major work of setting up camp had been finished. Now the expedition entered its calmest, and to some, its most boring and disagreeable period. Ronne knew that the men must be kept busy, either with expedition work or just hobbies. Left to himself, a man would probably start thinking about the friends and comforts he had abandoned at home. The Antarctic is a perfect place for just sitting and brooding. The empty spaces and the feeling of endless time undermine a man's determination to get on with the job. Ronne has found that Amundsen was right when he said, "Keep the men busy and you keep them happy." So he made sure that the expedition's routine chores—kitchen duty, melting ice for water, hauling coal—were rotated so that everybody had some daily task. But the men still had a lot of free time. Ronne encouraged them to read or work at handicrafts. Nearly every man was engaged in some sort of hobby such as woodcarving and model building. Ronne himself constructed a perfect 12-inch replica of one of the expedition's dog sleds.

Halfway through May, the sun made its last appearance for two and a half months. Twilight, however, would still come once a day as the sun climbed almost to the horizon. Then the sun's rays turned the sky sunset red and the red light spread eerily across the icy landscape. This twilight gradually shortened and finally stopped. The expedition was left in perpetual night. The men lived solely by the clock, as they might underground or aboard a submarine.

The Antarctic night, however, is not a blackout. On the contrary, a weird glow lights up this majestic world. The stars shine down through the smokeless, dustless air with a brilliance most people never see. Clouds do not appear very often. The luminous starlight glitters down on the white snow, which seems to magnify the cold light. When Ronne walked outside, he could see the sharp outlines of distant peaks and cliffs. The moon sometimes added its own light to this dazzling night scene.

The entry in Ronne's diary for June 17, 1947, describes a winter day:

> The temperature was minus thirty-four degrees F. [The temperature rarely got up to −10 degrees Fahrenheit in these months. This is a good deal colder than the freezer compartment in most refrigerators. Ronne would not allow his men outside to work in temperatures below −55 degrees because their lungs might freeze.] It was unusually clear, and the short twilight hours revealed a wonderful assortment of fluffy, multicolored rainbow clouds above the glacier, which were caused by refractions of the rays from the sun on its white surface. It was an unusual experience and sight for the men to watch. McClary and Wood slept outside with their sleeping bags in the snow last night and continued their testing program. Thompson spent the day outside working on his tidal gauge and then took some terrestrial magnetism recordings. Robertson skied out to the ship to work on the planes. The dog teams were out hauling coal and various

small items in from the ship. McLean, Hassage and Smith were doing the driving. Both the teams and the men seem to be coming along fine. Dodson and Owen spent the day in the blubber shack rendering oil for the dog pemmican. Kelsey, Lassiter and Adams removed a heavy collection of hoar frost from the rhombic antenna wires. Peterson, as usual, was busy on meteorology, and Fiske, when not helping him, sewed some dog harnesses on the machine. Gutenko was in the galley working on the trail food, and Nichols worked on his lists of equipment needed for his trail trip. Latady developed seven rolls of negatives of some of our indoor activities, and they all turned out quite well. My wife wrote an article for N.A.N.A. on a roundup of our activities thus far, and I spent part of the day working on the trail sleds, then came in to do some more figuring on the gasoline consumption and the weight loads the planes would have to carry for our program. This becomes more and more complicated, and each time I figure it out the enormity of our undertaking frightens me. We had a movie tonight about the life of Wilson; it was excellent, and some of the fellows came in for some coffee and cake before we turned in.

The expedition held its next party on midwinter's night, June 22. From now on the sun would be climbing back up to the horizon. There was also another reason to celebrate: Ronne and the British leader, who had brought his men to the party, discussed pooling resources on some of the sledge trips. The cook again served up a feast, this time for an international gathering. In the decorated bunkhouse, the explorers joined in singing songs and toasting their progress.

Most of the explorers were pretty shaggy by this time. Ronne had told them that showers and shaves would be optional. "They could be as filthy as they pleased," Ronne says. For the most part the men looked forward to the weekly shower. But the hair and beards of many had reached exotic lengths. Ronne kept himself clean-shaven.

One lesser reason for Ronne's neat appearance was that he was a civil servant—Postmaster Fourth Class, to be exact. The United States Government had made Ronne the Antarctic's first postmaster. The United States established the post office at Stonington Island to reinforce its territorial claims. In honor of Ronne's birthplace, he was given the postmark, OLEONA, the name of a Norwegian settlement in Pennsylvania. But, to spare Ronne the job of hauling sacks of letters for stamp collectors, the public was not told until after Ronne had reached the Antarctic. So Ronne canceled only six official letters during his year in the Antarctic, making OLEONA, ANTARCTICA, the rarest cancellation in United States postal history.

As winter gave way to spring, the camp's pace quickened. Despite the blizzards of July and August, the men completed their preparations for the coming months of exploration. The mechanics worked over the airplane engines and the aerial cameras, while the pilots, Lassiter and Adams, calculated how many miles they could get out of the three planes with the available fuel. The men who would go on the trail parties inspected and mended their tents, clothing, sledges and equipment. The expedition's two women helped sew the hundreds of orange tail flags which are sometimes dropped by a surface party to mark the path it has chosen. Ronne, meanwhile, worried over the broad logistical problems: how could he best use the men, dogs, machines and fuel to cover the most ground?

Ronne tackled the expedition's first mission when the midday period of twilight was lasting only three or four hours. He wanted to establish a weather station 20 miles from camp on the high plateau that runs down the center of Palmer Peninsula. From this outpost his spotters could radio when the weather was right for flying. If he were ever to complete the mapping of the peninsula, Ronne knew that he must take full advantage of the few dozen clear days they could expect in the months ahead.

Ronne set out for the plateau with five men and two dog teams on the morning of July 15. The eerie, starlit ice fields stretched silently away. The sleds were loaded down with tents, sleeping bags, stoves, cooking utensils, mountain climbing gear, radios and a large supply of food for men and dogs. The trail party advanced slowly up the glacier, dodging crevasses and trying not to get lost in a world that looks pretty much the same in all directions. Several times an avalanche thundered down a nearby slope. Except for lunch, the men never stopped, yet they covered only 13 miles that first day.

The next day the party assaulted the glacier's steepest section. As they climbed, the men gained a wider and more striking view of the peninsula and the coastline. But the ascent was tough. Sometimes when the surface was very steep, they had to relay the sledges up. They attached both dog teams to one sled, hauled it up and then brought the dogs back down to drag up the second sledge. Still there were some unexpected rewards. A fantastic display of aurora australis brightened the dark southern skies. Swirling colored curtains of light danced across the heavens.

But nature also knew other tricks. After the men had turned in on the evening of the second day, the freezing wind mounted to a shriek. The snow whipped against the thin tents, then covered them over. The blizzard lasted five days. The men had no choice but to stay in their sleeping bags and hope the 90-mile-an-hour winds would not blow away the tents. They ate when they got hungry and passed time by talking to the base over the radio. Aside from the death of one husky, the party came through in fine shape.

Ronne and his men lived through the blizzard in fair comfort because the expedition had brought only the finest equipment. The effective clothing, tents and sleeping bags had evolved from the experiences, sometimes unpleasant, of earlier expeditions. Polar explorers often found that clothing and tents which looked warm and sturdy in the United States turned out to be worthless against the Antarctic's relentless cold. Ronne himself had been the victim of poorly designed gear, and out of his own experience he helped to design many of the items used by his own expedition: the ski boots, for example, were made to his specifications.

Snug in his blizzard-bound tent, Ronne recalled an earlier expedition made unforgettable by faulty equipment—the Second Byrd Expedition. In March, 1934, Ronne and several other men were sent out on a sled trip to set up Byrd's advance camp. Ronne, the ski expert, led the party. He recalls trying to read the compass with the icy wind howling in his face. After fighting the freezing wind all day, Ronne could still find no comfort at night. Because the zipper of his sleeping bag had broken, he had to sleep in his parka. But he still shivered. Not alone, however. "Everyone suffered on that sled trip," Ronne says. "Our food was inadequate, our sleeping bags not right. There wasn't one thing right. We froze and we suffered. When I look at a map of the Antarctic, that's what I think of—thirty days of suffering." Today, 33 years later, he still has numb spots on his nose and cheeks from the ordeal.

That experience made him think twice about another trip to the Antarctic. But the pull was too strong. "Back in civilization," Ronne says, "you think about the beautiful, glorious, bright days when you see all that magnificent scenery. No worries. A community of good friends who have congenial times together. When you're back in civilization, with all its troubles, you say, 'My God, let me see if I can't get back to the Antarctic again.' "

When the weather cleared over the plateau and the weather base was established, Ronne and three of the men started back to the base. Harries-Clichy Peterson, the physicist, and Bob Dodson, a geologist and Harvard man, remained behind to report the weather. Before Ronne left, he asked the men if they had everything they needed. Did they feel confident?

"Sure," Peterson snapped, "you're talking to a Marine."

Ronne led the party back to the base. Knowing they were going home, the dogs pulled eagerly. And on the downhill route, the trip took just 11 hours. Toward evening, clouds gathered and the sky darkened; the explorers moved, ghostlike, through the night.

Ronne planned to send back more supplies and a second shift of men to take over the tedious duties at the weather station. But foul weather grounded the planes and stymied the relief party. The weather-spotters reported that the wind was keeping them indoors also; otherwise they were well. That was the last news the radioman heard from Peterson and Dodson.

Four tense days passed. Finally the skies cleared on July 26 and Adams flew the scout plane up to the plateau and buzzed the tent. The two scientists did not appear. Unworried by the radio silence, Ronne now began to imagine the worst. That evening, while most of the men were watching a movie, Dodson lurched into the bunkhouse. He was exhausted and almost incoherent. Peterson, he said, had fallen down a crevasse. While Ronne gave orders to prepare the sledges and get the rescue equipment ready, Dodson told the story.

The day after the others left, Peterson's sleeping bag got wet and froze. Then the tent began to sag and rip. The men decided to make a run for the base. Struggling to pull the tent pegs out of the hard-packed snow, one of the men stepped on the radio. Dodson and Peterson were not concerned; they thought they knew the way back. At noon, just as the sun peeked over the horizon, they set out on skis, not even stopping to eat lunch.

Halfway down the glacier they got lost in the maze of crevasses. Gaping holes seemed to lurk everywhere. The light faded. Each man had a close call, falling halfway into a concealed crevasse. After several hours of cautious poking and dodging, they decided they had skied clear of the crevassed area. Eager to reach the base, they foolishly took off their skis—the best protection against falling into a crevasse—and walked. A few minutes later, Peterson disappeared in the snow.

Dodson yelled into the small black hole. Peterson called up for a knife and Dodson tied his to a rope and lowered it down, 120 feet. But Peterson did not take the knife. Nor did he say anything more. Frightened and cold, Dodson marked the spot with his skis and hurried off to camp.

Soon after Dodson arrived, a search party moved out of camp. They raced to the area and the men spread out, searching the rough terrain yard by yard. The temperature was 20 degrees below zero. In the beam of his searchlight, Ronne could see scores of crevasses. Just as Ronne was thinking that Dodson and Peterson should never have come through such a dangerous stretch, the first two dogs of one team broke through into a crevasse. The men pulled one back up, but the second dog twisted around, chewed through her traces and plunged down into the crevasse. Ronne feared that Peterson, too, had fallen into the crevasse.

After three hours, Dodson at last found the skis he had left behind as markers. The other men clustered around the small hole. Butson, the smallest man in the group, offered to go down after Peterson. Sitting on the edge of the crevasse, he hooked a climbing rope to his harness. Ike Schlossbach beamed a searchlight into the crevasse. Ronne looked on grimly as Butson dropped out of sight. Peterson had been in the crevasse for 12 hours.

When the Englishman had descended 110 feet, he shouted back, "Here he is! He's alive."

The men smiled as they passed down another rope. After a lot of jiggling on the lines, Butson called up, "All right, pull!"

It took eight heaves before Peterson came unstuck. He had fallen headfirst and gotten firmly wedged between the converging sides of the crevasse. To add to his misery, both arms were pinned against his body. He had resigned himself to a slow, lingering death.

Miraculously, Peterson now found himself being carried to a warm tent. Doctor McLean's examination showed that Peterson had no broken bones. But the deadened nerves in the pinned arms would take weeks to mend. Ronne could only hope that the impatient Peterson had learned his lesson: men cannot survive in the Antarctic without taking all the "tiresome precautions."

Two days later, on July 28, the weatherman sighted the sun over Adelaide Island. Spring had come to the Antarctic. Smiling through ragged beards, the men went out to see the red ball rise briefly over the horizon. The sun would stay up longer each day until, four months later, it would remain in the sky constantly.

During August and September, Ronne ordered the final preparations for the intense exploration ahead. The aviators hoisted the two planes off the *Beaumont*, attached the wings, tuned the engines, added extra fuel tanks and, after dozens of small modifications demanded by the cold, took both planes up for test flights. Soon these planes—a single-engine cargo carrier and a two-engine Beechcraft C-45—would work together with the sledge parties in the exploration and photographing of new land.

The pilots and the sledge parties would work together in other ways. The pilots would reconnoiter unknown terrain to find safe routes for the men traveling on the ground. In turn, the sledge parties would pick suitable spots along these routes for the planes to land. The sledge parties could also leave emergency supplies at scattered points in case the pilots should be forced down. Once a landing strip was selected by the sled parties, the pilots could then shuttle supplies from Stonington Island to these strips, which would function as advance bases. Working from these new bases, both the sled parties and the pilots could make further advances.

Ronne sent out the first sled party on August 30. It consisted of four men, three sleds and 2,200 pounds of carefully selected supplies—radio, hand-cranked generator, tents and food for 100 days. The party's mission was to establish two advance bases in George VI Sound, 130 miles to the south. When the geologist, Robert Nichols, and his men had completed this assignment, the planes would follow with more supplies. A snow tractor would arrive last. But the party never got more than 20 miles from Stonington Island. The four luckless and not very experienced explorers ran up against fresh snow, sludge and thin ice. At one point, one of the three dog teams broke through the sea ice, and Nichols, running to help drag them out, fell in too. After 10 unproductive days in the field, the men gave up and, more bitter than ashamed, returned to Stonington Island.

This failure forced Ronne to replot his strategy. At the same time that Ronne was drawing up new plans, the British suggested that the two expeditions combine their huskies, an offer which Ronne gladly accepted since he had lost so many of his own dogs in the distemper epidemic. With Major Pierce-Butler, Ronne made plans for two sled trips, the larger to be a joint British-American venture, officially called the Joint British-American Weddell Coast Sled Party. It left on October 9 with four men, three sleds and 27 huskies and headed east across the Palmer Peninsula and then south along the edge of the Weddell Sea ice shelf. This route would take the party along the world's last unexplored coastline.

The smaller trip would consist of just two men, Robert Nichols and Bob Dodson, the geologists and leaders of the party which had been forced to return. They rested up for two weeks, then repacked and started out again toward George VI Sound at the end of September. They particularly wanted a leisurely trip, with plenty of time for collecting rock samples. At the same time they could note the coordinates of the mountains and glaciers along their route.

Ronne could not have gone on these trips even if he had wanted to: he had to work at Stonington Island, organize the sledge parties, and be navigator on the photographic and exploration flights.

The Weddell Coast group covered 1,180 miles over the next 106 days in one of the longest sled trips ever made in the Antarctic. The men often traveled at "night" when the sun was low on the horizon and the surface more likely to be frozen. They reached their farthest point south 12 days before Christmas, 1947. When they returned at the end of January, 1948, the men described the wonders of the Antarctic landscape: the red sun brooding over the western ridges, silhouetting the icebergs and mountains; low clouds that gave off a weird blue light. They described, too, the pleasures and hardships Ronne knew so well—the camaraderie, the struggle with the dogs, the hard days of work, the fear of frostbite, the occasional plunges through the sea ice or halfway into a crevasse. Every man who made the long sled trip agreed that it was reason enough for having come to the Antarctic.

Nichols and Dodson also found on the trail the uncomplicated but arduous, even dangerous, life they sought. During a break in the stormy weather of December, Ronne flew down to visit them. On their own since the end of September, the two bearded men greeted him warmly. Tanned and hardened, they appeared fit and healthy. Nichols, the robust, diligent scientist, and Dodson, the enthusiastic Harvard graduate who had been one of the first to volunteer for the expedition, had gotten on well together. They had also filled their sled with hundreds of pounds of rock specimens. They did have some problems. At one point, when a month of bad weather grounded the supply plane, their food almost ran out. They were down to a cup of lemonade and a half-cup of seal beef each day, and their dreams focused entirely on banquets and exotic foods until the plane arrived. And Dodson had been the victim of a unique Antarctic affliction. The cold air contracted the metal of his dental fillings and they fell out, dropping into his mouth. But the two men were full of high spirits, not complaining, and they indignantly rejected Ronne's suggestion that they return with him. Hitchhike on an airplane? These veterans of the Antarctic ice kingdom would not hear of it. Like Ronne, they loved the hard life, the overwhelming landscape of white plains and mountains and the often total silence.

"We'll get back under our own power," Nichols said. But the geologists did allow Ronne to carry their rock samples back to the base on his plane.

Ronne's pilots also stayed busy, flying up, down and across Palmer Peninsula. From October through January they flew reconnaissance, photographed the country and brought supplies. The two pilots, Lassiter and Adams, logged a total of 39,000 miles in the expedition's three planes. With the aerial cameras mounted in the bottom of the two-engine Beechcraft, the aerial photographer, Bill Latady, took 14,000 pictures. These provided Ronne with an over-all view of Palmer Peninsula and the area to the south, while the sledge parties provided the latitude and longitude of the major terrain features. Ronne also took bearings on mountains and other distinctive topographical points whenever a landing was made in the field. Ronne says: "An aerial photograph may be beautiful to look at, with mountains and glaciers and water and so forth, but it is worthless for mapping purposes unless some of the features can be located in relation to accurately establish control points on the surface." From 10,000 feet the wide-angle cameras can photograph a lane 150 miles wide. Since the pictures are distorted at the horizon, they must be overlapped to make accurate maps.

By making full use of both sledge parties and aerial photography, Ronne's expedition explored and mapped more than 450,000 square miles of Antarctic territory, more than half of which had never been seen by man before. These distances and the scope of Ronne's exploration are not easy to grasp. If his main base had been New York City, he would have been sending dog teams out as far as Ohio and his planes would have been exploring down the eastern coast to Florida. An area of 450,000 square miles covers the states of New York, New

Jersey, Pennsylvania, Michigan, Ohio, Maryland, Virginia, West Virginia, North Carolina, South Carolina and Georgia. Even this great achievement, however, covered only a corner of the massive Antarctic continent. Palmer Peninsula is but a finger of land jutting off the nearly circular land mass.

On one of his last flights, Ronne and two of his men finally photographed George VI Sound and Alexander Island, the same area Ronne and Carl Eklund had explored together. The Beechcraft C-45 cruised at 10,000 feet beneath a clear blue sky. Wrapped as usual in their heavy parkas, the men craned to see the distant peaks. Ronne could remember which ones he and Eklund had camped by and which ones they had sledded around six years before.

Some 300 miles south of Stonington Island, where George VI Sound makes a right-angle turn from south to west, the Beechcraft lost radio contact with the base. Ronne knew that if the plane were grounded they would probably never be found. But he insisted on flying farther. The region beyond the Sound had never before been seen or photographed. Ronne could not pass up a chance to explore this unknown place. They flew on over the vast white plain, now called the Robert English Coast. New mountains came into sight. One of the tallest of these, 10,500 feet, subsequently named Rex Mountain by Ronne, is today a common feature on even the smallest maps of the Antarctic. Ronne wanted to land so that he could obtain accurate "fixes" of this major landmark. They all knew that a landing so far from the base, with no radio contact, was dangerous. But Ronne was willing to take the chance. The plane glided gently down onto the deep snow.

Despite the bright sunshine and the peacefulness of the setting, the men were uneasy. "From the air," Ronne recalls, "we had commanded a wonderful view over hundreds of miles of unknown territory. On the ground, however, we were merely specks in the middle of a vast whiteness, over 500 miles from any other human being. It was a lonely feeling. With only the softly coughing engines of the airplane for sound and the suggestion of a mountain in the distance to break the monotony of the plain, I don't believe I ever felt so helpless in my life." The moment Ronne had taken a "sighting" on Rex Mountain, he hurried back inside and the plane lifted away from the snow, the three men all feeling the same sense of escape.

In naming newly discovered spots, such as Rex Mountain, Ronne used the names of expedition members and financial backers, all of whom can now find their names somewhere on a map of the Antarctic. In all, Ronne named 120 new features—mountains, glaciers, capes and shorelines. He suggested his wife's name for an area the size of Texas—Edith Ronne Land (now called Ronne Ice Shelf).

Flying home from Rex Mountain, Ronne encountered a heavy overcast 100 miles from Stonington Island. At the same time the base radioman announced, "Visibility zero in twenty minutes." Weather in the Antarctic is almost totally unpredictable. A blizzard can come from nowhere. The pilot, an Air Force officer named Jim Lassiter, went down to 3,000 feet, beneath the thick clouds. There he could see land. Over the radio they heard warnings that the winds would increase to 80 miles an hour. The dark mass of clouds settled lower and lower on the land. Still 50 miles from base, they had to come down to 400 feet and then to 200 feet as the weather closed in. But Lassiter said that he knew the way. Skimming along close to the half-frozen waters of Marguerite Bay, he dodged icebergs and banked away from cliffs. A sudden down-draft caught them and the plane dropped to within 50 feet of the dark slush. Ronne's plotting board, resting on his knees, jumped up in his face as the plane fell. Ronne thought that his good fortune had ended at last. But Lassiter remained cool and pulled the plane up short of a plunge into the bay. Finally he sighted solid ice and brought the plane down only four miles from the base.

The radioman had thought he might have to call for a rescue squad. Instead, he sent for a tractor which would tow the Beechcraft back to camp. The 70-mile-an-hour winds made this job rough going. Two men had to lie on each wing to keep the plane from flying into the air like a kite. Ronne found himself thinking that while mechanized exploration was more comfortable than dog sleds, it presented more opportunities to get hurt.

By January 1, 1948, the Ronne Research Expedition had run out of objectives. They had explored nearly half a million square miles of land. Now there wasn't an unknown square mile within 1,200 miles of Stonington Island. In addition, the expedition's scientists were completing their comprehensive, year-long study of the Antarctic. For the next seven weeks the men dismantled and packed away equipment as soon as it was no longer needed and moved supplies aboard the ship. By January 22 the last sled party, the Weddell Coast group, had returned. Now, even though most of the men spoke enthusiastically about coming back to the Antarctic someday, they were also wondering what they had missed back in the civilized world.

The weather almost prevented anybody from finding out. Contrary to Ronne's expectations, the ice in Marguerite Bay never quite melted. As February came, bringing the Antarctic's warmest weather, the ice stayed several feet thick. The men began to worry that they might have to spend another winter at the base. Ronne would not have minded in the least. But he let some of the men experiment with dynamite to see if the expedition could blast its way out. It could; but this would take time.

Then, on February 11, the radioman received a message from a United States Navy icebreaker. The captain, an old friend of Ronne, wanted to pay a visit. Reluctant to leave before a full 365 days were up, Ronne felt he must take the ice-breaker's help while it was available. When the men heard that an icebreaker was on its way, their faces showed how eager they were to return home. Then the sleek gray Navy ship churned up alongside the dowdy *Beaumont,* and the explorers had a look at the clean-cut sailors with their creased parkas and cameras. Civilization had come to the Antarctic. At that moment many of the men began to feel nostalgic about the year that had passed.

On February 23, 1948, the *Beaumont* steamed north, away from Stonington Island, in the jagged wake of the icebreaker. Soon the Antarctic's high cliffs fell below the horizon. Ronne did not regret leaving. He knew he would return.

After the 1947–1948 expedition, Ronne did return to the Antarctic five more times. Promoted to the rank of captain in the Navy, he was military commander at Ellsworth Station during the International Geophysical Year (IGY) Program in 1956–1958. In 1961 he was invited by the Chief of Naval Operations, Admiral Arleigh Burke, to the Antarctic to take part in the celebration of the 50th anniversary of Amundsen's expedition in December, 1911. But he was never again in command of his own expedition. "The government has taken over," Ronne says. The extent of this "take-over" is illustrated by the fact that the United States is currently spending $27 million each year in the Antarctic. Helicopters and snow trac-tors with electronic crevasse detectors have replaced dog sleds. Government-organized or government-sponsored expeditions, composed of thousands of sailors and other servicemen, now make Ronne a part of the Model "T" age of polar exploration. Exploring the Antarctic has become something a man does not tackle on his own.

Now 68, retired from the Navy and living in Washington, D.C., Captain Finn Ronne has probably spent as much time in the Arctic and Antarctic as any man who ever explored these regions. On his eight Antarctic expeditions, he lived there for a total of six years, longer than any other man, and he lived in the Arctic for 12 months in all on his four trips to that region. Ronne would love to go back. After all, 25 percent of the Antarctic is still unknown—the last major unexplored territory in the world. But he has outlived an age. Now he must sit back and watch other men carry on. He does find satisfaction in knowing that his work smoothed the way for them. The pioneering old explorers had to do it the hard way. And, as Finn Ronne says, "I am the last of them."

three

The Manners of Monkeys

C LARENCE RAY CARPENTER is a professor of psychology and anthropology at Pennsylvania State University in University Park, Pennsylvania. He teaches primatology to graduate students, devoting a good deal of his lecture time to explaining how to make field studies of monkeys and apes.

At 63, Carpenter is a large man with a full face and gray hair combed straight back. I imagine that in his youth, in North Carolina, he would have been described as "strapping." He grew up as a farm boy, and he still has a country flavor: he moves and talks slowly, and has a rural courtliness, disposing him, in conversation, to let the other person have his say.

When he talks he is serious, not in a pedantic way, but in his earnest attempt to cover the subject. He says of his teaching: "I don't lecture, I just talk." Sometimes he speaks in the jargon of the scientist, but his studies are as free of "academese" as any scientific reports ever written.

When he is not at the university, Carpenter often works in the garden and woodland surrounding his modern home. As a hobby he makes wine from the grapes he grows, adding imported pure culture yeasts. His other hobbies are photography, golf and squash. He was a lieutenant colonel in the Air Force Reserve, and is currently on an awesome number of commissions and media boards, serving, for example, as a member of the Board of Advisors for Media Programs of the United States Office of Education, and a member of a special Presidential Commission for Instructional Broadcasting. He is a director of the State College Federal Savings and Loan Association and also does a good deal of work as a consultant for educational technology companies.

In contrast to this well-ordered existence, Ray Carpenter has also been involved in more exotic pursuits. At various times since 1930 he has left the university classroom and laboratory and journeyed to such places as Japan, Thailand, India, Sumatra, the Panama Canal Zone and the small Caribbean island of Santiago, where, for months at a time, he has devoted himself to the passionate and sustained study of the natural behavior of monkeys. Trekking through forests, climbing trees, hiding in blinds with field glasses ready, he has spent his days stalking such species of primates as the howler, the spider and the rhesus monkeys and the small anthropoid, the gibbon. The results of these observing expeditions have established him as one of the world's most brilliant primatologists, a pioneer in the field whose own studies are of immense value and whose work has stimulated other scientists to follow his trail-breaking example.

Earlier primatologists tended to be specialists in small areas, working in the laboratory and confining their interest solely to an animal's appearance or its skeleton or its parasites or its diseases or its reproductive system. Until Carpenter came along, no one had crossed these boundary lines or attempted to learn everything possible about a species in the environment where it developed.

Carpenter did just that. He was particularly interested in behavior and he formulated an approach which would allow him, by observation of a species in its natural setting, to gather information about the animal's ecology, behavior and social relations. His formula had five basic elements: (1) systematic observation and reporting, (2) of all behavior, (3) of a large number of animals (rather than one or two in the laboratory), (4) in the wild, (5) over a considerable period of time. He insisted on the natural setting because he felt that many kinds of behavior in the species would be distorted or suppressed in the laboratory or zoo. His aim was to obtain a complete picture of how the animal acted when living alone in his chosen, undisturbed habitat.

Carpenter started his monkey-watching career on December 25, 1931, on Barro Colorado, an island in Gatun Lake in the interior of the Panama Canal Zone. Fresh from Stanford University graduate school, where he had completed work for a Doctor of Philosophy degree, Carpenter spent six months observing howler monkeys—large, bearded monkeys with prehensile tails, given to uttering loud roars and howls (the obvious source of their name). In his report on the Panama study, Carpenter described aspects of the howlers never before recorded. He had made detailed observations of their hands; their manner of fighting; their territoriality; the extent and speed of their wandering, their social organization; their behavior within groups; the relations between different groups of howlers; and the behavior of howlers toward other species. Carpenter remembers that the four other primate specialists, on a joint expedition to the Rio La Vaca area in northern Panama, looked askance at his observational approach. "These distinguished gentlemen felt that it was kind of spurious to have a behaviorist in camp—perhaps a throwback to the methods and interests of the naturalists of the 1860s and 1870s," Carpenter recalls.

Very quietly, Carpenter's Panama study made history. A recent book, *Primate Behavior*, a collection of essays on behavioral anthropology by eminent men in the field, is dedicated to Carpenter. Its editor, Irven DeVore, declares that "virtually nothing systematic was known about the natural behavior of a single monkey or ape until Clarence Ray Carpenter began his study of the howler monkey of Panama in 1931." Carpenter's report, in fact, told man more about the howler monkey than he knew about any other species besides himself.

Carpenter's work in Panama had its direct antecedents in work he did while he was acquiring his advanced degrees. At Duke University, working on his master's degree, Carpenter raised a loft of pigeons. He watched them continually, trying to describe and test patterns of monogamy. When he went to Stanford to work on his Ph.D., Carpenter stepped up his pigeon-watching. At Stanford he had about 100 pigeons in study cages. He wanted to discover whether there was any relationship between a pigeon's behavior and the amount of male sex hormones in its blood stream. For more than a year he spent three hours every day watching his pigeons—ideal training in the observational skills needed for his study of monkeys.

Carpenter was not planning ahead for the Panama trip when he began to work with pigeons. He was simply interested in their behavior, which prompted him to put in long hours observing them. After he had finished his studies at Stanford, he became involved, almost accidentally, with the Yale Laboratory of Comparative Psychobiology, and this organization actually assigned him to do the study of the howler monkey. But, as Carpenter says, his experience with the pigeons meant that he was "well prepared" for the kind of work he did in Panama.

Carpenter's earlier life may provide further insight into why he should have produced pioneering animal studies requiring years of patient work. He grew up on a farm in Lincoln County, North Carolina, where his family raised dairy cattle, poultry, grains and cotton. There was no surplus of money, and as Carpenter says, he "grew vegetables" to get money to go to college. Besides accustoming himself to hard work, Carpenter learned to approach animals in a straightforward, realistic way. This disposition gave him an advantage over many scientists working in the area of animal behavior. And he always loved the outdoors. "Most farm boys hate it," he explains, "but I would still be there if I hadn't felt an urge to know more, to learn, to become a teacher."

Intrigued by his Panama field work on howlers and its results, Carpenter went on to study the spider monkey, also in Panama. Next, in 1934, he did a study of two captive mountain gorillas at the San Diego Zoo. Normally averse to observing animals removed from their wild condition, Carpenter judged that a study in his comprehensive style on the only two mountain gorillas in captivity could still yield valuable information and prepare for a field study of this magnificent anthropoid. Then, in 1937, Carpenter went to Southeast Asia to study the orangutan and the gibbon, and, incidentally, the elephants and rhinoceroses in The Atjeh of Sumatra. In 1938, he traveled to India to collect 100 rhesus monkeys, which he transported to Santiago Island off Puerto Rico. He regards this experiment as his most productive, since it created a colony that still thrives. Through 1938 and 1939 he made continual observations of this colony, which was also used for various medical experiments and for wartime research.

In the early 1950s Japanese scientists who had read about the Santiago Island experiment recognized the value of their own 400 monkey colonies scattered throughout Japan's islands. The Japanese are, in fact, today's most industrious primatologists. Their response to Carpenter's experiment helped spark the strong current interest in non-human primates. At an earlier date, however, the Japanese army, marching across Sumatra in 1940, had halted Carpenter's plans to conduct a study of the orangutan there. World War II and Carpenter's induction into the Air Force, where he wrote jungle survival manuals and helped operate Army universities, diverted him from wild monkeys. After the war, though he was still concerned with primate research, he shifted his energies from the field to the classroom.

Looking back over his many expeditions, Carpenter regards as his most fascinating experience the six months he spent in Thailand in 1937 studying gibbons. Gibbons, Carpenter declares, are the most charming species of ape. And the backdrop for this highly successful scientific venture was a storybook one of Buddhist temples and opium runners.

As co-leader of the six-man Asiatic Primate Expedition (APE) and only member of the Behavior Research Division, Carpenter arrived in Singapore aboard a steamer early in 1937. He and the expedition's other scientists watched nervously as the natives unloaded their tons of supplies and transshipped them by train to Bangkok, the ancient, sprawling city of 1,000,000 people that is dominated by scores of temples and is a favorite holiday spot in the Far East. Here their equipment was transferred again to the Royal Siamese Railroad for the 150-mile trip to Chiengmai near the Thailand hill country. In Chiengmai, medical and educational missionaries helped the expedition get oriented. The scientists told the residents that they were looking for wild gibbons and asked for suggestions. They then made side trips to check a few recommended spots. Finally, however, they chose as the most promising location one they hadn't investigated. Chiengmai was at the end of the railroad line, so they had to load their gear onto buses for the 50-mile ride to the end of the road toward Doi Intanon, a 7,000-foot mountain. The scientists hired 70 porters to carry their equipment another 12 miles up the mountain. Here they established the Main Camp.

Most of the men on the Asiatic Primate Expedition had come to collect specimens and skeletons of various primates. Carpenter wanted only to observe gibbons. He moved two miles farther along the trail, 500 feet higher up the mountain, and made a second camp. In a naturalist's paradise, a beautiful valley forest with bears, deer and hundreds of birds flying around, and with the cries of gibbons filling the air, Carpenter pitched his tent. "It was exciting," Carpenter remembers. "I was very anxious to get in there and go to work."

Carpenter was up each morning with the sun to observe gibbons. Wearing khakis, boots and a sun helmet, Carpenter had two pairs of field glasses around his neck; a watch and a compass on his wrists; a camera slung over his shoulder; a pack containing first-aid kit, snake bite antidote and sandwiches on his belt; a .38 pistol on his hip; notebooks and pencils in his pocket and a machete in his hand. Thus equipped, he was ready to make the forest his laboratory.

The object of Carpenter's curiosity was the hairy, relatively small (15 pounds), rather man-like ape, the *Hylobates Lar*. Gibbons have thin bodies, long arms that touch the ground when they stand up and no tails. Two to three feet tall, they are black, gray or buff-colored, according to the species, and are found in Thailand, Sumatra, Burma, Malaya, Borneo and the Himalayas. Carpenter calls gibbons "beautiful animals, the most interesting I've studied, including the gorilla and the chimpanzee." They are included in the select group of higher primates—the great apes, the gibbons and man. Like men, they have no special breeding period and a wide range of facial expressions, from mild to vicious. Gibbons sometimes "smile" and greet each other with an embrace and a faint little squeal. Gibbons live almost exclusively in treetops, swinging with wondrous dexterity from branch to branch. "Their movements through the trees are awe-inspiring," Carpenter says. "When they really take off, their speed is fantastic and they may make jumps of 50 or 60 feet." Fully 90 percent of the time gibbons travel by swinging (scientists describe this as "brachiating"). Sometimes they rest by hanging from a branch with one hand. They often sit or stand with their trunk almost erect. The old ones who are in their thirties age like humans—their skin wrinkles, their mouths sag and usually their teeth are chipped. They make excellent pets, if trained when young.

Not even these basic facts about the gibbon were known before Carpenter went to Thailand. This ignorance is peculiar, yet revealing. Why should scientists have avoided studying man's primate cousins? The answer, it would seem, lies in the gibbon's similarity to humans. "It's almost as if man were embarrassed to study them," Carpenter points out. "We knew a lot more about insects than about primates. We didn't want to realize the relevance of primate studies to human behavior. There's also another reason. The evolutionary controversy comes in here. We have religious opposition to the concept of evolution, and this inhibited the study of primates as contrasted with the study of safer animals like insects or birds. Man sometimes appears to fear what he might learn. Watch people at the zoo looking at monkeys. I think people are somewhat am-

biguous here. If you mention a monkey to a man he wants to laugh. His laughter serves to cover up his embarrassment because the monkey exhibits a lot of human-like behavior. These are similarities which are embarrassing to the human."

For these reasons, science in the early 1930s knew very little about nonhuman primates. In preparation for his expeditions, Carpenter made a list of missing information about primates, reading dozens of books and noting every aspect of their life that was unknown or controversial. The long list that resulted guided and drove him on his expeditions. Do they have territory? Do they migrate? If not, why not? Do they live in groups? What is the composition of the group? Do they have mating seasons or not? How do they reproduce? Do they cooperate, that is, help one another, work together? Do they have anything like tools? Who are their enemies? What is their life span? Do the young have distinctive patterns of behavior? How do the mothers raise the young? Do young and old play? What kind of play? What is the function of play? Why do animals stay together in groups? How many males and females are there in a group? Are there solitary males? Do they have dominance, as in certain other animals? Do they fight? Why do they fight? What do they fight over? Is there competition for receptive females? What kind of food do they eat? Do they eat any meat? How do they get protein food? How do they protect themselves from weather? These and hundreds of other questions, Carpenter noted, needed answering.

"You can't predict when you will get the answers to questions like these," Carpenter says. "So you just continue to work hard and constantly. You know you'll *never* find all of the answers."

Part of Carpenter's genius was that he went to Panama and later to Thailand with many questions and an open mind—

nothing else. "I didn't have any preconceived hypothesis. I didn't set out to prove anything. I went there almost like a tape recorder, prepared to observe and to record what was there, then write it up and make limited interpretations."

But the gibbons in the forests of Doi Intanon refused to co-operate. For the first two weeks Carpenter's questions went unanswered. He had as a guide an elderly member of the Karen tribe, very unexpressive and perhaps mentally retarded. He came from a dark, shy hill people who dressed colorfully, wore silver necklaces and raised opium as a cash crop. Carpenter and his guide communicated solely through gestures. Gibbon calls echoed through the thick trees, but Carpenter could not seem to get close to the animals. "Time and again," he wrote in his report, "I pushed hurriedly but cautiously through the forest toward the place from which I could hear gibbons calling, only to arrive and get just a glimpse of the apes as they disappeared among swaying leaves and branches." And Carpenter was a man with long experience in stalking monkeys. He knew the importance of moving slowly and deliberately. He had developed special observational skills: walking cautiously; raising hands slowly; use of concealment. But the gibbons swinging through the trees of the Doi Intanon valley were more than a match for Carpenter. They quickly demonstrated one fact about themselves: their eyes and ears are much better than man's. Carpenter found that he sometimes disturbed them at distances of 300 yards. Even when Carpenter thought that he had been very clever, he would look through field glasses only to find the gibbons staring back and then bounding off. "I heard gibbons all around me and I saw limbs trembling," Carpenter says. "Two or three times I got glimpses of gibbons. This was rough. I always knew there was a possibility that the animals would somehow completely avoid me. I became pretty frantic. 'Okay,' I said after a few weeks of frustration, 'I can't study these gibbons. They are here but I can't see them. They are completely wild and afraid of men because hunters have shot at them. Only another gibbon could get close to them.' "

Carpenter grimly acknowledged that the situation at Doi Intanon was hopeless. He realized that he might go home empty-handed and a failure. But he wasn't ready to abandon his basic premise—gibbons, he still insisted, could be studied in the wild—somewhere. He decided to move his camp 70 miles northeast to another mountain-village-temple, Doi Dao. Here he was more successful than he had dared hope.

This success pointed up one fact: the selection of an area for study was more crucial than Carpenter had thought. Doi Intanon, from all reports, had sounded ideal. Actually it was too wild. Doi Dao, on the other hand, was not so far removed from people. There were a few villages and a few hundred Thais about. More important, there was a Buddhist temple and a priest. The Buddhist ethics that forbade the killing of animals was respected by the Thai people. Unlike their cousins at Doi Intanon, the gibbons around Doi Dao had not learned to avoid men as the wild ones did. They were certainly not friendly. But they were not so tense and excitable as those at Doi Intanon and could, with skill, be studied.

In addition to gibbons conditioned to humans, Doi Dao also offered a travel-poster setting for Carpenter's second camp. Doi Dao is a great jutting rock of a mountain, densely covered by forest. During the dry season, which lasts into April, the mountain and the nearby fields are hazed over with smoke from trees burnt by the farmers to clear the land. Doi Dao has an underground stream, a clear spring at its base and large caves which are sacred to the Buddhists. The neophyte priests came to the mountain to spend their "forty days in the wilderness," and pilgrims came too, even from as far away as Bangkok to visit the holy temple at the foot of the mountain. Every day the temple priests chanted, sometimes for hours at a time. It was on the temple grounds, in an open guest house, that Carpenter established his second camp. He was, in fact, a guest of the temple. Gibbons could be heard all around.

Carpenter quickly discovered that the countryside around Doi Dao possessed assets more important to him than its beauty. It was made to order for field studies, with rice fields carved out of thick forest, and bamboo groves scattered throughout. The cultivated areas of rice alternated with vertical walls of forest, so that an observer could look into the forest world of the gibbon. Furthermore, the ground was often uneven. From the valleys, cliffs rose higher than the trees below. Stationed on these cliffs, Carpenter had an excellent view of the gibbons in the treetops. The area was crisscrossed by paths, which simplified Carpenter's treks. The gibbons' food and water tended to be concentrated in a limited area, which made their movements more predictable. Yet Doi Dao's great virtues were the area's sanctity, which had protected the gibbons from hunters, and the presence of people, which had conditioned them to the sight of man.

Living in the priests' guest house, which had a concrete floor and a roof but no walls, Carpenter set to work. He had to hire three of the natives to take care of the camp. There is a strict caste system in Thailand, and under its code, Carpenter had to have three servants: a cook, a coolie and a first boy. "The first boy," Carpenter remembers with some amusement, "can't do the cooking. The cook can't clean house. And neither the cook nor the first boy can carry away the garbage." The three natives brought their mattresses and built lean-tos close to

Carpenter's shed. Beyond the camp, Carpenter preferred to work alone. Here he did not need a guide as at Doi Intanon.

Now, at long last, Carpenter was ready to study the gibbon. On the first day, March 23, he managed to get within 30 feet of a group of gibbons. "After weeks of frustration, this was pretty exciting," Carpenter says. The gibbons he found lived in trees at the foot of cliffs only a hundred yards from Carpenter's camp. They lazed in the treetops, eating fruit, grooming themselves and each other, stretching, looking about (which behaviorists call "exploratory activity"). If Carpenter got too close, they gave various alarm calls and swung away quickly.

Carpenter designated these gibbons Group 1. He soon discovered that Group 1 consisted of an adult male, an adult female with a baby and two teen-agers. (Gibbon sex is very difficult to determine at a distance because the skeletons of the male and female are identical and the average size is about the same.) There were obviously other gibbons in the vicinity but Group 1 kept to itself. Carpenter began to conjecture what he eventually confirmed: gibbons, like most humans, live in families. Previously scientists thought that gibbons, like many other monkeys, either roamed in herds or grouped themselves in the harem system of the baboons. But no, the gibbons have settled on a very civilized arrangement. As the young gibbons near maturity they begin to take an interest in the young adults of other groups. There is usually some visiting or courting, and eventually a young couple will split away from the parent groups, forming a new family. By the time he ended his study, Carpenter was observing 21 families—about 75 gibbons. Always the family groups had one adult male, one adult female and from none to four children. Rarely was there an extra young female or old animal in the group.

To make his observations, Carpenter spent 90 consecutive

days studying gibbons constantly. Obviously, he needed patience. "Field observation taxes the observer's capacities to the limits," Carpenter notes. "But it's marvelous training and I think it should be part of every scientist's background, whether he ends up in the laboratory or not."

Carpenter's trailing and observing lasted from sun-up to sunset every day, and the course of his day was shaped by what the gibbons were likely to be doing at any given hour. By the end of his study, Carpenter had recorded their day in great detail. They awoke in their lofty perches at 5:30 A.M. and stretched for an hour. For almost two hours after that the groups would exchange calls. These morning calls apparently served to announce their presence to other groups of gibbons. Calls and hoots reverberated back and forth between all the groups. Carpenter would often plot the calls and establish the location and sometimes the identity of different groups.

A little after 7:30 the animals started traveling, a kind of morning stroll in which they move from tree to tree. Carpenter calls this "group progression." Carpenter furtively followed along on the ground, or moved ahead to hide in a blind near where he thought the gibbons would settle for their morning meal. At 9 o'clock the gibbons stopped their progression and, for the next two hours, ate breakfast. Their diet was of great interest to Carpenter. He carefully noted the food, mostly fruit, that they preferred. After they had thoroughly stuffed themselves, the gibbons moved to other trees. Finally, at noon, they quieted down for a midday siesta, which often lasted three hours. Only the youngsters moved around much during this siesta period.

Carpenter got good views of some gibbons through his field glasses. For better observation, he arranged several simple blinds on the cliffs overlooking Group 1's forest range, near ponds and favorite fruit trees. Once a family came within 30 feet of one of his lairs. At that distance, the gibbons completely filled the field of his binoculars. "What a thrill after my experience at Doi Intanon," wrote Carpenter, with something less than the cold detachment usually ascribed to scientists. Outside the blinds Carpenter often found himself in unorthodox positions. Sometimes he would be duck-walking through bamboo, other times lying on his back beneath a tree full of gibbons, or perhaps sitting high in a tree himself.

Carpenter believes that the observer's skills and behavior are the most crucial elements, aside from the location, for a successful study of free-ranging primates. "An untrained observer may not see anything, or he may frighten the animals. Quick motions are frightening. Slow, deliberate movements are not. Being partly concealed works well. Learning how to use cover, moving quietly through the forest—these are needed skills. An observer must move slowly, particularly when he tries to get close to a group. The field glasses should be raised slowly. The general strategy is be there but don't disturb the animals. Adjust to them."

Occasionally Carpenter went out with a 35-mm. reflex or 16-mm. movie camera. He always carried them ready to shoot. He rested the movie camera on his shoulder, with the tripod along his chest. He could extend and position the legs, focus and adjust the diaphragm and press the button, all in 30 seconds. This, too, must be done silently and without attracting and disturbing the gibbon.

As for animals that might be stalking Carpenter while he was stalking the gibbons, they turned out to be rather small and unimportant. "I didn't worry about the large animals that are popularly thought to be dangerous, such as snakes and predators. It was the darned insects. This is one of the tough parts. Some seasons they're awfully annoying. Swatting them tends to interfere with observations. In Barro Colorado Island it was ticks, bedbugs and mosquitoes. These insects come up your pants leg. I've still got scars around my waist from bugs of various kinds. They come up and stop under your belt. I think the seed tick is the nastiest thing. You may go out in the morning with a clean suit of clothes and then around 9 o'clock you run into a nest of them. It breaks open and they spray over your clothes—dozens of them. They're very difficult to get off. In Thailand it was the sweat bee. They collect around your eyes and nose and mouth. They don't leave when you swat at them. You have to actually rub them out of your eyes where they collect and feed on the moisture."

Unfortunately for Carpenter, effective insect repellents were not produced until World War II. During his field trips, insects were one more test of his patience. One day he sat down on a nest of what he described as "malicious wasps." "Observations," he noted in his report, "were concluded for the day."

Man-eating beasts were no problem, but Carpenter's work was dangerous for other reasons. As Carpenter says: "I have been in situations where if I had broken my leg nobody would ever have found me. I might have been only four or five miles away but this is tropical forest. I couldn't tell anybody where I was going because I didn't know. Gibbons determined the course of travel and I was alone. Fortunately I got by with it. But I wouldn't recommend working alone to anyone else."

Carpenter recommends a two-man team as the ideal observing unit, and the men should be equipped with walkie-talkies so they can work up to 500 yards apart. One man could rescue the other if necessary, and they could corroborate each other's observations. This is important because observations when first made are seldom clear-cut and conclusive. As any courtroom trial shows, the same event can be witnessed and interpreted in many different ways. Carpenter always tried to resist the impulse to make absolute conclusions from a few observations. He filled his notebooks and then made "limited interpretations." Field observers have to be especially careful of what is called the "single dramatic incident"—a striking but fortuitous and atypical occurrence. Carpenter, for example, once saw gibbons in a nest and was excited about the possibility that gibbons build and use nests. Carpenter noted the observation, later examined the nest closely and saw that it was a bear's nest. His cautiously-arrived-at conclusion was that gibbons do not build nests themselves, but they do sometimes rest or play in deserted bear nests.

While the gibbons slumbered through their long midday siesta, Carpenter wrote in his notebooks and ate his lunch, consisting of a sandwich or peanuts and raisins. After the gibbons were well rested, they traveled some more and ate some more. If it rained they all stopped, hunched over in a furry ball and waited until the rain passed. At about 5 o'clock in the afternoon, the gibbons started moving toward where they would spend the night. During the day they had covered perhaps 1,000 yards. Although not nest-builders like all the other non-human primates, the gibbons do have favorite trees, usually dense and protected from the wind. Having picked a tree, the gibbon family settled for the night. As the sun set, Carpenter would see them curling up or even stretching out on their backs for the night. When the light faded and the gibbons went to sleep, Carpenter's long day was also over.

Although Carpenter was doing what he liked best, he does not hesitate to say that field studies "can become pretty hard work." Having cast himself as a relentless recorder, Carpenter had to stay stubbornly at the job. He never gave himself a day off. "One can't just go out and sit a few days and shoot a couple of animals and come back and write the natural history of that animal," Carpenter says. "One must literally live with them for months at a stretch."

On the fourth day of his first week at Doi Dao, Carpenter found his second family of gibbons. He wrote: "I had climbed into Observation Post No. 5 anticipating the approach of Group 1, which I had just seen in the valley. To my left I heard the clank of bamboo, a sound produced by animals jumping from one stalk to another and making the swaying stalks strike together. Turning, I saw a buff-colored gibbon of adult size. A few minutes later, the whole of the group [designated by Carpenter as Group 2] came into view in the following order: buff male, buff female, buff young juvenile, and black young juvenile. I could see them all very clearly."

As the weeks passed and Carpenter learned his way around the woods, he found more and more new groups until he eventually had 21 under observation. In April—the month when spring rains erased the smoke that had lasted since February—Carpenter began to realize that each group or family had its own territory. Group 1, he noted, always stayed within a certain sector of the forest. Group 2 stayed in a different sector, and so did all the other groups. Each territory averaged about 60 acres and had rough, overlapping boundaries. But each family knew when another family was intruding in its territory. Then the calling, and possibly fighting, began. Territory, Carpenter learned, is always affecting the gibbon's behavior.

Carpenter's discovery and analysis of territoriality were a major contribution. Scientists had already found that some birds, fish and reptiles show territorial behavior during their breeding seasons. The male trout, for example, will defend a certain area of the bottom, in which one or more females may then lay eggs. The concept of territoriality for mating was well formulated before Carpenter began his work. But after months among the gibbons and other monkeys, Carpenter saw that territoriality did not occur as sporadic, seasonal behavior. On the contrary, a gibbon group displayed a constant, lifelong concern for their territory and guarded it from other gibbon groups.

Carpenter often watched gibbon families protecting their territory in the strips of forest between their respective territories. Hanging and sitting about 25 yards apart, they indulged in "vocal battles," uttering calls, shouts and high-pitched notes. After they had finished threatening each other, the groups edged closer, moved awkwardly, mumbled and after a few minutes separated. Such a confrontation, Carpenter noted, would be "a favorable situation for fighting between groups, and I have no doubt that fighting does occur." The gibbon families, in other words, acted like primitive warriors or street gangs who confront one another, talk tough, look each other over and then either fight or part with under-the-breath curses.

Carpenter had seen captive gibbons engage in short, vicious battles. But in the wild there was little fighting, except perhaps when young adults were splitting off and looking over other groups. Typically the male drives away intruding males.

The gibbons appeared to reserve whatever pugnacity they possessed entirely for their own species. They do not fight with any other animals. And Carpenter saw gibbons and other species of monkeys eating together in the same trees. The gibbons would never have tolerated strangers of their own species.

But even among gibbons, the "fighting" comes down to mostly talk, or, more exactly, screeching. These vocal battles became even more tense when there was something more than territory to fight over, such as food or water. Many times Carpenter saw one group marauding on another's territory. The home group would immediately become very excited and race out to ward off the intruders. The group always stuck together in a kind of mutual-defense pact. The invaders, having seized a few grapes, usually retreated. Carpenter discovered a very interesting fact: the family that won these encounters was inevitably the one nearest the focus of its own territory. In human societies also, the home team is always considered the likely winner in an otherwise equal contest.

The gibbons resented Carpenter's intrusions into their territories. Sometimes they immediately fled. But on many occasions they shrieked their indignation and rage from the high treetops down at the unwelcome visitor. More dramatically, they broke off branches and dropped or threw them at Carpenter. The meaning of this gibbon behavior is a controversial subject. Some scientists apparently do not wish to credit gibbons with enough intelligence to think of using an object as a weapon. Carpenter's impression was that the branch-throwing gibbons decidedly were aiming at him. Carpenter dodged their missiles, and the gibbons never managed to hit him. "You just have to outsmart them," Carpenter says, complimenting the gibbons' intelligence.

The concept of territoriality has itself become controversial, at least as applied to human behavior. In *The Territorial Imperative*, Robert Ardrey, paying repeated tributes to Carpenter's findings, maintains that men occupy, defend and view their property and country just as gibbons and many other animals do. He feels that we could better understand ourselves if we would face the fact that much of our behavior, including our commitment to territoriality, is rooted in our dim evolutionary past. Ardrey suggests, for example, that when the Japanese bombed Pearl Harbor in 1941, they totally misunderstood the elemental passions that are unleashed when one nation trespasses on another's territory. Japan thought that America was lethargic, isolationist and divided, and we were—until the foreign intruder galvanized us into united action. In the same manner, Ardrey believes that territoriality accounts for the difficulty America has experienced in Vietnam.

Carpenter himself has never tried to apply his conclusions about gibbons and howlers so directly to humans. But he has always assumed that such connections may be possible. A chief motive for his work, in fact, was the realization that since man and monkey are evolutionary cousins, knowledge of monkeys might provide insights into human behavior and social interaction. In the introduction to his study of gibbons, Carpenter notes that, since man and the higher primates have physical similarities, they probably also share emotional and behavioral traits.

Dominance, another of the concepts which Carpenter helped formulate for primates, ties in with territoriality. The dominant group is the one which can control and defend the largest territory. Although gibbon territories are normally equivalent, Group 2 dominated 50 acres while Group 3 often ruled over 100 acres.

Group dominance does not depend, as one might expect, on the group's number and the strength of its members. Rather, a group's power depends primarily on the forcefulness of its strongest, most dominant member. The difference in dominance is not so great among individuals or groups of gibbons, but among other animals Carpenter studied, especially the macaques, the degree of dominance varies greatly from one group to another and among individuals within each group.

For example, Carpenter did experiments with macaques on Santiago. When he had charted a group's structure and defined its most dominant member, he captured the leader, "Diablo." Then he observed the group for a week. Previously, the group roamed the whole island. Now, as the Number 1, 2 and 3 dominant males were removed, it gradually reduced its range to a small coconut grove. Without its three most dominant leaders, the group's power declined enormously. Territoriality and individual dominance, as this experiment showed, are very definitely related, since dominance helps to determine a group's range.

Within each group there is a scale of dominance. The leader is the most dominant and the rest of the animals rate below him. The more dominant animals have more rights and privileges than the less dominant ones. The parallel among chickens is the so-called "pecking order." Since gibbons live in small families, dominance does not operate so strongly among them as it does among the monkeys that group themselves in large herds. The degree of dominance possessed by a member of the gibbon family roughly corresponds to its age, as is generally the case in human families. Carpenter made the interesting discovery that the gibbon male and female are about equal in dominance. The male will rush out to face a threat, but the female will often lead the family on its travels through the trees.

Each day at Doi Dao Carpenter learned something about the gibbon. Exhilarated at his success, he had the further pleasure of enjoying immensely the comforts of his camp site. His three servants looked after him well. Outside his guest house a bubbling spring flowed by and eddied in a clear pool, which delighted Carpenter. He laid bamboo poles across the pool to make supports for orchid plants which he bought from native boys and girls for 25 cents. "What luxury!" Carpenter recalls. "A private orchid garden of 200 plants!"

Dr. Sherwood Washburn, a scientist friend from the Doi Intanon camp, visited Carpenter for two weeks. Dr. Washburn, an anthropologist at the University of California at Berkeley, spent the time helping to collect entire groups of the gibbons that Carpenter had studied. Washburn then skeletonized the animals. This was the first time this kind of work, which complemented Carpenter's behavioral studies, had ever been done in the field.

The gibbon skeletons provided useful information. Studies by Professor Adolph Schultz, emeritus director of the Anthropological Institute in Zurich, showed that a high percentage of gibbons had mended bones, which meant that they must sometimes miss their spectacular jumps. (Carpenter suspected that the breaks could also have resulted from fights.) Again, Professor Schultz discovered during an autopsy that a gibbon had eaten a nestling bird. This meant that gibbons do not live only on fruit.

Carpenter's wife, Mariana, and her sister, Helen Evans, who were on a trip around the world, arrived at Doi Dao about two weeks before the camp was closed. Carpenter did not stop his observations. "One day off," he insists, "and you lose touch with many of the families." Both women went to work, too. Mariana Carpenter helped transcribe and edit notes. Helen talked to the natives and taught the children American songs; these "public relations" efforts helped Carpenter in his collecting activities.

When guests arrived, the old cook proudly produced his one dish for special occasions—caramel egg custard. Along with the egg custard he prepared wonderful rice dishes. The cook was highly qualified for his duties. His great trade secret was the formula for making bread rise—and he guarded this carefully. He had learned this "magic" from his father and he was taking no chances on letting it fall into the hands of the first boy, who could become a cook if he had it. He kept his yeast in a special chest and would let no one see how he made the bread rise. With good bread on the table, plus good brown rice and egg custard, the visitors were well fed.

Carpenter's most unusual visitor came unannounced in the middle of the night. He woke up to hear loud stamping noises. Listening in the dark, he mistily realized that an elephant was standing near his mosquito net. "Yes, I was scared," Carpenter says. "I didn't know what he might try to do. My heart pounded noisily. He could have torn the shed apart. But he decided that there was nothing there so he went on off."

The natives use elephants for the heavy work of harvesting teak logs up behind Doi Dao, and they are brought down for a few days' rest every month. The lead elephant is chained, but the other eight or so in a group are allowed to wander around, which accounted for Carpenter's elephant—and also for some good trails, made by elephants foraging in the dense underbrush, throughout the territorial ranges of the gibbons.

Diversions of this kind were few. In the four months he spent at Doi Dao, Carpenter had ample time to work, and his diligence produced valuable results. At Doi Dao, he made a pioneering contribution to the study of gibbon communications. He was the first man to use disc recorders for recording and analyzing primate "vocalizations" in the field, and with the information he gathered, he was able to formulate a correct approach to understanding these complex and varied sounds. Carpenter plotted the numbers of calls during each day. He distinguished 11 types of gibbon vocalizations, ranging from hoots and squeaks to cries and growls. Gibbons are noisiest in the morning when they sound off, apparently for the benefit of their neighbors. During the rest of the day they are fairly quiet. But they will respond loudly to intruders at any time. And the young have their own cries and chirps which can be heard throughout the day.

Carpenter used his recorder to make samples of the different types of calls for scrutiny in the laboratory and also to test the gibbons' reactions to their own voices in the field. From the United States, Carpenter brought a parabolic reflector which he used to focus the distant sounds on a microphone. Sometimes he mounted this on a platform in a clearing, standing underneath to record the gibbons' cries as the reflector gathered them in. He also took this equipment up to his observation posts on the cliffs so that he could pick up all the sounds coming from the trees. When he played back their recorded voices, Carpenter was interested to learn that the gibbons reacted in the same alert, curious and defiant manner they used to greet other groups of the species *Hylobates Lar*. The gibbons seemed inclined to copy some of the calls they heard and Carpenter even found that he could make them answer his own rough imitations of certain calls.

Interpretation of the many gibbon sounds is difficult. One might dismiss the calls as meaningless on the grounds that the gibbons are just animals and not capable of making useful sounds. On the other hand, the calls could be interpreted in facile human terms. If a gibbon whimpered, you could say, "He's obviously upset." Carpenter avoided both pitfalls in favor of another attitude. "My concept," Carpenter says, "was not to make inferences about the experiences and 'feelings' or 'affectional systems' of the animal. You see how gibbons respond to another's calls. The key is to observe. This is the key to the understanding of all animal communications. It's not what the animal says or the gestures that it makes. It is not what the animal 'means' or feels. It's the response of the other animals of the same species, usually in the same group, which reveals the functions of communication patterns in a species. I don't try to read the animal's mind. I simply observe what the other animals do. For example, there is a little, high-pitched cry made by young howlers: 'Aaahh! aaahh!' If you heard only this, you'd say, 'Well, the animal is in pain.' But then you hear, 'Umm,' from another animal up the line, from the mother. They approach each other and the infant might climb onto the mother's back. Now what the young howler was saying was, 'Where are you?' And the other howler answering, 'Umm, here I am.' The function of the exchange was to coordinate the behavior of the animals. If the infant were completely separated from the group, his call would have been more intense, a very different kind of call, which would have resulted in the female, and possibly the male, coming to his defense. But this call 'Aaahh! aaahh!' is always used to coordinate separated females and their infants or juveniles. And the response to 'Aaahh' is 'Umm.' It's almost a language."

After months of gibbon observations, Carpenter knew which gibbon was saying what to whom in what situation and, generally, why. For example, Type IX vocalization, as designated by Carpenter, is a chatter or series of cries made by the leading adult to the rest of the family as they are traveling through their territory. Judging from the actions and sounds of the other gibbons, Carpenter decided that the function was most likely that of directing the family's walk through a forest on a sunny afternoon.

Despite the sophistication of these calls, Carpenter points out that gibbons and other monkeys do not have a real language. "It's not speech," he says, "it's a signaling system.

Speech is abstract. It means you can talk about something that is at a distance, or remote in space or time. Their behavior is more like a pointing system." Yet Carpenter's studies showed that the sounds made by gibbons and our own languages were not so far apart as had been supposed. Carpenter tried in the 1930s to relate his research on animal communication to human language studies, but at this time, linguistics experts and scholars had done little work with animal sounds. The communication of monkeys, it was assumed, had nothing to do with human languages. Today, Carpenter notes, "Scholars and scientists are becoming interested in what they call the 'design characteristics' of animal communications." Scientists like Stuart Altman, of the Yerkes Regional Primate Research Center in Atlanta, Georgia, are beginning to realize that animals and man use sounds in somewhat similar ways. Work of this kind on the porpoise has been especially well publicized.

Studying gibbon communication, Carpenter found that the Thais have their own version of what gibbons are "saying." Buddhists believe in reincarnation after death and they believe that the gibbons were human beings in a past life. More specifically, they believe that gibbons are reincarnations of humans who were disappointed lovers. The Thais think that this is why there are so many gibbons. They believe that of all the different human conditions, the class of those disappointed in love has the greatest number. The natives also believe, mystically, that gibbon calls somehow help their crops of rice and corn to grow, and for this reason, as well as their horror of killing, they hate to see anyone kill a gibbon.

When Carpenter, with Washburn's help, did "collect" studied groups of gibbons, he found himself invited to leave his fine guest house near the clear pool over which the orchids grew. "I was so anxious to get clear and accurate data on the composition of the groups," Carpenter recalls, "that I decided to collect whole groups and study the specimens. The skeletons of the members of the groups were to be measured by Professor Schultz, so that we could determine the composition and the growth stages of the animals. It's sometimes very difficult with the gibbons to tell which is male and which is female, or to tell the age of the animals. Anyway, I violated the Buddhist code of ethics, and I was driven out of the Buddhist temple. In retrospect, this was a horrible thing for me to do. In my zeal to know, I failed to realize how inappropriate my behavior was in a Buddhist culture."

When the *ompur* or mayor of the village heard what Carpenter was doing to the gibbons, he insisted that Carpenter leave the temple guest house. Abashed and momentarily homeless, Carpenter had to move just before his wife and sister-in-law arrived. Luckily for the lawless scientist, a neighboring *ompur,* whose leg wounds Carpenter had cared for, opened the doors of his temple. Carpenter moved his camp up on a red clay hill. He could finish studying the same groups of gibbons in the forest, and he did so for the remaining three weeks of his stay in Thailand, with deep regrets that the two women could not enjoy the blooming orchid garden he had prepared for them.

In assessing his own work, Carpenter is most proud of the comprehensiveness of his results. His aim was to develop evidence and information about the gibbon and to present the whole picture, rather than any one particular part. "I didn't go out, for instance, and study just the sexual behavior and forget everything else," he says. "I also studied mother-infant relations, the development of families, territoriality, group relations and interactions of other social and ecological factors. I tried to become an anthropologist and an ecologist."

Aiming for a comprehensive view, Carpenter, in Ardrey's apt

phrase, "imposed the mathematics of the laboratory on the confusion of the jungle." Carpenter tried never to overlook any form of behavior. To guide himself in the study of groups, for example, he sometimes made use of a simple mathematical formula which quickly tells the number of possible interactions within a group. The formula, $\dfrac{Nx(N-1)}{2}$, indicates that in a family of four animals there are six "potential interactions": $\dfrac{4x(4-1)}{2} = 6$. (An "interaction" occurs when an animal performs any action—touch, gesture, look—in relation to another animal.) A group of 18 members has 153 different interactional probabilities. "Using this formula, the potential can be compared with the actual," Carpenter explains. "Actually, the interactions with the infant are limited because the mother is intervening, acting as a buffer here. But this kind of detailed interactional description tells an observer, in fine perspective, what the complexities are. It's better than just describing group behavior in general terms, which was previously the case. The approach that I helped develop was both *systematic* and *analytic*. And this approach, I would say, is being used increasingly these days, whether the animal in question is the langur of India or the baboon of the Serengeti Plains."

Carpenter did achieve an unprecedentedly complete picture of the monkey species he studied. And, valuable as his work was in itself, it took on even more importance because it stimulated other scientists to follow his lead. But not immediately. Despite his pioneering studies, few of Carpenter's fellow scientists rushed to emulate him. As late as 1954, in fact, Carpenter felt that he had to be defensive even about the basic idea of conducting field studies of animal behavior. Then the scientific community, especially anthropologists, began to change its opinions. A new interest developed in the natural behavior of animals, especially the more intelligent species, and expeditions into the jungle to study these animals became more commonplace. In 1967, for example, there were at least nine expeditions in the field seeking to observe, in the fashion Carpenter pioneered, such animals as the lion, the chimpanzee and the gorilla.

In fact, wherever there are primates today, there are likely to be primatologists studying primates. In northern India, Charles Southwich has been studying the population and group structures of rhesus monkeys, while Phyllis Jay has been recording the social behavior of the long-tailed langurs. Thomas Strusocker is in the Camaroons, Africa, watching vervets. Jane Goodall is also in eastern Africa, where she has long been studying the chimpanzee. Recently she has been using tape recorders and movie cameras to determine if the chimpanzee's facial expressions and the sounds it makes are related, and just what each communicates. George Schaller is known for his great books about mountain gorillas, deer and lions. Irven DeVore and S. L. Washburn have worked together studying the behavior and social organization of baboons. K. Imanishi and many other Japanese scientists have studied the Japanese macaque in a colony on one of Japan's small islands. David Horr is in Borneo attacking the difficult task of studying the rare orangutan, which lives in this country and in Sumatra.

Essentially the condition for this change in view is the growing evidence that man can never fully understand himself until he understands the entire animal kingdom. This direct observation of animal behavior, which is now called ethology, has as its leading theorist Konrad Lorenz, whose studies, such as *On Aggression* and *Evolution and the Modification of Be-*

havior, seem to confirm many of the Freudian theses about the influence of the early environment on both human and animal infants. More recently, Robert Ardrey, in *African Genesis* and *The Territorial Imperative,* and Desmond Morris, in *The Naked Ape,* have explored the larger and important implications of the relationship between animal and human behavior.

In his own studies, as has been noted, Carpenter implicitly advanced this view, indicating his belief that animal behavior, seen in its entirety, would be found to have many similarities with man's behavior and social interactions. Today scientists increasingly discuss man and animals as though the behavior of both had much in common. Behavior patterns such as aggression, territoriality, communication, sexual behavior or feeding are linked together by scientists to explain both human and animal conduct. It would be an exaggeration to say that Carpenter alone is responsible for the strong current interest in the comparative analysis of human and animal behavior. But Carpenter's studies stand as the pioneer model for the work of many scientists today, and concepts which he introduced are being refined and expanded. By approaching gibbons with a detached, rigorous, I-am-here-to-learn attitude, Carpenter saw clearly as few before him the biological basis of human behavior. In seeing clearly he brought back much valuable information and thus opened many new doors of research for scientists who followed him.

On June 18, 1937, Carpenter left Doi Dao and rejoined Harold Coolidge, the leader of the Asiatic Primate Expedition in The Atjeh of Sumatra. He was, he recalls, "sorry to go home. A field study is never finished, you know. There are always things you would want to do if you had more time. I'd allow a year for the gibbon study if I were to do it again."

four

The Evidence of
Yesterday

T HE DAY starts precisely at 3:45 A.M. Someone knocks
loudly and hurriedly on the door. Dr. Philip C. Hammond rolls over on his cot and blinks. Outside, the summer sky
is dark. He has been asleep for only a few hours and he does
not want to get up. But duty calls—and Hammond approaches
archeology in something like a military fashion. A slender man
of average height who is an associate professor of Mediterranean Archeology at Brandeis University, he pads over to the
bureau and dunks his head in a basin of water. He dries off
easily: his gray-brown hair is cut down to a practical quarter-
inch all over. His well-trimmed mustache and pointed goatee
are a shade longer. He is standing in his office-bedroom; nearby
are a desk and filing cabinets covered with charts, maps, notebooks, tape recorders, pieces of pottery and a few bones.
Hastily he pulls on his khaki pants and shirt. On the shoulder
is a patch with the letters "AEH"—the American Expedition to
Hebron. More befogged than rested by his few hours of sleep,
he still moves with a brisk precision, holding his shoulders stiff,
his back straight. A few minutes after four, Hammond slams

the door behind him. Crossing the courtyard in the half-light, he joins several of his assistants shuffling over to breakfast.

They walk across a dusty courtyard, enclosed on two sides by two stories of classrooms, on the third by a kitchen and dining room, on the fourth by a high wall. His Majesty King Hussein of Jordan has granted Hammond the use of this school for the summer of 1966. In September, young Jordanian girls will return to the school to study home economics. But now the classrooms are home and laboratory for the AEH. Even though the 37 members of Hammond's expedition sleep on mattresses on the floor, everyone considers the accommodations luxurious. After all, they have a roof and, most of the time, water and electricity. They are lucky, they know, not to be waking up in tents—a more common shelter for archeological expeditions.

In the dining room the scramble has started. The first shift— 20 area and site supervisors—is hurrying to finish breakfast and move on. They have to be on the "dig" by five o'clock. In the rapidly growing light slanting in through the windows, they find two fried eggs staring up at them, oatmeal on the side and plenty of coffee to wake them up. Nobody is in the mood for talk. Besides, they have work to do. Hammond answers a few questions from supervisors. The scene—the bare tables, the khaki uniforms, the early-morning, bleary-eyed urgency—re-minds one of an army mess hall. The troops come, eat on the run and rush off to their assignments. Hammond is himself tense and tireless, and he runs a fast-paced, demanding expedition.

On the narrow street in front of the school, some of Hammond's men are already loading the hired buses with supplies carried out from the school building. One of the site supervisors, an American college boy who is at Hebron to learn how to *do* archeology, hauls out a large box of food for the midmorning break. Two supervisors follow with a water container. Arab boys lug out baskets of unwanted pottery shards collected the day before. Older men, college professors, pace about studying their clipboards. A few specialists tinker with their cameras or their surveying equipment. The Americans shout at each other to hurry.

The sun is just clearing the low hill to the east of Hebron, and its glare spreads across the sleeping city. The white buildings of stone and plaster brighten as the men work. A slight breeze stirs, blowing in from the Mediterranean 40 miles to the west. At 4:45, Hammond's "dig" staff boards the buses and they roar off to the southwestern edge of the city, a mile away. There the archeologists are digging up the past. The goal of the American expedition to Hebron is, in fact, the full reconstruction of Hebron's copious history.

Hebron, located 15 miles west of the Dead Sea, is one of the world's oldest cities. For at least 5,000 years the sun has peeked over that same eastern hill and spread its morning rays across Hebron's clustered buildings. And even before houses and streets were actually built, the legends say, Hebron's slight valley figured prominently in mankind's first days. When God created Adam, He is said to have found the red clay here. The legends say also that Noah started the first vineyards after the Flood on the slope where Hebron now stands.

Hammond has not yet determined exactly when some nameless people first gave up their nomadic life to build a city on this sacred ground. But the biblical chronology indicates that Abraham came here—to "raise an altar to the Lord"—about 1750 B.C. Abraham and other patriarchs were buried in the city's Cave of Macpelah. Much later, the Moslems built their sacred mosque, which stands today, directly over Abraham's grave. The Arabs, in fact, now call their city "El Khalil" ("The

Friend") after Abraham (who was often called "The Friend of God"), rather than Hebron, the biblical name.

From the time of Abraham on, the Bible mentions Hebron every few pages. Isaac and Joseph lived there. Moses assaulted the city and captured it. The descendants of Aaron inherited it. Samson brought to Hebron the gates of Gaza. But the city reached its greatest glory in the time of David, in 1004 B.C. "And the time that David was king in Hebron over Judea was seven years and six months." Later, when David made Jerusalem, 20 miles north, his capital city, Hebron lost some of its importance.

In biblical times, Hebron's citizens raised olives, figs, nuts, pomegranates and grapes in the stony soil, as they do today. Then, as now, the same two ancient pools and some 25 springs supplied water to its residents. Then, as now, travelers came to Hebron from Egypt and Lebanon.

Time and two hundred generations of men have had their effect on Hebron. The life and people, the buildings and streets, the tools and jewelry have changed since biblical times, though the city itself looks much as it did 3,000 years ago. Archeologists are, of course, interested in these changes. Since archeology is the scientific study of the life and culture of ancient peoples, it attempts to explore the past and to discover how men used to live by excavating ancient cities and tombs to recover their history and artifacts.

Hebron spent several thousand years at the crossroads of history, and its past is as rich as that of any city in the world. A bewildering variety of peoples ruled or lived in Hebron, passed through the city or traded within its walls. All left their mark. Before the time of Christ the Canaanites (3000 B.C.), the Hyksos (1750 B.C.), the Israelites (1100 B.C.), the Assyrians (700 B.C.), the Babylonians (600 B.C.), the Idumeans (400

B.C.), the Greeks (300 B.C.), and the Romans (50 B.C.) were the chief occupants or overlords. The most warlike of these residents built Hebron's walls about 1750 B.C., and it became more a fortified refuge than a city. Judas Maccabaeus tore down most of these fortifications in 164 B.C.

As one of many Roman provinces, Hebron received special attention from Herod the Great (King of Judea) who had many buildings erected. Some of the distinctive Roman masonry still stands today. The Roman emperor Hadrian built a road to Hebron in 270 A.D., making the city a famous marketplace, and Constantine, in 350 A.D., built a basilica in honor of the patriarchs.

Through all these years the people of Hebron built houses, knocked them down, built new houses, leveled them, took stones from a deserted house across the street to build a new house on top of the old—and so the city rose, one level on top of another. One man's roof became another's foundations. The boundaries and layout also changed. The city expanded and contracted and spread in new directions. The aristocrat's district of one century became olive groves the next. On demolished slums, kings erected their vaulted baths. Proud walls and towers, fought over for generations, crumbled into little hills topped by fig trees.

In the city of Hebron, history is frozen beneath one's feet. The record, however, is accidental, chaotic and cryptic. The citizens of ancient Hebron thought no more of 20th-century archeologists than we do of archeologists who may unearth our remains in 4500 A.D.

In the seventh century the armies of the Prophet Mohammed marched irresistibly over Hebron and all the Near and Middle East. Hebron entered its First Islamic Period (635–1200), becoming a major holy city for that religion also.

In the 12th century, the Crusaders wrested Hebron from the Moslems, calling it the Castle of Abraham. Islam soon won out, however, to become the dominant religion, as it is today. Though an important holy city for both Christians and Jews, Hebron is Islam's fourth holy city, after Mecca, Medina, and Jerusalem.

Hebron's sanctity has been largely responsible for its modern decline as a center of trade. Its citizens practiced a fanatic orthodoxy, unmatched in the rest of Jordan. They considered anyone a foreigner who came from beyond the city limits. Zealously religious, the Hebronites saw no virtue in being kind to strangers, including fellow Moslems. They were, in fact, always hostile. Businessmen as well as tourists learned centuries ago that they would do well to avoid Hebron. Similarly, no archeologist tried to excavate Hebron before 1963, the year of Hammond's first expedition. It is the last major biblical site to be explored.

Hebron's reputation for hostility to strangers was forbidding even in academic circles. When Hammond announced his intentions, his colleagues seriously predicted that the expedition members would be murdered in their beds. "It can't be done," the prophets of doom said. "It should be," answered Hammond, intrigued by the challenge. He approached the Jordanian Department of Antiquities, soothed over objections and made a summer survey in 1963. Since Hammond is a college professor, his digging is always confined to the summer vacation. He brought a staff of 22 in 1964 for the first groundbreaking, returned with a planning staff of 10 in 1965 (they surveyed but did not excavate), and went back to the trenches in 1966 with a staff of 38. He has enjoyed cordial relations with the Hebronites, much to the surprise of the pessimists.

Hammond is uniquely qualified to insinuate himself and

several large expeditions among the suspicious Hebronites. First of all, he is a learned man and a Christian scholar, attainments which these people respect. With a Bachelor of Arts in Biblical Literature from Brothers College, a Bachelor of Divinity in Old Testament from Drew Theological Seminary, a Master of Arts in Semitics from Yale University, and a Ph.D. in Near Eastern Archeology from Yale University, Hammond could hardly be considered a boorish foreigner. Second, he speaks fluent Arabic. Third, Hammond is shrewd enough to know that if he wants to come back each summer, he had best maintain constant harmony between his expedition and the citizens of the city.

So Hammond works hard to avoid even the slightest friction. He briefs his people on the local customs and insists that they conform. For example, no excavation is allowed within 1,000 yards of the holy mosque. The Arabs, as far as Hammond is concerned, are always his hosts and he is only a guest. And finally, Hammond enjoys rather than fights the ticklish setting. As a latter-day Lawrence of Arabia, he takes delight in "one-upping the locals." Staying one jump ahead of the most orthodox in town is for Hammond more than a necessity, it is a pleasure. He admits that he relishes the intricate diplomacy, role-playing and image-making required to gain respect from Hebron's citizens. Because of Hammond's personality and good sense, the American Expedition to Hebron, far from being merely tolerated, is liked and respected. Even in Jerusalem, 18 miles north, a merchant told one of the Americans, "Oh, you can charge it, you're from the Expedition!"

Hammond turned to archeology rather belatedly. He celebrated his 30th birthday on his first expedition—hanging from a rope ladder in a cistern in the Moabite Desert. But as a young man growing up in Brooklyn, New York, Hammond had not been interested in archeology. He thought he might go into biology or criminology. World War II interrupted these plans. Enlisting at 18, commissioned a lieutenant at 19, Hammond fought in the Normandy Invasion from the eighth to the thirty-eighth day and, after recovering from a wound, found himself a civilian again at 21. His religious inclinations now became dominant. Hammond's family was not especially pious, and he does not know how to explain his own zeal. He studied biblical literature in college and seminary, thinking he might like to teach languages or serve as a minister. He went on to be ordained and did preach at several New England churches in the period from 1951 to 1957. At the same time, however, he was working on his doctorate in archeology at Yale, and his dedication turned increasingly from religion to archeology. He soon found his ministerial duties confining; he felt that he had "outgrown" formal Christianity, and in 1957 he changed his vocation: he became a full-time teacher of Semitics and archeology, first at Lycoming College from 1957 to 1960, then at Princeton Theological Seminary from 1960 to 1966, and now at Brandeis University. Immediately after the shift to teaching, he began to spend his summers excavating in the Near East—first in Jerusalem, then in Petra, where his small expedition lived in the famous tombs (1959–1962), and finally at Hebron. Now Hammond's life revolves around archeology—his teaching, his writing, his plans, his hobbies. During the summer he digs, and during the rest of the year he figures out the significance of what he dug up. Hammond jokes that "even his family is archeological," since his wife and three children are asked to help whenever possible.

Now the kitchen clock is ticking toward five o'clock and Hammond's "dig" supervisors are reaching the various sites. Hammond finishes his breakfast. He is the man responsible for

the progress of the whole expedition and so he spends most of his day at the base while his assistant director oversees the "dig." Later in the morning Hammond will drive out for an inspection. But in the day's early hours he devotes himself to administrative duties. There is, after all, more to an archeological expedition than digging holes.

Walking back to his office, Hammond threads his way through a string of about 20 late risers—the camp staff—and greets them enthusiastically. He is not genuinely pleased to be up so early, but he likes to radiate purpose, drive and, if possible, good humor. The five o'clock breakfast shift—mostly college girls, with a sprinkling of older male specialists—are not all so devoted; they nod grumpily. The expedition's 13 girls, like all the men except Hammond, live six or eight to a room on the school's second floor. They straggle to the kitchen across the courtyard, now filled with that bright, almost painful glare which is the most striking feature of the Jordanian landscape.

These campside workers—the expedition's secretaries, record-keepers, photographers, laboratory technicians, architects and pottery cleaners—back up the work done on the sites. Their job is to handle the endless stream of artifacts flowing in from the several sites. All these archeological finds must be cleaned, classified, processed and recorded; in the case of the more important artifacts, an architect-artist draws them and a photographer records them on film. Hammond insists on complete records. Half the expedition is needed to process and record what the other half finds.

Most of the expedition's 37 members come from various American colleges—eight in all, including the University of Southern California and Princeton Theological Seminary. Almost three-quarters of the expedition are students; most of the rest are teachers. Then there are a few people with special skills, such as photographers and architectural draftsmen. With the exception of these specialists, no one is paid for spending his summer vacation working in Hebron. In fact, they usually have to pay their own expenses, which total almost $1,500. Getting to Hebron presents the main difficulty: a round-trip plane ticket costs $890. Some of the students resort to desperate stratagems to whittle down this amount. One boy took a steamer to London and hitchhiked 2,000 miles to Hebron. The members have to put up an additional $600. Three hundred dollars of this is for clothes, side trips to other excavations and personal expenses. The last $300 is designated as a "camp fee," and Hammond uses it to pay the local help and buy the food. In return for this outlay, the students and teachers have the opportunity to work 15 hours a day for six weeks, from June 27 to August 13. Some lucky ones, however, receive grants from their schools. Baldwin-Wallace College of Ohio set an example, which Hammond hopes more schools will follow, by underwriting its eight representatives. The high cost of going on a "dig" is a touchy subject. Would-be archeologists (as well as teachers who want to advance in their profession) need field experience; therefore, they must go on expeditions. But many of them can hardly afford the cost.

Actually the whole expedition squeaks by financially. While each member has to pay his own way, Hammond has the onerous problem of paying for the entire operation. The AEH is his project and he has to scrape up the money if he wants to keep it going. He plans to excavate at Hebron until at least 1972, but so far nobody has offered him a "blank check." His own university permits Hammond to raise funds, but only if he stays away from their prospects. Hammond has to work almost as hard finding the money—over $27,000 for 1966—as he does excavating. He does not like to complain and only says, "It's not a pleasant part of the work."

Back at his desk, by 5:05 A.M., Hammond studies a map of Jebel-er-Rumeide, the low rise on the city's southwestern rim. The expedition is digging at some 15 sites scattered over a quarter square mile of this rocky, vine-covered hill. While the supervisors direct the excavation, a geologist and a specialist with an electronic sounding device search for promising spots to open new trenches. Recent tests have indicated the presence of a wall under an untouched field and Hammond is trying to figure out how to distribute the men to handle the new site.

Before Hammond can solve the problem, the camp administrator comes into his office. She has kitchen problems. Then a girl from one of the labs pops in. She has been cleaning a skeleton unearthed the day before. But now she fears that she has mixed the bones from two skeletons. Hammond hopes not. He makes a note of the administrator's dilemma and goes off to the lab with the girl. He looks at his watch—already 6:45.

In the three laboratories, the camp crew has been at work almost an hour. Several people work in each lab, on an assortment of projects. The lab space is assigned rather haphazardly. If the pottery cleaners need more room, they settle where they can find it. But one lab is basically a darkroom. Since Hammond insists on photographing each artifact—and there are thousands of them—the technicians are kept very busy. Another lab houses the record-keepers and their typewriters, gamely trying to keep the artifact entries up-to-date. In a corner the photographers have set up a little studio for photographing pieces of pottery and jewelry. At a side desk, a girl is working with a coin-cleaner, which is an ultrasonic bath. When dropped into it, encrusted pieces of metal suddenly show their true form and color. Hammond always seeks out helpful electronic gadgets. The girl also makes use of electrolytic and chemical cleaning. In the third lab, the expedition's architect is working on a drawing of a recently uncovered floor. Unfinished maps hang on the walls and the surveyors have stacked charts and diagrams on the side tables.

Hammond's morning passes quickly. Before he has time to decide which men will work at the new site, it is 8:30. He remembers that he has to visit a local official at the city hall. He could have written a letter but he knows that a personal appearance will help him in the future. Hebron's bureaucrats have taken good care of his transportation problems; when the expedition is to go on a side trip, half the taxis in town appear at the camp. Now Hammond climbs into his Land Rover—nicknamed "Baby"—and rides off to thank the right people.

Diplomacy practiced, Hammond heads out to er-Rumeide. To keep his morning almost military in character, he likes to make his inspection promptly at 9:30. Parking "Baby" at the site, he starts his tour. In his left hand Hammond carries a swagger stick, tipped with half the jaw from a horned viper, which has been a part of his image for years. He insists that the stick is a sort of magic wand: a man with a swagger stick is far more likely to be admitted to inner offices and come away with all requests granted.

The 15 sites on Jebel-er-Rumeide are scattered over an area 500 yards across. Although they are usually within shouting distance of each other, the workers on one site can seldom see any other site. The hill undulates through a variety of ridges and knolls. Dozens of farmers have built their houses here and they have planted vineyards. Across this rock-strewn expanse, Hammond pursues his meticulous archeological campaign.

Hammond stops first at Area 6, the summit of Jebel-er-Rumeide. The supervisor, a college professor, greets him and reports on how the work is going. Area 6 covers three sites, each of which includes several trenches more or less side by side.

The digging is organized along military lines. Hammond's senior staff is made up of five area supervisors, older men who usually teach in American universities. Each of these men has a staff of his own, consisting of three to six male college students who supervise the sites in each area. None of these 20 or so men wields a shovel. Hammond has hired about 175 natives to handle the picks and shovels and carry the baskets. A work crew of eight natives is assigned to each trench—one pick man, two hoe men, and five "basket boys," who may be anywhere from 16 to 60 years old. In military terms, the staff consists of one general (Hammond), six officers (the area supervisors), 14 sergeants (the site supervisors) and 175 privates.

Once this efficient excavation machinery has been organized, the question is: where to dig? Hammond's expedition came to Hebron because they felt sure the ground contained numerous remains of the cultures and races that had lived there. But certain areas, obviously, may be more fruitful than others. Sometimes likely spots exhibit surface clues. If there is a crumbling wall jutting out from a hillside, then it is sensible to uncover the rest of it. If the ground is covered by stones of the size used to make house walls, it is reasonable to expect a basement to reveal itself only a few feet down. If the soil is filled with bits of pottery, it seems wise to look farther down for bigger pieces.

Often, however, there are no clues on the surface. Usually archeology requires educated stabs in the dark. The first excavations are actually "test trenches" or "soundings." The surveyor measures off a square five meters (16 feet) on each side. The work crews dig straight down, keeping the sides of the square perfectly vertical. If, after five or ten feet, the supervisors can find no pottery, no house remains, no bones, no evidence of human habitation, the trench is filled and forgotten. When an entire area yields only "negative soundings," it is crossed off the list; presumably the land has been used only for farming.

When Hammond first excavated at Hebron in 1964, he split his men among three major areas. One of these was Jebel-er-Rumeide. The second lay at the northeast end of town, near a major crossroad. The third, at the north tip of Hebron, was called "the Mountain of the Patriarch." Since nobody knew what was in the ground, the expedition had to feel its way. After extensive testing, Hammond eliminated both areas to the north of Hebron. The crews at Jebel-er-Rumeide, however, hit pay dirt. Nearly every site, nearly every trench, yielded a variety of sherds, bones and parts of houses. Now Hammond had to pinpoint the underground remains as precisely as possible. If a trench reveals the walls of a house running straight across, the next step is to sink two new trenches—one on each side of the first—to find where the walls go. But if the wall is huge, perhaps part of a city wall, it is more efficient to start digging 100 or 150 feet away, in the direction the wall seems to run. As Hammond's team dug more and more trenches, Jebel-er-Rumeide became like a huge jigsaw puzzle. Each trench represented a new piece in the puzzle. And the object was to find out what the whole buried picture looked like.

The process is slow and laborious. The pieces fall into place over weeks or even years. On a good day a crew can deepen a 16-by-16-foot trench by only three feet. And there are only a limited number of supervisors and crews. Hammond has to bide his time. Much of the summer is spent planning the next move, the next trench. These decisions are not made rashly. As the days pass, Hammond weighs what the supervisors tell him, what the artifacts reveal and what the surveyors discover, and then he decides where the next trench will go.

Area 6, the summit of Jebel-er-Rumeide, does not, however, require any decisions for the moment. The professor tells Hammond that the work is going well. The trenches in Site A, the first opened, have gone down through 130 distinct levels or strata (they are numbered from the surface down). Each stratum—usually only a few inches thick—reveals something about the past human presence which created it. Hammond assumes that every period of human occupation, or lack of it, leaves its own distinct stratum or strata. For example, stratum 64 might be a floor of rock; 63 might be fine sand blown into the deserted ruin; 62 might be the caved-in roof, indicated by masonry if the beams had rotted away; 61 might be the stone walls which fell over on top of the roof; 60 might be dirt fill brought in by the next owner, a farmer; 59 might be black soil left by a fire, perhaps from burning over a crop; 58 might be a stone foundation; 57 might be a layer of grain if the floor happened to belong to a miller; and so on. These layers are often squashed down and barely detectable. Archeologists develop a fine sense for changes in the color, texture and appearance of the soil. Hammond once distinguished 10 plaster floors, one on top of the other, all within a space of two feet.

At Area 6's Site B the diggers have uncovered a complex water storage system, and the work has gone down through 121 strata. The number of strata, or even their depth and thickness, tell nothing about a site's age. If an aristocrat built a marble house and his descendants maintained it for 500 years, that house's floor, only one stratum, would represent five centuries. But if the house had fallen into ruin, and the neighbors had used it as a garbage dump, and then wandering thieves camped there, there might be 25 different strata representing a period of only 25 years. The different levels in any site are left by hundreds of generations of mankind, engaged in hundreds of different activities. One level may be only a day in human history, the succeeding one a century.

Archeologists do assume that when there are two strata in the same trench, the lower one will be the earlier one. If one stratum can be dated—perhaps by a coin minted and used only for a few years—the ones below it are presumed to be earlier, the ones above later. The exceptions to this rule are often humorous. A rat might dig a hole down through 80 strata and leave a bottle cap next to a Roman bracelet. Archeologists have to be alert for such false clues.

From Area 6 Hammond walks quickly down the slope, through olive groves, to Area 7. The supervisor hails him by the Arab name "Mudir." It means "director" or "boss." All members of the AEH and the workers use this title. There are practical reasons for calling Hammond "Mudir." Hammond takes seriously the responsibilities of a command position and wants his authority recognized. But his senior staff would find it awkward to address him as "Dr. Hammond." They are his friends and themselves Ph.D.'s. No matter what name they used, Hammond would be reduced to one of the gang in the eyes of the students, the workers and the natives. To avoid such problems, Hammond asks that everybody simply call him "Mudir." Then too, Hammond says that the name is "part of the image." He insists that the distinction—the mystique, perhaps—bestowed by the word is a valuable asset in an Arab country. Hammond has to hire and fire the laborers: these actions are most easily accomplished by "Mudir." Hammond has to visit numerous officials: they are more inclined to be polite to "Mudir." Hammond has to keep a 37-man expedition out of trouble: the townspeople are inclined to forgive the friends of the "Mudir."

A minor incident in town suggests that Hammond is right. Two girls went to the post office to pick up the expedition's mail. The clerk would not allow them to take a package, valued at $50, which belonged to one of the college boys out in the trenches. The girls had on their official AEH khaki uniform (shirt and culotte), another one of Hammond's devices for marking his group as distinguished, serious archeologists, not tourists or worse. Both girls argued, in Arabic, that they should be allowed to take the package, and one girl became quite angry. Finally the other girl realized that the situation was hopeless. Backing away from the window, she said in English to her indignant friend, "Never mind, we'll send the Mudir to pick it up." At this point the clerk, who could have understood only one word in the sentence, "snapped to." He almost forced them to take the package. He had no desire to get mixed up with the "Mudir."

Hammond learned about Arab psychology mainly during his summers at Petra from 1959 to 1962. This first-century theater lies deep in the barren wastes of the Jordan desert about 70 miles south of Hebron. The nomadic, camel-riding Bedouins still live in these wastelands just as they did 1,000 years ago. To proceed with the excavation of Petra, to get the workers he needed, Hammond had to gain the respect and cooperation of the Bedouins. As it turned out, he had no trouble, because he thinks the way they think. The Bedouins are complex and subtle people who appreciate both hardness and cleverness. They admire horsemanship and skill with a rifle. Fortunately, "being something of a ham," Hammond likes "to be able to outride and outshoot" everybody else. He grew up on horses and took readily to the camel, showing a dexterity which impressed his hosts. The Bedouins also appreciate "a citizen who can make a play on words or give a long speech." Hammond also passed those tests. The Bedouins further complicate human relations by subscribing to a strict code of custom and ceremony—what might seem like senseless formality to an outsider. But Hammond enjoys these intricacies. "It's all very appealing," he says, "if you enjoy playing a role." The swagger stick and the title "Mudir" are the visible symbols of the role Hammond enjoys. But Hammond's success in handling the Arabs is not just stagecraft. He and they appreciate many of the same skills and virtues.

Now, still inspecting Jebel-er-Rumeide, the "Mudir" sees that Area 7 is going well. Site A, with 58 strata, has gone straight down into numerous pottery factories built by the Hellenistic Greeks about 300 B.C. Historians have maintained that there was Hellenistic occupation in Hebron. Now this site has yielded the first tangible evidence of their occupation. These long-cold kilns contain thousands of chips and pieces of pottery, a treasure which has kept the camp workers busier than they might have wished. Hammond likes the results so well that he decides to extend the trench. The same site supervisor, a college student, will have responsibility for another 265 square feet of excavation. This boy, like many of the Americans, wears a *kufiya*, the Arab's traditional headdress, while working in the summer sun.

In Site B, with 38 levels, the archeologists have uncovered a rich man's house, complete with cobbled courtyard. Most important, they have come upon a segment of the ancient city wall, presumably the one King David walked upon. This huge wall is one of the expedition's great discoveries. During the 1964 season the archeologists exposed the front face of an obviously massive wall. But until 1966 nobody knew how wide it was. Hammond had to wait two years to confirm his guess that the wall represented the main fortifications which David had defended when Hebron was his capital city.

Hammond moves on to Area 3, where the wall was originally discovered. The supervisors have been excavating their way across the top of the wall. Behind the outside face, the part of the wall an enemy would see, lie great boulders. Finally the team has reached the back face. The wall turns out to be an amazing 36 feet thick. Much of its original height—it's impossible to say how much—has crumbled down. Hammond immediately orders new trenches at all points likely to intersect the wall. His tentative conclusion is that the hill of Jebel-er-Rumeide used to be the main city and that the wall probably runs all the way around.

Judging from the artifacts, the wall was built around 1700 B.C. That date ties in nicely with the biblical chronology. But this fact, though pleasant, is not critical to Hammond. "We are interested in biblical tradition. But we are not trying to prove anything. We have discovered that the city of Hebron existed at the date implied by the Bible. But had it been a different date, I wouldn't have cared. I call them as I see them." Though an ordained minister, Hammond insists that in archeology he is secular.

The excavation around the wall provided one of the expedition's great surprises. Trying to pin down the wall's direction, Hammond had ordered the workers to dig a 100-foot trench which he thought would certainly cross it. But after weeks of digging no wall appeared. On an inspection, Hammond examined the trench. He complimented the crew on the precision of their excavation: the walls were vertical, even and on line with the strings put down by the surveyors. One of the cardinal rules in excavation is: no burrowing outside those lines. Hammond joked that now they knew where the wall was not. Then he told the workers to clean the sides so they could be photographed; after that the trench would be filled in. Hammond walked off to the next site.

The young supervisor went to the side of the trench, barely touched it with his pick and saw a layer of dirt fall at his feet, like plaster off a wall. He had found *the* wall! Hammond's trench had missed it by just one-half inch. The college student wouldn't soon forget that event. At that moment he became a great archeological discoverer. He experienced the same elation felt by Heinrich Schliemann when he found the lost city of Troy, by Sir Arthur Evans when he discovered the Minoan culture of Crete, by hundreds of other archeologists who have made major discoveries. The weekend archeologist very likely feels the same excitement when he finds an Indian arrowhead.

Strictly speaking, however, the student's discovery was not supposed to happen—not on Hammond's expedition anyway. The wall was not where Hammond had decided to dig, so it should not have been found. If the wall had been uncovered in the trench, Hammond would have found only what he expected, and he would not have been particularly elated. Hammond does not thirst for the discoveries which the layman probably regards as archeology's most exciting aspect. Hammond's passion is thoroughness. The important thing is to follow the plan. "My concern is that everything continue routinely." Still, more than most sciences, archeology is a reach into the unknown. Naturally one will often encounter the beautifully unexpected—even when an expedition is run in a highly organized way.

The wall's future excavation is uncertain. Before Hammond can dig up land, he must pay for the right to do so. Since he has little money, he usually starts in empty fields, which are cheaper. Complications arise when he makes a major find, such as the wall, which, unfortunately, disappears under somebody's house or vineyard. Hammond cannot proceed unless he has the money to buy the farmhouse and hillside. So he must dig his trenches somewhere else. King David's wall, so close to total discovery, will remain a mystery for a while.

The wall so far uncovered has been left open as a tourist attraction. This is unusual, done only with the most striking or valuable finds. Usually Hammond's expedition opens a trench, excavates to bedrock, records the discoveries in great detail, then fills the trench up. When the AEH leaves in August, the villagers can hardly tell where the Americans have been digging. This procedure is sensible, since there is nothing dramatic to see in most trenches. Hammond actually has little choice; he only rents the land for a few months, on the condition that he leave it as he finds it. In the case of the uncovered wall, Hammond now has to pay a yearly rent to the landowner. Hammond does so to insure cordial relations with the Jordanians.

A dramatic find presents another problem. The archeologist may be happy to discover a courtyard or well-preserved plaster floor, but he is also a bit dismayed. A great archeological discovery, if it is to be preserved in its natural setting, is an automatic dead end. Excavating beyond the courtyard means tearing it up. A major find has the practical result of making further excavation impossible.

Archeology is necessarily a destructive pursuit. The pick men and the hoe men cut their way carefully into more ancient strata only after destroying the strata above. This destruction weighs heavily on the minds of modern archeologists. Hammond is particularly concerned about it, and has tried to devise new recording techniques that preserve the appearance, at least, of anything discovered. The expedition's photographers, surveyors, artists and architects make it possible for Hammond to know how every trench looked at every single stratum.

This obsession with thorough records marks a departure from archeology's earlier, more carefree days. In archeology's "swashbuckling era," from 1850 to 1920 (and in some cases, continuing to the present), archeologists simply dug for loot. They excavated with the single-mindedness of grave-robbers. Their aim was to find statues, columns, jewelry, pottery, anything which might look impressive in a book or a museum. These archeologists—many of them tinkerers and amateurs in the field—simply cleared away dirt until they found something, put it aside, cleared away more dirt and so on. They paid little attention to strata, nor did they know precisely where in the past they were operating.

Hammond views such practices with a scientist's scorn. His own methodology is as precise as the swashbucklers' was sloppy. The approach used at Hebron, Hammond says, "is the closest to a scientific method that has as yet been devised."

Archeology as pursued by the AEH is a very slow and painstaking affair. Once the surveyors have marked off a 16-by-16-foot square, the workmen begin the test trench by making a cut three feet by 16 feet along one side. This long, thin trench is a window into the past. The supervisor kneels in the trench and studies the wall until he has distinguished the various strata. Each stratum is then marked with yellow cards held in place by three-inch nails stuck into the dirt. Once the supervisor has discovered the thickness of the first stratum, he directs the workers to remove that layer, and only that layer, from the rest of the 16-by-16-foot square.

Any artifacts found are tagged with identifying information: the area, site trench and stratum number. Ultimately the recording card will list also the artifact's size, date of discovery, condition, description, illustration and photo index number and its disposition. If a skeleton or a floor turns up, the photographer takes a picture on the spot. For positive identification, the thousands of AEH photographs always include a slate board marked with the date, area number, site number, trench number and stratum.

Only when stratum one has been fully cleared, examined, recorded and photographed, do the workers move on to stratum two. Again the artifacts are collected and recorded. By now the trench bottom may be uneven since the strata can undulate and slope under a surface that is perfectly flat. So the crew descends, layer by layer, in a process that is like pulling one blanket at a time from a large stack.

When the diggers reach the depth of the initial test trench, they probe down another three feet on one side of the trench. Again they clear away the whole 16-by-16-foot area, one stratum at a time. When they reach bedrock and can go no farther, the supervisor does an exact scale drawing of the trench side, showing each of the strata and its appearance. The drawings tie in with the photographs, the supervisor's notes and the clues provided by the artifacts.

In the end, therefore, Hammond does not have just an empty hole. On the contrary, he can easily describe the appearance of every stratum, tell what objects were found there and, most likely, what the people were doing when they lived at each of the levels. The positions of the trenches are recorded so exactly and the digging done so precisely that Hammond could come back in 25 years, dig a trench next to the one he filled up 25 years before, and tie in the new trench with the old, stratum by stratum. The records are complete. There are no loose ends.

Hammond's satisfaction lies in "getting the last ounce of data out of the site." He can accomplish this only by the rigorous, scientific means he has helped to perfect. "Efficiency," he has said, "is next to godliness. And, who knows, it may be closer."

Hammond's next visit in his morning inspection reminds him of the expedition's major disappointment. One four-man group has been looking, without success, for tombs, either natural caves or man-made hollows. Tombs are especially valuable finds because ancient people were often buried with jewelry and other artifacts. Also, the skeletons often provide clues to the society—the state of dentistry, for example. Hammond smilingly refers to skeletons as "citizens" or "incumbents." The 1965 team enjoyed great success in finding tombs. But in 1966, the expedition did not find even one.

This failure was surprising. The expedition's secret weapon —a proton differential magnetometer—had predicted that the site did have tombs. The magnetometer, nicknamed "jazz-eye" by the expedition, detects buried objects which break up the earth's magnetic field. The magnetometer can't tell the difference between a rock and a wall. But several soundings can suggest an object's shape and size. The magnetometer crew has to guess the rest. Of course, "negative data," the absence of objects, is valuable too. At Hebron, a small crew of electronics experts worked most of the summer testing likely tomb sites. Hammond takes help where he can get it, and he has made more extensive use of the magnetometer than most archeologists.

From the tombs, "Mudir" moves on to Area 2, on the western slope of Jebel-er-Rumeide. More active than the other areas, this one boasts five sites, with four more already excavated and closed. The artifacts date mostly from the comparatively recent Greek and Islamic periods. The important finds include an Islamic house, a cemetery with 30 burials and the only stratified evidence of Roman occupation found so far on Jebel-er-Rumeide. The supervisor asks Hammond to have a look at the test trench: is there one stratum or two? Hammond can see two. Now he walks down to where he parked "Baby." His two-hour inspection at the dig is completed. Turning the jeep around, he heads back to the school.

He has almost reached the door of his office when he is intercepted by girls with problems in the labs. He is in a hurry: he wants to get back to his maps again before deciding how to distribute the men who will handle the new site. Still walking, Hammond holds a few impromptu conferences in the hallway. Then the photographer reminds him that he has to order a table from the carpenter and describes exactly how it must be made. On some days Hammond finds time for a second inspection of the sites. But he knows that today it will be impossible. Besides, the "dig" is progressing well. Hammond jumps back in "Baby" and heads into town to order the table.

The carpenter greets Hammond with a smile and a cup of coffee. Hammond knows that the coffee is hospitality, not a business gimmick. He also knows that you refuse it only from dire necessity, and then in the most tactful manner possible. You can't say, "I don't care for any, thanks." An Arab will be offended by that. The week before, one of the expedition's girls had declined with the explanation that the Mormon religion forbade her to drink coffee—that was considered an adequate excuse. As for Hammond, he is always ready for another cup of coffee.

Hospitality, in fact, emerged as one of the expedition's major problems, a surprising and almost comic one. Once Hebron had decided to accept Hammond and the expedition, they did so completely. Suspicious at first, the Arabs turned out to be full of a generous spirit, so much so that they almost swamped the expedition with snacks and kindness. On the sites, the nearest farmer always brought trays of coffee and cake. Hammond knew that the hospitality couldn't be refused, but he hated to see his supervisors stop working.

While Hammond is at the carpenter's shop, work stops on the "dig." Precisely at 1:30 P.M. Hammond's assistant director blows the whistle. The rocky landscape is bathed in the incandescent light of midday. The last few hours in the heat have passed slowly. But the day, on the sites at least, is over. The supervisors round up their equipment. The dozens of baskets of pottery are loaded on the buses. The workers start off on foot to their homes. The archeologists fall wearily into their seats on the bus and the "dig" staff returns to camp.

Hammond himself gets back just in time for lunch. This two-o'clock meal is a more lengthy, dignified affair than the rapid-fire breakfast nine hours before. The students and teachers discuss the problems encountered on the sites. With a joke about "skulduggery," one mentions a warrior burial he once found, complete with sword and armor. Outside, the shadows of afternoon appear. The members of the expedition unwind a little.

But not too much. At the meal's end, Hammond makes his official announcements, suggestions and reprimands. Speaking energetically, he describes the next side trip to another archeological site. On the expedition's "day off," Hammond "hauls everybody around" to visit other digs in that part of the world. Friday, their only free day, is the Arab holy day, so they can't work anyway. The students learn a lot by seeing the other excavations. As Hammond says, by the time he "gets through with them, Friday is rougher than a normal working day."

Hammond continues his announcements, his voice taking on an ironic, darkly humorous tone as he chastises the delinquents. He mentions no names but the guilty know whom he's talking about. Like all expeditions, the AEH has a few problem cases. Some of the students thought they had come for a European holiday, only to find themselves faced by a backbreaking work schedule. The misfits have not always been properly briefed by their schools. And Hammond, totally caught up in the work, shows little sympathy. When one girl tried to sleep late, saying she was sick, Hammond ordered that she stay in her room, with no visitors and nothing to eat but rice. She soon improved. Hammond does not expect that everyone will be as dedicated as he is. But he does insist that each person do his share. The vacation-minded soon come to regard "Mudir" as a man with a whip.

Hammond is relentless simply because there is so little time. To some, the "dig" might seem to last forever. To Hammond, the six weeks are all too brief. He has the responsibility of advancing the excavation on all fronts. He also has to train 15 to 20 students who have never been out of the classroom. "Everything we do," he says, "is set up on SOP," an Army phrase meaning "Standard Operating Procedure." "We get more work done because everybody knows where we're going and what they're doing. The work is very complex. But we can begin with completely untrained students and by the end of the season they know how to do it. By following the book, I run a fairly GI dig."

Hammond, however, sees beyond the work and the rules. He does make allowances for morale. He hires a staff of eight Arabs to look after the school. They clean, make the beds, wash the clothes and cook. Hammond insists on excellent food. This service leaves the expedition free to concentrate on archeology. He also arranges trips into Hebron's market quarter, where the Americans can shop for Bedouin jewelry and inlaid wooden boxes. And he decrees that three o'clock to four-thirty each afternoon is free time for everyone. Not surprisingly, most of the expedition members take a nap.

Work starts again at four-thirty in the courtyard. All the pottery collected that morning is washed and laid out to dry in the sun. The Arab boys lay the pieces on 10 large rectangular mats. Since the supervisors bring back 40 baskets, each containing perhaps several hundred pieces, the courtyard is covered by over 10,000 sherds. The pottery assistants, mostly girls, or as Hammond coolly refers to them, "girl types," begin sorting the sherds into three piles—rims, handles and bases. After this preliminary sorting, they attempt to classify the pieces. Hammond has to go through these innumerable piles, giving the final verdict on a piece's age or type. To Hammond these pottery sessions are "the most excruciating event of the day. You are faced with 25 students circling you, saying, 'What is it? What date is it? How do you know?' " But the sessions are necessary. Sometimes dozens of pieces turn out to be from the same vase, a bit of luck which makes the day worthwhile. All the important pieces must be catalogued to show what sort of people lived in what stratum. The students learn the subtle art of looking at a few inches of clay and rattling off, "tenth-century Islamic" or "obviously Greek." All the while the natives grin at the curious proceedings.

The pottery sessions last until six-thirty. Then Hammond and his senior staff—"the Senior Citizens"—gather to discuss "top-level problems," Hammond's ironic nomenclature for small talk and cocktails. Since orthodox Islam forbids alcohol, Hammond is careful to partake behind closed doors. While the "officers" discuss, the students carry the pottery back into the laboratory and tidy up the equipment for the next morning.

The day's final meal is at seven. Like lunch, it is full and leisurely. Sometimes there are lectures. But always Hammond ends the day with his announcements and suggestions.

At eight, the expedition's day is officially over. The members can do as they please. Most of them are asleep by nine. A few try to squeeze in a little social activity. On some occasions, everybody stays up to entertain guests, such as local journalists and United Nations officials. Or the AEH may have been invited out to a party.

Usually, however, Hammond heads straight back to his office. He is ready for another five-hour stretch of work. He calls himself a "night person." "I go through the day in a happy mood because I'm not 'with it.' About nine o'clock I wake up and then I'm good for the rest of the night." Hammond works on the theory that "a twenty-four-hour day is flexible and if you work hard you can get an eight-day week." Hammond's disdain for sleep is really a part of his love for archeology. Like Lawrence of Arabia, he feels that "if you're going to do something, you must do it completely. Success depends on whether you are willing to put in that much time."

But Hammond, unlike Lawrence, does not fancy that he is pushing himself for the perverse joy of going beyond his own limits. "No," he says candidly, "I know what my limits are. I caught a mortar shell during the war and I know just about how far I can go. I know exactly where to stop. When I need sleep, I go to sleep." Out of dedication to his work, Hammond simply tries not to need much sleep.

In his office Hammond dictates to his recording machines for several hours. The important discoveries have been left on his desk. He describes each artifact with archeological precision. He does not mind the monotonous work because he is "ultimately responsible for every piece."

These objects—the jewelry, coins, bowls, jugs, vases, tools, mosaics, parts of houses—are debris retrieved from the maw of time. Though the makers and users died 10, 20, 30 maybe 40 centuries ago, these bits and pieces remain, mute testimony of an extinct people and a way of life. Finding these artifacts and knowing what to make of them is Hammond's science. His rigorous approach, he believes, is the only way to take full advantage of a site. The reward for this thoroughness is a better, clearer picture of humans who lived, worked and raised families so long before ourselves.

"This methodology is the only way we'll get the complete data and thus an insight into the technology and chronology of the ancient cultures. It sounds pretty dead. But it really isn't. Out of this mass you can eventually build a picture of how man lived and what his daily life was like. And that, I think, is what we're after. It used to be artifacts themselves that were very important. You filled up the museums. Now we're more interested in what they tell us about human development. One might almost call it anthropological archeology. Sometimes you find things that are inexplicable and you have to sit down and say, 'What was this used for? What did they *do* with it?' Or you find a combination of things together that tell you a little bit about their life. For example, we found a house, or a cave that was being used for a house. It had been hit by an earthquake and the pottery was still on the floor and you could just see the people scrambling out as the ground shook. You get insights into the life of the people and eventually you build this into a composite so that you can see how life was actually lived in that time. We dig because there is something there and it is ancient life and we have to find out as much as we can about that ancient life."

But until the puzzle falls entirely into place, Hammond finds his satisfaction in "doing the job properly, in getting the last ounce of data out of the site." His obsession is "the stratigraphic history of this place from beginning to end."

A little after one in the morning, Hammond turns in. Outside his window the stars blink and twinkle just as they did when nomads first camped at Hebron, when Abraham came to worship, when David wielded kingly power, when the Greeks and Romans brought their dominion to this land and when Islam installed Allah in the hearts of the people. Beneath these same faraway stars, life went on at Hebron for 5,000 years. But now archeologists have come and time stands still as they look into the past. The job at Hebron is hardly begun, however. Hammond goes to sleep thinking of all that he must do tomorrow.

five

The Past Tense
of Man

INSIDE the explorer's small tent the greatest headhunter sat serenely on a camp stool. The oldest and most loving of his four wives, wearing only a short fiber skirt, rested at his feet. The chief appeared to be completely relaxed. His placid, rather gentle face would never suggest that he had killed 58 men. Yet all Jivaro Indians—warring tribes that live in the thick Ecuadorian jungles to the east of the Andes Mountains—acknowledged his prowess and feared him accordingly.

Lewis Cotlow, a rugged-looking, 51-year-old man dressed in khakis, studied the chief closely. He had traveled to the headwaters of the Amazon to meet this legendary figure. Now he wanted to understand him. For years Cotlow, a life insurance agent who devoted more time to visiting primitive peoples than to working at this occupation, had wondered why one man cuts off another's head, shrinks it and then dances around it. But Utitiaja seemed content to smile silently down at his wife. A woman in her fifties, she gazed back at him with an expression of profound tenderness and pride. The explorer's usually animated face was pensive and he tried to break the silence diplomatically.

"How old are you, Utitiaja?" Cotlow spoke in Spanish to his translator, Shuara, the fourth person in the tent. The young man listened respectfully to the chief's answer and replied, "He is not sure. Fifty-six or fifty-seven."

Cotlow sat on a camp stool a few feet away from Utitiaja. He leaned forward as though he could get closer to the chief's mind. At once aggressive and friendly, Cotlow talked with an impassioned directness. Although this trek into Jivaro country was only in its fourth week, his handsome, tanned face showed how taxing his life away from civilization had been.

"How old were you when you went on your first raid?" Cotlow asked.

"Ten." Shuara again translated the chief's quiet reply into Spanish. This plain-looking young Indian, whose parents had been slaughtered in the ceaseless jungle wars, had wandered into the territory's Catholic mission at Sucua, Ecuador, when he was still a child. Now 23, a Christian and no man's enemy, he was welcomed by all the tribes.

Cotlow, a resourceful man at both survival and diplomacy, continued to probe. "Were you afraid?"

"Yes, I was very frightened. But not as frightened as when I took my first head." Utitiaja smiled at the memory, his smile exaggerated by the harsh light from the lantern overhead. Outside the brown Army tent the deep Amazon jungle rested in the forbidding darkness. The rest of the Indians had gone to sleep. The other world—the one with cars and skyscrapers and movie theaters—was far from this tiny Jivaro clearing.

"How old were you when you took your first head?" Cotlow asked.

"Seventeen," Shuara gave back the answer.

Cotlow was a veteran explorer of the most primitive regions in Asia, Africa and South America. He had heard and witnessed many strange things. But Utitiaja's answer startled him nonetheless. For an instant his mind flickered back to his home in New York City where teen-agers lead quite different lives.

"Who taught you how to be a great hunter and warrior?"

Cotlow had always used the man-to-man approach. Not a trained scientist or an anthropologist, Cotlow traveled and explored for the satisfaction of finding and actually getting to know rare breeds of men. He was never content to know them as statistics and lifeless facts. He wanted to know them personally. But so far Cotlow had not been able to get close to Utitiaja. Could one just dismiss Utitiaja as a savage? A madman? A murderer? Cotlow was not ready to accept the civilized man's easy answers to things he did not understand.

For the past three days Utitiaja had been helping Cotlow make movies of Jivaro dances and ceremonies. They had worked together closely. During those three days, while Cotlow ran his cameras and Utitiaja acted and directed his warriors, Cotlow had studied the Indian closely. He had chatted with Utitiaja on many occasions. But Utitiaja was an unusually self-possessed man, and he never offered any information about himself.

Cotlow felt grateful to have these few hours alone with the most famous, most feared of South American headhunters. Utitiaja and his warriors were planning to return to their home territory at dawn the next day, so this was Cotlow's last chance to ask the right questions.

Now Utitiaja began to talk at greater length. "My father taught me to be a warrior, as all Jivaro boys are taught if their fathers are alive. My father lived until I was thirteen so he taught me much. He showed me how to hunt, how to aim the blowgun, handle the lance, move through the forest like the jaguar. When I was seven I started going on hunts with him. I listened and watched him, and so I learned."

Utitiaja spoke with dignity and a quiet confidence. When Cotlow had first seen Utitiaja, three days before, he had been surprised. He had expected the headhunter to be a big, fierce man. Instead, Utitiaja was smaller and less muscular than most of his followers. His face especially amazed Cotlow. No barbaric cruelty, not a hint of ferocity showed. Cotlow saw instead a gentle, almost vulnerable-looking man. Nevertheless, Utitiaja moved with an easy authority, an inner assurance that said, "I am the leader." The chief's unexpected appearance and bearing intrigued Cotlow almost as much as his reputation. What, he wondered, could be the source of such confidence?

"And every morning," Utitiaja continued, "he sat me down in front of him, even before he ate, and told me what I must do when I grew up. He told me who our enemies were, who had killed my brother and his father and his brother. Each time he told me exactly how each man caused their deaths. Every morning he told me that my most solemn duty would be to take blood revenge against those who had killed members of my family."

Shuara translated Utitiaja's recollections. The Jivaro language had a singsongy, Chinese sound. The only noises besides the voices of the three men were the chirps of the crickets outside and the fluttering of the lantern flame.

Cotlow had first heard about Utitiaja in 1945, when he was on his second expedition to the Amazon jungle, the most extensive wilderness left in the world. Peruche, a famed chief himself, had told Cotlow, "I am not the greatest warrior. Today the greatest is Utitiaja. All Indians have heard of Utitiaja." And just before Cotlow returned to Jivaro country for the third time in August, 1949, he read about Utitiaja in *El Commercio,* a newspaper in Quito, Ecuador. An article by a missionary lamented the horrible increase in wars and revenge killings. The padre said that Utitiaja was largely responsible.

"I can still see my father, serious, stern, speaking softly but with great force. If I did my duty I would have good wives, good hunting, and long life. If I failed, my crops would spoil and my aim become poor. And he was right. I have had a good life because I have always performed the most sacred duties of a man."

Cotlow remembered that he had heard his own people, his civilized neighbors, talk about "sacred duties." Sometimes they too demanded the death of an enemy.

"But there was more than my father's talks in learning to be a warrior. When I first accompanied him on a raid, at ten, he kept me close to him throughout the fighting. When he had killed his enemy with the lance, he called me to his side and gave me the lance. Then he told me to plunge it into the dead man's body so that I would know the feel of it and learn how hard I must thrust. He wanted me to do this, also, so that I would not be afraid."

The 10,000 Jivaros, Cotlow had learned, were divided into small, scattered tribes. Even a great chief like Utitiaja might command only 25 warriors, plus their women and children. These 100 or so Indians were further split into loose family groups of about 30. Each of these families lived in a jivaria, or communal house, which was built of logs and thatch in a jungle clearing. The other families lived about five miles away. If the members of the tribe lived closer together, they would compete for the animals they hunted for food and would wipe out the supply. The nearest other tribe, usually an enemy, lived two or three days' march away. In the endless Amazon jungle, property is not very important. No Indian ever killed for land. The Jivaros had more spiritual reasons.

"On my first raid," Utitiaja went on, "I killed the man who had killed my father. I had sworn to my father that I would avenge his death so his soul could rest in peace. I was thirteen when he died. It was four long years that his soul was restless and unhappy because I could not take blood revenge. When I killed him, I could say, 'See, my father, I have brought your soul peace.'"

When a Jivaro warrior takes an enemy's head, and after he has retreated a day's march, he shrinks it. After removing the skull, he boils the skin down to one-third its original size and shapes it with hot sand. Soon after this almost ritual procedure, the warrior begins a long fast as a prelude to a great *tsantsa* feast which lasts four or five days—the most significant event in the Indians' lives.

"What is the *tsantsa* feast like, Utitiaja, when you are the victor celebrating the destruction of your enemy and his spirit which keeps trying to hurt you?"

"It is a wonderful thing," Utitiaja answered. "You feel that you are good, that you have done what you are supposed to do in this world. You have triumphed over your enemy by killing him. You now triumph over his evil spirit and make it a good spirit to help you more. And you tell the souls of the people you loved that they can stop wandering unhappily. These are all splendid things to feel. It seems that you are soaring high, like the condor. I wish I could have more *tsantsa* feasts."

Cotlow liked these celebrations himself. The *tsantsa* feasts, in fact, had brought Lewis Cotlow back to the Amazon jungle for the third time in nine years. On the first two expeditions (in 1940 and 1945) Cotlow had taken thousands of feet of documentary film. Now, in 1949, on his third trip, he wanted to complete a full-length feature movie, "Jungle Headhunters," for which he particularly needed a colorful, dramatic ending.

Cotlow thus had some frankly commercial reasons for this third trip. Aside from finishing his movie, he had also gathered enough new material for a book about his expeditions to South America (*Jungle Headhunters* published in 1950) and for the lectures he gives in the United States. But Cotlow does not go into the jungle simply for the money he might make from films, books and lectures. He could earn more in New York City in various business ventures. A man would be ill-advised, he says, to think of exploring for profit. The financial returns are definitely secondary.

But to Cotlow, the *tsantsa* dance was far more than a perfect scene for a movie. As the climax of the warrior's revenge killing, the dance was the focus of all of Cotlow's questions: Why did the Jivaros kill each other? Why did they cut off heads? Why did they then dance so joyously around the shrunken heads? Cotlow had come back to the Amazon to find the answers to these questions. At least he had told himself that was why he returned.

I suspect, however, that there is a more fundamental explanation for his return—one that applies as well to all 13 of his expeditions. Cotlow is such a complex man that even his own insights sound disturbingly as though they come from several different men. The central fact is that Cotlow has been unable to resist going back to the stone-age world of the primitive man. After each trip, when he is exhausted and perhaps actually sick, he swears he will never do it again. But a few months of rest always dull the pain and whatever forbidding memories he has, and back Cotlow goes. He often tells people that he is part primitive. The truth may be that he wishes he were. I think Cotlow explores in order to communicate with cultures more appealing to him than his own. By exploring he can partake, as much as a 20th-century white man can, of the vitality, simplicity and integrity of the primitive world.

Cotlow's search—for his movie's ending, for an understanding of headhunters, for a personal enrichment—had begun three weeks before his conversation with Utitiaja. The DC-3 carrying Cotlow and his two cameramen, Bodo Wuth, a German from Quito, and Jules Bucher, an American from California, touched down on the tiny airstrip at the Sucua mission in the Amazon. Colonel Winstead, the pilot and head of the United States Air Force Mission in Quito, brought the plane to rest two feet short of the jungle. Cotlow had always found that the most frightening part of exploring was the "civilized" means of getting anywhere. Catching his breath, Cotlow hopped out to meet two missionaries, one Catholic, the other Protestant, both seeking to save the souls of young Jivaros.

Cotlow stayed with the Spanish padre because he had a more spacious mission building. They rode off in a jeep provided by the Ecuadorian government. The Jivaro boys who had accompanied the padre thought that a ride in a jeep was perhaps civilization's ultimate, most thrilling benefit. At his crude boarding school in the jungle, the missionary was educating some 125 Jivaro children, all of whom had lost their families in the jungle wars. Although happy students and good workers, the young Indians did not quickly forget the teachings of their fathers. In his two days at the mission, Cotlow noticed that the children of one clan would not play with children from enemy clans. The padre told him about one boy who graduated from the mission and, wearing a cross and a Catholic medal around his neck, returned to the jungle to avenge the murder of his father and brother by killing four men.

Cotlow quickly made preparations for his expedition into headhunter territory. The missionary recommended Shuara for a guide. He had no family, no enemies, no feuds: he was a true neutral. Like Cotlow, he wore the white man's khaki shirt and pants. But as a result of his years in the jungle, he needed no shoes. For the heavy work—carrying the supplies and hacking out a trail—Cotlow hired six half-breed bearers. Chief of these was Don Bodillo, a tough, beefy trader from the mountains. Cotlow also borrowed six worn-out horses for the first day's march. Cotlow always tried to travel light in the jungle, but he couldn't do without tents, sleeping bags, lanterns, insect repellent, first-aid supplies, movie cameras, some extra clothing, gifts for the Indians and, of course, food. The menu on this trip included many cans of beef stew, hard candy and Cotlow's favorite, canned sardines. The Indian children would get most of the candy. Soon Cotlow's food supplies would be exhausted and he would end up accepting native hospitality, as he did on most of his other expeditions.

Plunging into the heart of Jivaro country, the 10 men—Cotlow, Shuara, Bodo Wuth, Bucher and the six bearers—had to cut their way through dense jungle. Two bearers in front, swinging machetes, chopped a path out of the green tangle. The high, lush vegetation nearly shut out the sun. Gaudy butterflies darted through the shafts of light. In the distance, exotic birds trilled and screeched. Monkeys scampered around overhead. In this shadowy hothouse Cotlow felt the sweat pour off his body, and clouds of insects closed in for an unusual white-skinned meal.

On the afternoon of the first day, Cotlow's horse got so tangled in the bushes and vines that he toppled sideways onto Cotlow's left leg. The explorer felt severe pain up to his hip. He could only lie helpless as the horse kicked and floundered, trying to get its balance. The other men joined in lifting the horse and simultaneously prying Cotlow's leg out. The accident kept him limping for weeks, but Cotlow was grateful he had broken no bones.

Accidents and diseases had always been Cotlow's main fear. South America's headhunters and Africa's cannibals did not worry him as much; he felt that he could deal with them. But the constant possibility of contracting amoebic dysentery or breaking a leg did concern Cotlow. He knew that many explorers have not come back and that others have been emotionally or physically shattered for life. Cotlow himself usually returned to New York with his health run down. He readily admits that his many expeditions would have been impossible without modern drugs and his doctor's skill at patching him up after each exhausting trip. Out of vanity he never let his photographers take a close-up of him after an expedition—he didn't want people to see how much the jungle had debilitated him. Cotlow now feels humble about his good luck in avoiding any major disaster. An explorer, he says, needs "an instinct, a feeling for when to advance and when to retreat." Cotlow resolved at an early stage in his career that he would not play the daredevil. "You can get into trouble if you try to be too brave," he says.

The next morning Cotlow had his first look at a river they would have to cross, the Upano, 400 yards of swift, swirling water pouring down from the Andes. Cotlow thought that here was a time when he should retreat.

But Shuara was unconcerned. He began shouting across to an Indian clearing perched atop the 1,000-foot-high east bank. Don Bodillo added his booming voice. Finally the Jivaros noticed the visitors. Two of the Indians started down the twisting trail to the river bank. After a half-hour of lying in the shade and swatting insects, Cotlow saw the men reach the water's edge, near a 20-foot dugout canoe. More shouting. The Indians recognized Shuara. Across they came, paddling furiously against the onrushing current.

The two natives agreed to take the explorers across the river. Before crossing, Cotlow sent one of the bearers back to the mission with the horses, and then he, Bodo Wuth, and the Indians pulled the boat upstream 300 yards to offset the pull of the current on their return crossing. Cotlow and Bodo Wuth leaned on their knees and hung on for dear life as the Indians paddled like machines. Jules Bucher, the American photographer, filmed the hazardous crossing from shore. The dugout shot along, hitting the far bank only 10 feet from the bottom of the path leading down from the Jivaro camp. After three more trips, the natives had Cotlow, his expedition and the supplies safely at the base of the sheer cliff.

The steep ascent, rocky or muddy by turn, was extremely difficult for Cotlow. Slipping and stumbling, his leg still in great pain, his heart pounding, Cotlow finally had to admit that he couldn't keep up with the others. In fact, he wedged himself against a tree on the trail and went to sleep. Cotlow kept himself in top shape by daily workouts back in New York City. But he was still not a Jivaro. Nor was he a young man. At such exhausting moments Cotlow usually found himself swearing, "Never again, never again."

After his nap, Cotlow finished the climb and met the local chief, Take, in front of the tribe's communal house. This mountaintop jivaria had an excellent view and could be easily defended. But Cotlow was not so impressed with the camp. The clearing was too small for long photographic shots. And there weren't enough Indians for an accurate performance of the major ceremonies. So, after the proper formalities and a brief meal and a few pictures, the expedition moved on.

For the next two weeks, Cotlow traveled from jivaria to jivaria. He took reels and reels of fine shots. But he still had no grand finale. The constant fighting and killing among the Indians were the main problem. One group he visited was down to five men, hardly enough to unpack the cameras for. More urgently than ever, Cotlow felt he must film the *tsantsa* dance.

Cotlow headed north, looking for the Jivaros who lived near the Sepa River, an offshoot of the Upano. Here, at last, he found the perfect setting—a wide, level clearing, a large jivaria, and little hills nearby for long photographic shots. Cotlow was introduced to Nayapi, the chief. Though he was reserved, Nayapi agreed to call in the men and women from several other jivarias under his leadership. Soon Cotlow had 28 warriors assembled to act out the *tsantsa* dance for him.

Despite the tenseness caused by the wars and by the Indians' natural hostility to the white man, Cotlow had little difficulty in persuading Nayapi and the region's other chiefs to cooperate with him. His success in dealing with primitive people is one of the reasons Cotlow keeps coming back to the jungle. Cotlow was frankly surprised by the almost painless success of his first expeditions. A global traveler since his early twenties, Cotlow had decided in the mid-1930s to switch his attention from tourist meccas to the remote hinterlands. He went to Africa in 1937 and to South America in 1940. Among other accomplishments, he brought out the first color films ever made of both continents. And he managed to stay alive, a feat which Cotlow attributes chiefly to his diplomatic ability. At first he thought he would not push his luck by returning, but he soon decided that he had a flair for getting along with primitive man, a talent he should not waste.

Lewis Cotlow's approach to primitive men is basic: look them in the eye, treat them like men and bring love. He tries to practice the golden rule: he puts himself in the headhunter's place. He knows how to convince the Indians that he is not interested in their wives or their gold. But he also knows that he can't patronize stone-age people. Like intelligent animals, they see through pretense. If an explorer is condescending, he may, with luck, be tolerated, but he won't be helped.

Cotlow makes it a point to be more than just sincere. Cotlow firmly believes that "If you give love, you get love. How can I say that? I go among these primitive people and I give them love. In my own way. I love them. They know I love them. I put my arms around the children. And they love me. I get up in the morning and the kids are around me, the headhunter kids, they come and put their arms around me." Cotlow had proved the value of this idealism in the world's most primitive areas. Never armed, always open to attack by the natives, he has found that love is his best weapon.

Nayapi's warriors, unfortunately, lacked gusto. They wanted to help Cotlow, they dressed up in their feathers, necklaces and headdresses and they danced—but they were only going through the motions. Their dancing was too stiff to be convincing on film.

Cotlow and his cameramen discussed the possibilities. The answer, the explorer knew, was a dynamic personality, a leader who could really excite the warriors. Cotlow turned to Shuara. "What about the greatest headhunter, Utitiaja?" Cotlow asked. He had wanted to see this legendary man, who could perhaps explain to him the mystery of headhunting. Now it occurred to him that the much-feared warrior and leader might also be the answer to his movie-making troubles.

Shuara had objections. Utitiaja's clearing, he said, was too small for good pictures. And Utitiaja had only 25 men. Shuara then suggested a plan of his own. He would go to the larger tribes nearby and ask them all to come together and help the white man make a movie. Shuara knew that they would be impressed by the copy of *Life* magazine which Cotlow had brought. It contained several pages of bright color photographs (taken during Cotlow's second expedition) of Jivaros who lived only 40 miles away.

"You mean the clans are friendly enough to come together?" Cotlow asked.

"No, there are not many friendly clans," Shuara answered.

"Then why should they bury the lance for me?"

"They will do it," Shuara insisted, "because of the things I will tell them about you. I will say that you have visited the Jivaros of the Santiago and the Paute, and that you have shown their pictures all over the world. But now you have come back to the Jivaros of the Upano because you know they are the greatest warriors of all."

"No, they'll never do it." Cotlow shook his head.

"I will tell them," Shuara went on, "that it was you who came on the big bird the last time it flew over the jungle. I will say that you have many gifts and a great feast for them. And I will tell them about the magic tricks you brought. Every *wishnu* [witch doctor] of every clan will want to see your kind of magic. Besides, all Jivaros love a party."

Cotlow considers himself a practical man and he was skeptical. He did want to finish the movie, however. If Shuara's plan could possibly work, he had to try it.

Accordingly Shuara left the next morning, carrying the copy of *Life*, to round up the Indians. The bearers, meanwhile, were sent back to the mission to buy two or three swine, the customary fare at *tsantsa* feasts.

Cotlow and the cameramen, Bodo Wuth and Bucher, settled down to wait. The days passed pleasantly at first. The three men loafed. Cotlow noted down his impressions of the Indians and the incidents of the trip. Occasionally, they joined the natives in fishing or hunting.

Cotlow marveled on these hunts at the efficiency of the Indians' deadly blowguns. With a 10-foot tube and poison darts, the skilled hunter could kill birds, monkeys and even wildcats at distances up to 200 feet. Unlike a gun, which would have frightened away the game, the silent blowgun allowed the hunter to make numerous kills before the animals suspected anything. The Indians had also perfected various fishing techniques. They used clever traps as well as a variety of nets. Sometimes they would dam a river, stun the fish with a drug made from the roots of the *tempo* plant and then simply pick their catch out of the water.

As a guest of the Indians, Cotlow preferred it when they went fishing instead of hunting. Fish are enjoyable the world over, Cotlow has found. Monkey stews and other native delicacies, on the other hand, take some time to get used to, although Cotlow did like the many dishes the Jivaros made from bananas. Cotlow also made sure he had plenty of boiled water for drinking. The Jivaros themselves favored a more spirited beverage called *nijimanche*. The Indian women produced this by chewing up boiled yucca tuber and spitting it back into large pots. After a week's fermentation, *nijimanche* serves nicely to promote fellowship, instill courage and keep the body warm. Each Jivaro consumes four or five quarts a day. Cotlow drank *nijimanche* only to be friendly. All too aware of how the drink was made, he could never develop a taste for it.

Despite this pleasant existence, Cotlow became more and

more restless as several days passed. So did the Sepa Indians who had agreed, because of their trust in Shuara, to act as hosts for this unique meeting of enemy clans. Cotlow began to fear the worst: Shuara might be injured, the headhunters might be too busy fighting to take time out for his movies, or perhaps the tribes had so decimated each other that Shuara was unable to find enough warriors.

The decline of primitive peoples like the Jivaros has long worried Cotlow. He was deeply pained to see the Indians hastening their own end by fighting among themselves. And he felt that if they didn't eventually extinguish themselves, the white man would, with his diseases and so-called civilization. Even while the Jivaros continued their ancient feuds, civilization was bringing roads and airfields to the Amazon basin. Missionaries had come, and army and trading outposts. Unprepared, unwelcoming, the Indians were being dragged by the heels into a harsh new world. Even a convert like Shuara was a potent force for change. When he talked about his new religion, the Indians saw that he was happy and their own beliefs were undermined.

Cotlow felt that a certain glory was passing. His first expeditions into Africa and South America forced him to realize that primitive man is changing, even disappearing from the earth. Today there are few tribes in the world that have not had some contact with civilization. Once the natives grasp the scope and power of the white man's technological culture, they tend literally to give up. Cotlow has observed the loss of hope from one expedition to the next. Proud warriors have become listless and abject as they comprehend how completely powerless they are to stop the advance of a civilization alien to their own.

Most primitive peoples are, in fact, in a state of cultural decline: young Eskimos prefer pinball machines and cars to hunting seal; Australia's aborigines are often wards of the state; the aborigines of New Guinea, like most other primitives, are becoming dependent on the white man's tools and technology, a dependence which erodes their entire culture.

Knowing that each year primitive man is pushed closer to oblivion, Cotlow feels impelled to visit again these vanishing peoples and chronicle their lives. His aim is "to cover as much as I can and make a record of these wonderful people and their customs before the inroads of civilization desecrate them." This compulsion, nurtured by his surprising early success in getting along with aboriginal peoples, persuaded Cotlow that exploring the primitive was somehow his purpose in life. "I got the feeling after a while that this was my destiny."

Cotlow has followed this destiny with distinction. He has seen more of the remaining primitive cultures than any other explorer. He has seen African pygmies and cannibals, Amazon headhunters, New Guinea aborigines and polar Eskimos, and in June, 1967, Cotlow, aged 69, set out on his 13th expedition, to visit the bushmen of Australia.

The Jivaros were hardly extinct in 1949, however. On the sixth day of Cotlow's expedition, shortly after dawn, Shuara returned. After a few *whe-dee*'s—a friendly Jivaro greeting— Cotlow's enterprising guide trotted into the clearing. Tired but happy, he told Cotlow that he had succeeded. The Tutanangosa group was right behind him. The Cambanacas would be there by noon. And the great Utitiaja and his warriors would arrive at two o'clock. Cotlow could hardly believe Shuara's report, nor could the Sepas.

The assembly was, in fact, as extraordinary as a snowfall in the Amazon jungle. Aware that anthropologists and fellow explorers might doubt his story, Cotlow has always treasured his proof. The Protestant missionary at Sucua wrote a letter to the President of Ecuador in which he said: "This expedition proved singularly successful for several reasons. One of the unprecedented things accomplished was the bringing together of four distinct groups of Jivaros that have been enemies since time immemorial." Cotlow feels that the gathering together of the tribes was one of the great events of his career as an explorer.

Cotlow asked Shuara, "How did you persuade Utitiaja?"

"I told him you could not have a successful picture without the greatest warrior of the Jivaros."

Wondering what kind of man the chief would be, Cotlow hurriedly set up his camera. Soon Shuara returned with 25 warriors of the Tutanangosa group, accompanied by an equal number of women and children. Predictably the Sepas greeted the newcomers with icy formality. The Indians had promised not to kill each other, but that didn't mean they had to be friendly. After all, most of the Jivaros standing in the jungle clearing had lost relatives to warriors from the other clan. Handing out presents, Cotlow tried to spread a little cheer. Not particularly interested in civilization, the Indians still appreciated safety pins, fishhooks, mirrors, knives, cloth and beads. The Tutanangosas accepted the gifts politely and retired to the edge of the clearing. The Tutanangosa women were loaded down with large supplies of food and *nijimanche*. Cotlow noticed nervously that nobody smiled.

"Are you sure we won't have any trouble?" he asked Shuara.

"Yes. They have buried the lance. And no Jivaro would dream of violating a truce."

Cotlow had to admit that in his experience with them the Jivaros had always acted honorably. On the other hand, they had never been faced by such temptation.

The Cambanacas, with only 19 warriors, arrived at noon.

Their frosty greetings made Cotlow more apprehensive. The Cambanacas knew they were the smallest in number and they were scared.

At last Utitiaja, the great headhunter with the gentle face, strode in with his Chupientsa warriors. At his side were two bodyguards whose villainous faces made up for their chief's mildness. Quite unexpectedly, Utitiaja walked directly over to Cotlow, his arm extended. Cotlow knew immediately that Utitiaja was a rare and unconventional man. Etiquette required that Utitiaja speak first to the Sepa chief. But Utitiaja had come to perform in a movie and he wanted to see the man who would make it. Cotlow shook his hand warmly and thanked him. He explained, with Shuara translating, that he wanted to show the great Jivaro warriors to the world. Utitiaja answered that he thought he would enjoy himself. Evidently he thought the unlikely meeting of four enemy tribes an intriguing situation.

Since Utitiaja seemed willing to talk, Cotlow invited him to sit down on the camp bench. The great headhunter and the explorer chatted briefly about Utitiaja's home and the pictures in *Life* magazine and how many heads Utitiaja had taken. Cotlow knew that he would achieve the best results asking about the Jivaros and their lives, not by talking about his own problems. It was Utitiaja who returned to the subject of the movie. Cotlow said that he hoped to film the *tsantsa* dance. Utitiaja promised to help.

While the self-assured chief went to pay his respects to the other chiefs, the eyes of 70 enemy warriors followed him. They had heard about Utitiaja all their lives. He had killed that one's brother, another's father. Many were sworn to put their dead relatives at peace by killing Utitiaja. Although some eyes were filled with hate, Cotlow saw many that showed only fear. But

Utitiaja paid no attention one way or the other. He moved with a casual indifference to these lesser warriors.

Utitiaja soon came back to Cotlow and suggested that they begin. Cotlow accompanied Shuara as the guide explained to the different groups what dances he wanted. Along the way Cotlow picked out the strongest, most impressive warriors. Juantinga, who was Utitiaja's bodyguard and son-in-law, would play the lead. He looked the part of the fierce head-hunter. The Indians began to decorate themselves. They put red paint on their faces and arms, drew black lines on their foreheads, stuck bright feathers in their hair, put on necklaces made of teeth and topped off their splendid appearance with brilliant headdresses of monkey fur and multicolored feathers.

The 30 most impressive-looking warriors gathered in the flat, grassy clearing. Nayapi, the Sepa chief, provided the *tsantsa*, or shrunken head. Juantinga stuck his lance in the ground and put the shrunken head on top. Beyond the circle of warriors, musicians began to play flutes and drums. The stage was set for the victory dance, the ritual celebration of a warrior who has killed an enemy and brought his shrunken head back to the jivaria.

The warriors, holding spears, began to dance—three steps forward, a lunge at the enemy's head, three steps back, then a sideways shuffle, three steps forward. But the Indians were not in the mood. Their dancing, like that of the Sepas, six days before, lacked spirit and conviction.

Cotlow shook his head. Making movies was a soul-trying business. Getting into the jungle now seemed the easy part. Filming was another matter. The scene being recorded on film was the most significant ritual in Jivaro life. It should have been full of passion, excitement, a driving energy. But the Jivaros were performing their roles as if they were half asleep.

Cotlow grabbed a lance and waded into the middle of the circle. "Act just like you did at your last *tsantsa* feast," he told them. "Each of you has come back with a shrunken head. Remember how you felt, how you danced then. Thrust your lance hard as if you were killing an enemy," Shuara translated. Then Cotlow demonstrated. He leaped forward and stabbed into the air. Every man, woman and child howled with laughter. Cotlow knew that most primitive people have a wonderful sense of humor. Perhaps because they are far from civilization's rush and worries, they spend more of their time smiling and laughing. Still the uproar caught Cotlow off guard. He sheepishly realized that he had no business telling a Jivaro how to handle a lance. But he also knew he had broken the tension. As a rule, Cotlow never hesitated to look foolish if that meant getting along better with the natives.

Now the warriors put their hearts into the *tsantsa* dance. Cotlow himself was scared by their jumps and grunts as he and the cameramen moved around them taking pictures. The headhunters thrust their lances angrily at the *tsantsa*, showing how they killed, frightening the spirit which still lives in the shrunken head, particularly in the shiny black hair. A rhythmic chant of little muttered cries kept pace with the slap of bare feet. Their faces soon showed deep emotions as each remembered his own raids and victims. Finally the hero, Juantinga, conquered his enemy's spirit. The contentment showed vividly on his face.

Next Cotlow asked for the *hantsemale*, another important dance at the *tsantsa* feast. Utitiaja put the shrunken head around Juantinga's neck. The warriors joined hands in a circle. The musicians played their strange, throbbing music. Then the men began to dance in small steps, making grunting noises that gradually rose to an ominous pitch.

Shuara whispered a curious fact to Cotlow. "See those two men over there," he said, "the one with the yellow feathers and the other with the jaguar-tooth necklace. Well, the man with the feathers killed the other man's brother. But now they are dancing together."

The dance went on with gathering force. The warriors' bodies grew more tense, their faces showing clearly the triumphant, almost mystical joy felt by the victorious headhunter—the faces, Cotlow realized, of fulfilled men.

When Cotlow had shot enough film, he stopped the dance. Now he wanted to thank the Jivaros. Breaking the circle, he took the hands of two breathless Jivaros. But he never did finish the speech. Suddenly the musicians started up again, the dancers immediately picked up the beat and Cotlow had no choice but to join in. The onlookers chuckled but Cotlow merged with the Jivaros in the true spirit of the dance.

Shuffling sideways, forward, sideways, back, Cotlow immersed himself in the primitive movements and sounds. Soon he, too, was breathing in hoarse grunts. The steady rhythm stripped away his civilized veneer and transported Cotlow into an elemental rapture. On the other side of the circle, Juantinga, who had already taken 28 heads himself, had retreated into the private world of the happy hunter. The black and shrunken head bobbed on his chest. As the heavy pounding of the drums filled the air, Cotlow studied Juantinga's rapturous expression. The once-fierce face revealed an exultation that could come only from the depths of the soul. And Cotlow himself was sharing those emotions. For a few minutes the explorer understood the peace that Juantinga and the other warriors found in killing an enemy and dancing around a shrunken head—a peace which, according to Jivaro philosophy, extended to both the living and the dead.

The headhunters' quest for peace of soul was something Cotlow could readily grasp. He had planned his whole life so that he could capture the same elusive serenity. As a young man, Cotlow deliberately shaped a life in which the rewards would be personal satisfaction instead of wealth.

Born in Brooklyn, Cotlow grew up on Long Island. He studied economics at New York University and later, after World War I began, at George Washington University in Washington, D.C. The United States Army, through the Reserve Officers Training Corps program, was also preparing him for service in Europe. But the flu epidemic put a stop to both his academic and military careers. Cotlow contracted the disease and nearly died in Walter Reed Hospital. When he had recovered, he decided to stay in Washington; for one thing, he didn't want his girl in New York to see him looking so thin and haggard.

Cotlow, only 21, was appointed a representative of the United States Shipping Board. As a "super-cargo" on Government ships operated by private companies, Cotlow had the responsibility of traveling around the world from one exotic port to another, ensuring that Federal regulations were obeyed, and photographing harbor facilities. While the ships were laying over, Cotlow often hastened off to see the countryside. He also read and thought a great deal; he soon reached his guiding values: Be true to yourself and do all things in moderation (except exploration, it would seem). After three years the Government canceled the program and Cotlow had to look for another job.

Cotlow had already been seized by a love for travel and great curiosity about the world. He carefully chose his next job so that he would have the freedom to indulge this desire. Returning to New York, he became a life insurance salesman, a difficult profession in the early 1920s, before life insurance had become popular. Cotlow wanted to deal with people and he felt that if he worked hard he could earn enough for trips around the world. At the age of 29, Cotlow made the select Million Dollar Roundtable (by selling a million dollars' worth of insurance)—an achievement he still views with pride. Cotlow had an obvious knack for making money. But he had always disapproved of his society's over-emphasis on materialism. True to his values, he was content simply to satisfy his personal needs. He was already taking several months out each year for travel, mostly to famous capitals and tourist spots. When he was in his early thirties, he gave a successful series of lectures around the United States called "The Soul of Japan."

Then Cotlow began to encounter anthropologists and explorers who convinced him that he had seen only half the world, and not the most interesting half. They told him about fascinating and exotic peoples far removed from civilization. "Hurry," they said, "primitive man is fast disappearing." Cotlow began the research that necessarily precedes exploration, and, at the age of 38, he went on his first expedition, visiting the pygmies in the Belgian Congo. Four years later, in 1940, he journeyed to the Amazon basin and found his first headhunters.

Cotlow kept going back to visit primitive peoples because in exploring he found his own serenity. He decided to devote only a quarter of his life to business. Exploring was more rewarding than making money. In the jungle he met and came to know interesting people. And when he returned from an expedition, Cotlow saw his work praised and appreciated. His discoveries, his movies, this recognition—all are part of what can be called the "psychic income" that gives Cotlow his peace of soul.

Cotlow understood people who went to great lengths to put their souls at peace, but he still felt that he didn't wholly understand Utitiaja. He knew why he wanted to take 58 heads, but not why he was a man of such composure. Cotlow understood headhunters now, but not Utitiaja.

During the two days following the *tsantsa* dance, Cotlow had become convinced that Utitiaja possessed a nearly boundless poise and bravery. The gentle headhunter did not pay the least attention to the explosive situation Shuara had concocted. The Indians from the hostile tribes eyed one another with veiled fear and hate. But Utitiaja had no concern for anything but Cotlow's movie-making and showed evident enjoyment in observing it.

Late in the first day of the meeting, after the filming of the *tsantsa* ceremony was over, Cotlow gave the natives their promised feast. The explorer had hoped that the ancient enemies might now relax and celebrate together. But the fears and suspicions ran too deep. Each tribe backed away to its own little camp. That night Cotlow slept uneasily, worried that a real war might break out. Every noise might signal the start of a deadly free-for-all. In the morning Cotlow discovered that the Cambanacas, the smallest group, had departed. They were outnumbered and had apparently slept as badly as Cotlow. Utitiaja, however, looked completely rested and ready to serve as assistant director.

With Juantinga playing the lead role, Cotlow filmed scenes which might lead up to the *tsantsa* feast—preparations for a raid, saying goodby to the wives, crossing a stream, stumbling into a booby trap, taking an enemy head. The afternoon of the second day Cotlow gambled and asked Juantinga to do a scene that could be very dangerous: Juantinga and his men would attack the jivaria while another tribe defended it. The danger was that a realistic battle scene might excite the warriors to the real thing. But the headhunters honored their promise. They acted superbly, and the lance stayed buried.

Trying to act as calm as Utitiaja, Cotlow still felt he was sitting on a volcano. He had to practice his best diplomacy: chat with the men, be polite to the women, smile at the children. He also had to bolster his own morale. Keeping clean and getting enough sleep were Cotlow's first rules. If he didn't get to a river in the daytime, Cotlow made sure he took a sponge bath in the evening. Then he changed into his very civilized nylon pajamas. The Jivaros, whose own cloth is very rough, never tired of touching the silky material. Cotlow felt a lot like a British planter, stuck away in some distant province, who always wore a tuxedo to dinner. Like him, Cotlow knew that a little bit of home is an excellent morale booster. When Cotlow crawled into his covered hammock, designed to keep away all insects, crawling and flying, he was totally exhausted and ready for sleep, and he usually found himself wishing he were back home.

That second night the Tutanangosas left, as silently as the Cambanacas had the night before.

But Utitiaja had not lost any of his enthusiasm for Cotlow's project. He was full of suggestions and Cotlow soon found himself taking more pictures than he needed, just to please Utitiaja. First there was Juantinga shrinking a head. Then there were shots of Shuara and Cotlow encountering three Jivaros on the trail and being taken before Utitiaja, who decided they were friendly. In still another scene, Cotlow himself went before the camera with his magic tricks. Predictably enough, all the natives enjoyed them except the *wishnus* —they resented the competition. Later Cotlow presented the tricks to Utitiaja, so that he could mystify his own witch doctor.

Cotlow's cameras also recorded some of the Jivaro children playing with a mechanical turtle and a top the explorer had given them. And he filmed a mother washing her baby. She filled her mouth with water, and then showered it over the child in short bursts as she rubbed and wiped the baby clean. Cotlow had always found that children in primitive cultures were consistently well-behaved. "No shouting and no screaming," he says.

Cotlow was sorry to see the sun go down on that third day. He knew that Utitiaja would leave the next morning. In their three days together, Cotlow had failed to find out very much about this remarkable man. Though friendly, Utitiaja was in no hurry to talk about himself. He gave the impression that there was little to say. But Cotlow had a different feeling, and with Shuara's help, he finally persuaded Utitiaja to join him for a long, leisurely talk.

Sitting in Cotlow's tent that last evening, Utitiaja responded readily enough to the explorer's direct questions. "Other things," he went on, "helped me to become a great hunter. In the evening I sat in the jivaria with my father and my uncles while they talked of wars, of enemies they had killed and stratagems they had used to fool the enemy." Many times, half-asleep, Cotlow had heard these nightly sessions himself. Drinking *nijimanche* and swapping stories, the headhunters passed the time that civilized people devote to TV and movies. "I learned a great deal from this talk," Cotlow says.

Utitiaja smiled to himself as he thought of his youth, and he looked down proudly at his wife. "When I was thirteen and I became a man, my mother and father had a great feast for me which lasted three days. The *wishnu* squirted tobacco juice up my nose to strengthen me and I went into the woods to dream. I built a shelter. And for five days I drank only *maikoa* [a narcotic], which makes you dizzy and makes you dream of your ancestors. And they told me I would become a great hunter. I had many beautiful dreams. But one kept coming back. I was resting in the forest and a jaguar attacked me. But I leaped up and ripped him to pieces. Later I told my parents and the *wishnu*. I knew then that I had had a good dream, because they were so happy. It meant that I would grow up to become a great hunter and a brave warrior. If I could kill the jaguar I could kill anything."

"How did you feel?" Cotlow asked.

Utitiaja looked amazed. "I felt wonderful, of course. Like anyone who knows that he will be successful at life's most important things. I felt happy. I felt strong enough to kill real enemies."

"But were you frightened when you went on your first raid?"

"Yes, because it was my first. The enemy has spirits too. Sometimes they are very strong. But after the first raid I learned that my good spirits were stronger. You see, I had drunk *nateema* [another narcotic] before my first raid and my ancestors told me I would kill my enemy and take his head. So it had to be that way."

"What are the main reasons for your success?" Cotlow asked.

"My father gave me some of his strength and bravery. And he taught me well. But the main reason is that before any war or raid I always drank *nateema* or *maikoa,* and through the dreams I learned from the Old Ones whether my plans could succeed or not. If they said 'no,' I postponed the raid. If they said 'yes,' I went ahead, knowing that I was absolutely certain to win."

This was Utitiaja's secret. He had never doubted himself

because he knew the spirit world was taking care of him. From his earliest days Utitiaja felt that he had been chosen for great deeds; that conviction had been confirmed at least 58 times. Utitiaja was a man of destiny.

Now, at last, Utitiaja was coming into focus for Cotlow. Cotlow always assumed that men everywhere, even the most outstanding, like Utitiaja, can be grasped on an everyday level, in the familiar terms of civilization, no matter how exotic their lives are.

Cotlow compared his interview with Utitiaja to a sportswriter's interview with a star baseball player. Utitiaja's explanation of his success as a headhunter could easily be transposed into baseball, business or theatrical terms. "Yes, I did dream that I would be the greatest ballplayer. I told my priest about it and he encouraged me. Now I've got those pitchers fooled. They think I can smack the ball over the fence any time. So they're scared. That's why I can hit home runs."

Cotlow had another question—one he hesitated to ask: "You have killed fifty-eight men, Utitiaja. Now that you are getting older, don't you worry about it sometimes?"

Utitiaja bristled. "It's right to kill your enemies. Men who would kill you if they could. Even you *apachis* [white men] know that, for I have heard of your wars."

"But I mean the blood feuds, not the wars." Cotlow knew he couldn't defend his civilization's wars. He tried to put the discussion on safer ground. "When you think a man is responsible for the death of a relative, is it right to take the law in your own hands?"

"Who else could kill him?" Utitiaja demanded. "I have heard that in your country you pay certain people to do that for you. I think that is wrong. I am the one who has the right and the duty to kill him. And I have always fulfilled my duties, not tried to get someone else to take care of them for me."

Utitiaja then told Cotlow that the three days of film-making had very likely enabled him to fulfill another of these "duties." Several months before, he explained, one of his daughters had been taken away by one of the same enemy clans which had come to appear in Cotlow's movies. (Securing wives is one of the reasons why the Jivaros carry out raids.) Utitiaja thought he had figured out which man was the kidnaper. Now he could kill him and perhaps bring his daughter home. Utitiaja thanked Cotlow for helping him. At the mention of his daughter, Utitiaja's wife had begun to cry and Utitiaja comforted her. Cotlow's interview with Utitiaja ended on this unhappy note.

After their evening together, Cotlow had a frame of reference from which he could view Utitiaja. Cotlow felt that men like Utitiaja became successful wherever they lived. To Cotlow, there wasn't that much difference between a Jivaro chief in the Amazon and a corporation president in the United States.

The next morning Utitiaja, his wives and his warriors were gone. Cotlow was saddened to think that he would probably never see the man again. With genuine respect and affection, Cotlow calls Utitiaja an "exemplar of the primitive." But Cotlow could return to civilization content, because through Utitiaja he had been able to gain insight into the primitive mind that he had never before experienced.

Men like Utitiaja have convinced Cotlow that primitive man has many fine qualities. Most are hospitable and considerate. The parents are devoted to their children. The men love their wives. And most are honest and honorable according to their own beliefs. Certainly Cotlow's experience with the Jivaros had proved that.

Years of exploring and numerous friendships with people in remote areas have also persuaded Cotlow that primitive men would be better off if we left them alone. "The civilized man," Cotlow insists with passion, "has not resolved his problems. Why should we tell the primitive man what to do? The primitive man has his faults. But let him alone. Until we have learned some solutions to life, until we have learned how to get along with ourselves, how can we tell the other fellow what to do? How dare we be so presumptuous? Civilized man ought to stay home and clean up his own terrible mess."

six

Pockets in the Earth

R USSELL GURNEE, a tall, easygoing family man, is a spelunker. His favorite pastime—it can almost be called an obsession—is the exploration of caves. (Caves, of course, are pockets of empty space in the earth's crust, most of which have been formed by water seepage.) For the past 18 years, Gurnee has been devoted to this increasingly popular sport and is past president of the National Speleological Society and one of its most active members. Whenever he can take time off from his heating business in Closter, New Jersey, Gurnee goes caving, which is also called spelunking. He enjoys wandering, sometimes crawling, sometimes even swimming, through tunnels and caverns which even he would describe as damp, dark, unclean and occasionally dangerous.

There are 5,000 cavers in the United States, yet many people cannot imagine what they find so exciting about caves. Gurnee's own motivation for caving is complex. He likes the traveling he has to do to reach a new and different cave. He enjoys the companionship of spelunkers—not at all a loner, Gurnee prefers to cave with others. He feels that spelunking, more strenuous than hiking but ordinarily less demanding than mountain climbing, is a pleasant way to keep fit.

Then there are aspects of the caves themselves that please Gurnee. For one thing, he finds their unique beauty highly appealing. Many are decorated by icicle-like stalagmites and stalactites, stately columns or bizarre formations which can resemble anything from tiny men to giant scrambled eggs. A cave with extensive speleothems—the general name for cave formations—is a genuine fairyland. Gurnee is impressed, too, by the size of some caves. The Carlsbad Caverns of New Mexico, probably the world's largest, cover some 36 miles and contain a huge chamber called the Big Room which is 4,000 feet long and 600 feet wide. Caves also interest Gurnee archeologically. Primitive men sometimes lived and worshiped in caves, and their wall paintings and other artifacts can be found in caves today. And caves often have strange varieties of plant and animal life, some of which are rarely seen outside. Finally, Gurnee finds caving intriguing because of the hazards involved. He feels that caves are a little like haunted houses, and he enjoys the tingle of fear he experiences whenever he enters a cave.

Gurnee tells of his reasons for caving in a random way, suggesting that no one reason is more compelling than another. But when I questioned him about his motives, he came back most often to another reason for caving. Like most explorers, he is drawn to the unknown. More than anything else, he says, "The sense of exploring the unknown fascinates me. When I flash my light into a dark corner, I am exploring it. There's a sense of discovery. It doesn't make much difference to me if somebody else has already explored and mapped the cave. I am discovering it for myself."

Gurnee first became interested in spelunking in 1950, when

he was 27. As a teen-ager he had visited commercial caves (there are about 200 in the United States), and during World War II, when he was a 20-year-old metalsmith in the Navy in the Pacific, he saw caves in the Philippines and in Okinawa. The Japanese used these caves for bomb shelters and pillboxes, just as the Vietcong have done. But Gurnee did not become a spelunker until five years after the war. His explanation for his late start is that he simply did not realize caving was a genuine sport. When he learned that many people liked to go caving, he tried it himself and "became addicted." Soon he was taking off six weeks each year from his business and many weekends as well to go caving.

Gurnee is customarily relaxed and soft-spoken, and he pursues his interest in caving with an unusual blend of casualness and dedication. He is never melodramatic about his hobby, and he is not trying to attract attention to himself or to prove anything. He believes that caving must first be fun. He caves the way other people play cards, usually with his pretty, dark-haired wife, Jeanne, who is also an avid caver. And he sometimes takes his two teen-age daughters along. Gurnee caves because he enjoys it.

At the same time, he plans his caving trips with great care and directs them toward definite goals. "It's no good just to pack up and run off," Gurnee says. "You have to develop a project. Over the years we have managed to boil our trips down to a fairly compact period. In three weeks we can do a study of a specific area with good results. In that time we can find the caves, map them and, if necessary, do the preliminary work for a further, more thorough expedition." Gurnee makes notes on the caves he visits and writes up formal reports for the National Speleological Society and any other group which might be interested in some aspect of the caves. He also collects biological specimens and sends them to professors whose interests include cave life. For Gurnee, caving is purposeful fun.

An excellent example of Gurnee's approach to caving is his three-week expedition to Guatemala in November, 1961. With his wife, six friends and a professional photographer, Gurnee made a sweep through this Central America country, visiting scores of caves. This expedition was especially important to Gurnee because it was the third and final stage of one of his most ambitious projects—to make a complete survey of the caves of Guatemala. Gurnee and his wife, along with a few other cavers, had gone to Guatemala on two-week reconnaissance missions in 1958 and 1960. Finally, in November, 1961, Gurnee thought he could wrap up his Guatemala "project" with an intense three-week assault on the caves they had not yet seen. Gurnee went to Guatemala in 1961 with two main objectives. He hoped to see a shrine cave, which the Indians regarded as so sacred that no white man had ever been allowed inside. And, in the Cuchumatanes Mountains, he hoped to find the highest cave in the Western Hemisphere.

In pursuit of these and lesser goals Gurnee and his companions caved from breakfast to dinner—whenever they were not driving from one cave to another. Gurnee ran a fast-paced expedition, yet there was no tension, no sense of urgency. By and large, Gurnee returns from an expedition in much the same humor as when he set out, whether or not his specific goals have been accomplished.

One member of the 1961 expedition did want very much for it to succeed. Russ Kinne, a noted nature photographer, went with Gurnee because he hoped to bring back a good photo story. He felt that the trip offered many possibilities. At the very least, he could write up an important caving expedition.

Better still, the group might get into a shrine cave, giving
Kinne a chance to photograph it. And best of all, they might
find the highest cave in the Western Hemisphere. *Sports Illustrated* also thought the trip would be interesting, and they
agreed to pay Kinne's expenses.

The four other members of the expedition were, like Gurnee,
along for the sport. Ackey Lloyd, an engineer from Virginia,
came with his wife, Betty. John Spence, as easygoing as
Gurnee, was the retired president of a camera company. He
had sold equipment to cavers for 25 years but had never
walked into a cave himself until he retired. The youngest
member, Norm Olson, was an engineering student from the
Virginia Polytechnic Institute. These cavers were all amateurs, in that they paid their own expenses.

Gurnee and his expedition flew into Guatemala City on
Friday, November 6, 1961. They planned to pick up their
bulky supplies, which they had sent ahead by ship early on
Saturday morning and then head for the highlands of the
Cuchumatanes Mountains.

At dinner Friday evening, José Storek, a Guatemalan geologist, joined the cavers. He had helped Gurnee on the two
previous Guatemala trips. Storek was, in fact, the man responsible for Gurnee's Guatemala project. He had emigrated from
Europe 20 years before and was captivated by all of Guatemala's scenic beauty. He studied rivers, mountains, canyons
and caves with equal enthusiasm. Storek had been upset to
discover that nobody was paying any attention to Guatemala's
numerous caves, and he wrote to the United States National
Speleological Society in 1957, inviting them to send someone
down to look at his country's caves. "So," Gurnee says off-
handedly, "I went." Gurnee had traveled all over the world—to
France, Spain, Yugoslavia, El Salvador, Puerto Rico—to ex-

plore caves, and he was delighted to add a cave-rich country like Guatemala to his list. Storek became Gurnee's most valued contact in Guatemala, and during the 1961 trip, served as translator and guide, traveling with the group whenever he could get time off from his job.

Saturday morning, Gurnee's expedition suffered its first setback. They found that they could not obtain their supplies, including some of Kinne's photographic equipment, until Monday. But Gurnee had come to Guatemala to see caves. He quickly improvised a trip to Puerto Barrios, a seaport on the Gulf of Honduras. Storek had heard about a tidal cave on the Rio Dulce, a river near Puerto Barrios. The reports said that the small cave contained vampire bats, rare animals which several of the Americans had never seen. There were also other caves near Puerto Barrios. The cavers quickly loaded up their two rented cars—a brand-new Ford sedan and a Chevrolet station wagon—and started off for the seaport. Gurnee's third expedition to Guatemala was supposed to have gone straight to the mountain caves. But now it was headed in the opposite direction toward the Guatemalan lowlands. An unusually flexible man, Gurnee tries to find another way to accomplish a goal when setbacks occur.

Puerto Barrios was most memorable for its state of disrepair. The best hotel, where the Americans and Storek registered for Saturday night, was almost visibly collapsing. And when the party went to rent a boat on Sunday morning to take them to the tidal cave, they didn't see any that could have lasted through a storm. Storek finally rented a battered 20-foot fishing launch with a little shack for a cabin. The captain and his crew of one welcomed the gringos with hospitable grins, and Gurnee and the others were soon chugging up the Rio Dulce toward cave number one.

The sun was climbing into a cloudless tropical sky. Porpoises from the Gulf of Honduras followed the launch up the cliff-lined river, sometimes arching high out of the blue water. Occasionally another fishing boat, as paintless and decrepit as their own, passed by the cavers. The Guatemalans on board stared at the curious assortment of foreigners. Why had they come to the Rio Dulce so early on a Sunday morning, so far from the usual tourist spots? Certainly the cavers were not dressed like most Americans they had seen. Several of them wore workmen's overalls. And a few had on bright-colored hats—like World War I helmets.

The boat putt-putted toward a large black hole in the northern cliff. The cavers stood up and stared expectantly. The river flowed right into the oval-shaped entrance of the tunnel, but since Storek had heard that the water inside was only knee deep, the skipper docked his launch outside, against the cliff that rose ominously above them. Gurnee leaped intrepidly off the side of the boat to wade into the black 15-foot-wide mouth of the cave, called La Cueva de Las Conches by the natives, and the others followed.

All eight of the cavers now wore the protective "hard hats." Attached to the front of these was a miner's lamp which beamed a cone of yellowish light into the darkness of the cave. Gurnee, who wore gloves and carried a pad and pencil for taking notes, splashed ahead of the others as though he couldn't wait to find out what the cave held. Since the bottom might be full of holes, the rest of the party were content to let Gurnee, the tallest person in the group, do the trail blazing.

Storek had heard about this cave, but he had never explored it, so no one knew what to expect. The cave might be only a few yards long or, a short distance inside, it might balloon into a huge chamber. It might contain unique and beautiful formations or none at all. There might be hordes of strange animals or perhaps not even one vampire bat. The lure of the unknown, the anticipation of the unexpected, made the entry into the cave very exciting for Gurnee and the others.

A powerful stench struck Gurnee's nostrils—the putrid smell of decay. As they had expected, this damp, tropical cave had living things in it. But what kind of things? Gurnee wouldn't deny that he was on edge. He was wading through two feet of water. Then he heard a scuttling sound. He quickly aimed his light against the slimy, glistening walls. Sand crabs clambered over the jutting rocks at the water's edge. The crabs watched the eight intruders with tense bug-eyes. The cavers, moving forward again, churned the water, making ripples spread out into far reaches of the forbidding tunnel.

They noticed now with a shock that the walls of the cave were literally alive. Hordes of cockroaches, three inches long and larger, swarmed along the damp rocks. Obeying a strong herd instinct, the cockroaches ran and turned together when the beams of light hit them. These primordial creatures did not like light. Much as the cavers disliked walking through the black water, nobody was too eager now to get closer to the sides of the cave. La Cueva de Las Conches was no place for people who were afraid of insects. Nor was it a place for claustrophobes, or for people who liked sunlight and dry clothes.

Gurnee stopped suddenly. Above him, where he had not looked before, hung a colony of vampire bats. They stared down at him with their tooth-lined mouths hanging open. At night, such bats will fly out and bite chickens, cows, any creatures from which they can suck the blood, including humans if they can find any injured or asleep. Non-cavers think these sinister mammals lurk in every cave, but they are actu-

ally very rare. Gurnee signaled to the others. Kinne closed in with his camera and took pictures. The strange life in this tropical cave was something of a shock to the American spelunkers. As for the vampire bats, they merely looked unhappy, presumably because their solitude had been disturbed.

After wading 50 feet farther, Gurnee reached dry land and he stopped to make notes on the shape of the cave. He and every member of the party had certain assignments—notetaking, photography, mapping, collecting biological samples. Gurnee moved farther into the cave as the others chattered excitedly about the bats and the cockroaches. Gurnee noted that the cave got very small after about 200 feet. But no one in the group wanted to slide into the narrow "tubes" and "bellycrawls"—cavers' terms for very narrow tunnels—at the end of the cave. Gurnee made more notes, Kinne took more pictures and they started back out. The vampire bats and the crabs and the cockroaches stared as the cavers moved toward the triangle of light at the cave's entrance.

Back on the launch they took deep breaths of the clean air. Some yanked off their boots, hoping they would dry before they reached El Silvino, another cave in the area. The skipper, who did not really understand what the cavers were after, started up his ancient motor. The old boat coughed on down the Rio Dulce, back to Puerto Barrios.

Gurnee, a most straightforward man, remarked that La Cueva de Las Conches was "a filthy hole," a sentiment the others concurred in. Still, the morning had not been wasted. They had come to explore a tidal cave and they had done so. Their observations were duly recorded for the edification of anybody who might be interested, spelunker or otherwise. Among other things, La Cueva de Las Conches, being below sea level, was probably the lowest cave in Guatemala, and perhaps in the Western Hemisphere. Kinne might ultimately be able to report that the expedition had explored both the hemisphere's highest and lowest caves. And they had found vampire bats, one of the secondary goals of the trip. Now they were off to see the second cave of the day.

Before noon the expedition was back in Puerto Barrios. The eight cavers ate a quick lunch, then started off for El Silvino, 20 miles away. The sun was high, the breeze hot and muggy. The four-lane highway they took west from Puerto Barrios to Guatemala City was one of the few paved roads in this small country, which is the size of the state of Ohio. Curiously enough, the road builders accidentally created a second and more convenient entrance to El Silvino when they bulldozed away a chunk of mountain. So the cavers did not have to hike to the cave. They simply parked their cars off the road and walked in.

Gurnee, his wife and Storek had seen El Silvino before, on their 1960 trip. They were returning now so that Kinne could take pictures. Unlike La Cueva de Las Conches, El Silvino is, in Gurnee's words, "a beautiful little cave," with surprising formations and large caverns.

Gurnee had first heard of El Silvino some years before, when Storek described the cave as one in which the natives scooped up catfish in baskets from its pools. Gurnee had been in hundreds of caves but he had never heard of such a thing. Usually a caver is lucky to find a few small blind fish. "We thought," Gurnee recalls, "that perhaps this was just a story." But on his trip to Guatemala in 1960, Gurnee confirmed Storek's account. A river flows beneath one end of El Silvino, and in the flood season, catfish swim into the cave. When the water level drops, the fish are trapped. The enterprising natives then come in and collect them in baskets.

While Kinne clicked off several rolls of film, the group hiked deeper into the cave. El Silvino snaked one way and then the other but it was quite level. The walls often spread out to a width of 40 feet and the ceiling sometimes rose to 30. But at the halfway point, some 400 feet in, the cavers had to crawl uncomfortably through a chute only a few feet wide. Caving is frequently as strenuous as this. El Silvino had a great variety of stalactites hanging from the ceiling and stalagmites rising from the floor, as well as columns and other strangely curved formations. Asked why anyone would want to go crawling around in a cave, spelunkers often mention these magical shapes. In this subterranean world the scenery is always new and quite unlike anything seen above ground.

Like most caves, El Silvino was created by water seepage. Rainwater, made slightly acidic by the addition of carbon dioxide or organic acids, had simply cut through the rock. Such caves occur only in limestone or dolomite, since this type of rock is usually faulted and the water, following the path of least resistance, seeps or flows through the cracks, simultaneously dissolving away the sides of the fault and enlarging the opening. Over thousands of years the seeping water makes a cave. A good-sized river may ultimately flow through a cave which started as a paper-thin crack. Since the faults often occur in geometrical patterns, the cave may twist and turn in sharp angles. El Silvino, for example, extended more or less straight for 150 feet, turned 90 degrees to the left for another 150 feet and finally went left again for the last 250 feet. A cave stops growing when the water stops flowing. The water may stop because of a change in rainfall, a major geological upheaval in the whole mountain or a river's change of course.

Cavers always look for regions of limestone. "We like to pick out a country that has limestone," Gurnee says. "Then we do a speleological survey of the country. We take a geological map, find the limestone, and then go down and look for caves." When most people see a limestone mountain, they only see a large rock, but cavers know that on the inside the mountain is really more like a piece of Swiss cheese, full of holes. Or so they hope.

Stalactites and stalagmites are formed in an altogether different way than the cave itself. They develop in the second stage of a cave's growth, a stage which many caves do not reach. After a cave has been scooped out, it sometimes begins to fill up once more. Water—this time in small amounts—again does the work. Drop by drop, it seeps into the top of the cave. Minerals in the limestone are precipitated out by the action of the water, and these precipitates begin to form a column that builds down from the ceiling—a stalactite. Or the drops fall to the floor and build upward to form a stalagmite. Eventually the stalactites and stalagmites may meet and form columns stretching from floor to ceiling. The range of cave formations, or speleothems, is endless and unpredictable.

Unfortunately, "vandals," as spelunkers view them, had broken off many of the speleothems in El Silvino and carried them away. Like all cavers, Gurnee does not approve of souvenir hunters and would like to see caves protected from such irreverent visitors. Strollers and picnickers, most cavers feel, should go to commercial caves where the guards and the railings will keep them from disturbing anything. In the same spirit the *National Speleological Society News* commands its readers to: "Take nothing but pictures. Leave nothing but footprints."

After several hours in El Silvino, Gurnee's group returned to the bright sunlight of the outside world. In the cave, the headlamps had shone only 50 feet ahead and they could see detail up to only 25 feet. The yellow light of the headlamp also dulled parts of the color spectrum, making the cave a shadowy world. Without the cavers' lamps the cave was in perpetual night. Outside, at three o'clock in the afternoon, the spelunkers squinted in the bright sunlight.

Storek had heard about another cave in the neighborhood, only 10 miles away, and they set out to find it, first, stopping for lunch along the way. Their destination was the Doña Maria gas station, marked as the "town" of Doña Maria on the map. The large cave Storek had heard of was supposed to be a few miles off in the jungle. His information was sketchy, so Storek recruited some Indians to lead them to the cave. (Finding caves is frequently a caver's hardest work. The best method of attack often is to find someone who knows the cave's location. Lacking guides, many cavers, especially in the American West, do intricate detective work, using old newspapers, books and mining claims in an attempt to locate a cave.)

Mrs. Gurnee and Mrs. Lloyd decided to forego the Doña Maria cave and remain at gas station instead, where they could take a swim in a small stream. The young Indian guide— his father owned the gas station—led the men off along a lovely jungle path. The Guatemalan lowlands, which make up about one-third of the country, are thick tropical jungle. The trail led tediously back and forth across a stream. It began to get late and the sun settled close to the trees. Gurnee had imagined that he would just skip over to Doña Maria and take a look. The boy kept saying, "It's right over that hill"—but always they had to cross the stream again. With their rope ladders, knapsacks and other equipment held high, the cavers waded in up to their waists—ten times altogether.

At last they were rewarded. Gurnee always liked what he called a "psychological cave"—a cave he worked hard to reach but which fully repaid him when he went inside. The Doña Maria had a "wide, classic entrance" on the side of a hill, partly hidden behind a fallen tree, with vines and bushes growing thickly around the hole. Kinne quickly took pictures of the scene. To get in, the cavers had to climb along the tree as the bark crumbled in their hands. The vegetation extended into the "twilight zone," that part of a cave which receives only indirect sunlight. As the spelunkers entered Doña Maria, a strong stench swept over them. Since caves in the United States are mostly lifeless and odorless, the tropical lushness of Guatemalan caves continued to surprise Gurnee. He immediately noticed the hordes of cockroaches scrambling along the wall. Spindly daddy longlegs also hovered among the rocks. The ground felt like a luxurious carpet, but when Gurnee looked down, he saw that "the floor was actually moving"—millions of insects, worms and spiders seethed under his boots.

Gurnee always maps a cave as he goes in. Most cavers usually do this on the way out, but Gurnee believes that not making a map immediately increases the chance of getting lost. To map the cave, one man stood at the entrance, shining his light inside. Gurnee walked ahead as far as he could see the other man's light and took a compass reading on the light. A third man, meanwhile, measured the distance between the two men with a tape measure. The man holding the light then walked up and replaced Gurnee who moved farther into the cave for another sighting. "You can make a rough sketch map of a cave as fast as you can walk," Gurnee says.

For 50 feet, Doña Maria was a strange garden. Frail-looking white shoots grew in lush abundance from the ground and in nooks and crannies. Animals and the wind had undoubtedly brought the seeds into the cave. In the absence of sunlight, they grew into white "fairy gardens." When the nutriment in a seed ran out, the plant would shrivel and die. Still, with a humidity of 99 percent and a temperature of 75 degrees, Doña Maria was a flourishing hothouse. (Caves usually are the temperature of the mean year-round outside temperature.) Farther along, the rich growth gave way to bare rock formations. Then the tunnel opened into "a forest room," as cavers sometimes term a cavern where many vertical columns have formed.

As their beams of light darted through the pillars and flowed along the cave wall, Gurnee and his friends looked to one another like robots with antennae growing from their heads—the beam from their headlamps. The headlamp is, in fact, a caver's most important piece of equipment. Gurnee prefers the acetylene type in which water dripping on carbide produces a flammable gas. Other cavers use a lightbulb-and-battery pack. American cavers use the two types equally. Normally, Gurnee prefers carbide so that he does not have to worry about whether batteries are full strength or about to give out.

Suddenly Gurnee's light picked out a vampire bat, one of a colony. The bats became excited, scuttling like crabs on their thumbs along the walls and across the ceiling. Gurnee describes them as "filthy, quite treacherous little things." Where they had congregated in Doña Maria, they left huge pools of tar-like excreta, which suffused the cave with a strong, unpleasant odor.

In the little pools of water on the cave floor, Gurnee found something more to his liking: isopods—small, colorless, blind crustaceans. Gurnee collected specimens in bottles; he would later send these to biologists in the United States. Like most caves, Doña Maria was filled with pools and with tiny rivulets that flowed along the side of the cave. In the absence of cavers, when the bats are quiet, the only sound in most caves is the dripping of this water.

The cavers spent two hours in Doña Maria. The men reached the cave's end, about 500 feet from the entrance, made notes, sketches and measurements, and started back out, stopping to collect more specimens. Gurnee had always found that time passes quickly in a cave simply because you have so much to do—from keeping your footing on rough terrain to looking at the scenery, from searching for interesting passageways to avoiding holes in the ground. But if a man is lost in a cave, time seems to stop altogether. The silent darkness is beyond time and 15 minutes can feel like hours. But Doña Maria was not a large or complex cave and the cavers easily found their way back to the outside world.

It was dusk and the jungle was quiet. Gurnee looked up apprehensively at the sky where dark clouds massed and swirled. The group started off hurriedly, and almost simultaneously, the light seemed to disappear and it began to rain. Great drops bounced on the broad jungle leaves, and in minutes the rain turned into a downpour. Wet to the skin, the men waded indifferently into the first river crossing, their headlamps stabbing through the rain-filled darkness. Gurnee wondered if the Indian boy knew where he was going. On the next crossing Gurnee realized that the river had started to rise, and he wondered how high the water would get.

Hardly a mile away from the cave, Gurnee began to doubt that they would ever make it back. They stopped to talk over their options. It looked as if they might have to take shelter somewhere until the rain passed. None of them wanted to wander around the jungle all night. Then they heard a noise—the roar of a gasoline motor without a muffler. The Indian boy explained that his father had a generator at the gas station.

This must be the sound they heard, and they trudged happily toward it, knowing it couldn't be far away.

Back at the gas station, they tried to clean themselves up and assured the women that Doña Maria had been a fine little cave. They had brushed close to danger, but Gurnee was happy they had not passed up the opportunity to explore a new cave.

That night the group drove back to Guatemala City, a distance of about 130 miles. Gurnee wanted to be in the city early Monday morning to pick up the rest of their equipment. The expedition had been on an enjoyable detour for two days, but now they must get back to their planned route. Their main goals—to visit the shrine cave and to explore the highest cave in the hemisphere—lay ahead.

Monday, however, was unproductive. It took the cavers a whole day to obtain their additional equipment and get it through customs. Feeling quite frustrated, they returned to the Hotel San Carlo for another night, resolving that they would be up with the sun the next day. But Tuesday was hardly better than Monday. They drove 100 miles north on the Pan American highway to Quetzaltenango, which bears a name from the Mayan past, as so many of Guatemala's cities do. Storek had heard about a cave with hot springs near Quetzaltenango, but the crack they found with steam coming out did not live up to the rumors. Another cave nearby also proved disappointing. So the two-car convoy headed north again, across the high Cuchumatanes Mountains, to Huehuetenango, where they spent the night. The countryside was mountainous and desolate—raw, interesting scenery that was a splendid fringe benefit of caving.

At their first night's stopping point, Huehuetenango, the natives told the cavers they would never reach the isolated town of Santa Eulalia in their low-slung American automobiles. "They were right," Gurnee says, "but the cars didn't know that, so we went anyway." They wound around mountains, slid through long stretches of mud and even drove across a stream. They lost the muffler and the oil pan on one car, but pushed on. The road ended in the central square of Santa Eulalia, a secluded village 8,500 feet up in the Cuchumatanes Mountains. They arrived in the afternoon, and while Storek went off to talk with the mayor, Gurnee rented a little house with a thatched roof and the women went to buy food for dinner.

The people of Santa Eulalia are descendants of the highly civilized Mayan race. When the Spanish came to Guatemala, their forefathers retreated into the almost inaccessible Cuchumatanes. The peaceful natives kept to their ancient ways and each village evolved a distinctive costume. Soon, the Catholic Church sent missionaries to the region, and today native and European beliefs are curiously blended.

Gurnee had learned about this village and the sacred cave located below it from a book entitled *Santa Eulalia,* by Oliver La Farge, an American anthropologist and writer who lived in the village for a year in 1933 to study the Indian customs. Discussing the town's religious ceremonies, La Farge often mentioned a sacred cave called Yalan Na'. Each New Year's Day, he reported, the Indian "prayer-makers" descended into the cave to prophesy the future. In another ceremony, they left in the cave a gourd of blood from a sacrificial turkey as a gift to the gods. The natives often commanded La Farge to stay away from this cave. "Many of these warnings," he wrote, "were given out of a perfectly clear sky, when I had not brought up the subject in any way." The natives consider the sanctity of Yalan Na' and the sacred caves to be inviolable. The last uprising, in which 50 natives were killed, had occurred when a white man stole an idol from a sacred cave.

Gurnee naturally wanted to explore Yalan Na' and Russ Kinne wanted to photograph the cave. Gurnee felt that seeing Yalan Na' would be the pinnacle of the cavers' trip. But first they had to convince the suspicious villagers that they should be the first white men to be admitted to the caves. In anticipation of this problem, Storek had obtained a letter from the President of Guatemala stating that he and the others had been requested by the Guatemalan government to make a study of the cave and asking the natives to cooperate. "But frankly," Gurnee recalls, "we didn't believe it would be possible to actually see it." That night they went to sleep like children who are not sure that Santa Claus will come.

The next morning, bright and early, he came. Not the way anyone had expected, however. Gurnee feels that what happened at Santa Eulalia shows very well how unpredictable a caving expedition can be. But "unpredictability is part of the excitement of caving," he says. Since hearing about Yalan Na' many years before, the cavers had assumed that they would have to go through a long and involved ritual to get into the cave. The cave was obviously so important to the Indians that it seemed logical that any visit to it would unfold with a good deal of ceremony. This expectation proved false. The cavers walked 200 yards away from the village to the cave's entrance, which was an eight-foot hole in the side of a hill. The mayor of the village accompanied them and gave his permission for them to enter. Gurnee and his group were nonplussed. They had expected to be taken through the cave. Instead, they were turned loose by themselves. There was no fanfare; they simply went inside. The cave floor dropped away at a 45-degree angle, and the cavers climbed down a series of ladders—logs with crossbars—to reach the level area below.

Today, Gurnee and his wife view their experience in the cave—which nearly turned into a tragedy—as a funny anecdote. Mrs. Gurnee tells the story:

"By the time we got into the cave and down the ladders, the Indians were worshiping. They had candles lit and were talking in the Kechl language. They were not waiting for us. They were having their ceremony and we were to take care of ourselves as best we could. There were three priests and ten other men praying and talking. The altar was in a niche off the main amphitheater. Then they started to burn pom incense which gave off a heavy black smoke. Just like a smoke bomb, only jet black. The smoke began to fill the cavern, and by the time Russ Kinne got his camera and equipment out, we couldn't see anything. We started retreating into side passages, choking and with tears streaming down our faces. Then I fell into a 20-foot pit. I didn't even see it on the floor; the cave was completely filled with black soot so that nobody could see. I was down in the bottom for about 15 minutes. Fortunately there was a slope of mud at the bottom of the hole, so I slid about the last seven feet. Even down there, I could still hear the chanting of the priest. Then I didn't hear the Indians worshiping any more, and, looking around, I found that I could climb up the other side of the pit."

With the Indians gone, the smoke began to clear, but even before it did, Gurnee started mapping the cave. "We had to map it by feel," Gurnee recalls, "but nobody could have dragged me out of there until I had finished. Actually the smoke didn't slow us down too much. Most caves resemble each other. One of the things we've found in our travels is that the people are different, the homes are different, the way they work the land is different. But once we get down in the cave, we're on familiar ground. Caves all over the world have the same configurations, the same stalagmites, the same formations, and they've been formed in the same way."

Searching around in the haze, Gurnee made some surprising discoveries. The walls of the cave were covered with soot almost an eighth of an inch thick from the burning of incense and torches. Thousands of burned-out torches on the floor made the footing very tricky. These pieces of wood, probably discarded by the Indians for hundreds of years, had built up to a depth of six inches in some places. There were also candle stubs and incense on every ledge and stalagmite. Gurnee found Santa Eulalia fascinating. He has always been interested in the way man affects caves. Of course, he had seen the famous cave paintings at Lascaux, France, and Altamira, Spain, where evidence of man goes back 20,000 to 30,000 years. But he doubted that the walls of Santa Eulalia had ever been clean enough—at least not for hundreds of years—for cave painting. Still the human artifacts (or trash, depending on one's viewpoint) deposited in this little shrine cave exceeded, in quantity anyway, anything Gurnee had ever seen.

The cavers were in Yalan Na' for several hours before they returned to the village of Santa Eulalia for lunch. When they talked over their experiences, they wondered why they had worried so much about getting into the cave. That had turned out to be the least of their problems. None of them could remember an expedition that had ever faced a smoke storm in a cave. Still, Gurnee was able to bring back a detailed map of a cave no white man had seen before. He and the other cavers counted the morning as both successful and memorable. But Russ Kinne viewed Yalan Na' with less enthusiasm. "It was," he remembers, "a dirty, messy place to work."

For the next three days the expedition remained at Santa Eulalia to look for new caves. In these limestone mountains, they eagerly concluded, there would certainly be more and probably larger caves. La Farge's book had mentioned another sacred cave into which the natives lowered a man, holding him by his feet while he piled stones on a crevice of ice, thereby ritually sealing away the winter each spring. The cavers also had read of a "dead man's cave" in the area, and they heard from the natives about other nearby caves, always described as "spectacular."

At eight o'clock each morning the group marched off into the hills. There were no roads, so they left the cars behind. Loaded down with gear, they hiked all day, looking for caves, often without success. Any shadow on a hillside can look like a cave, and the natives often led them up and down miles of mountains, only to point to a hole that went nowhere. Non-cavers think that a big entrance means a big cave, but actually this is not so. Gurnee wasn't hoping to break the world's record for the longest cave (62 miles); finding just one cave of a few thousand feet would have made him happy. When he didn't find such a cave, all the hiking began to seem like work.

They did find "six little caves" each a few hundred feet in depth. One was the "dead man's cave" they had read about. And when the Indian showed them a skeleton lying in a side passage, the cavers could not help remembering that dozens of spelunkers had died in caves, often from falls and drowning, but sometimes from losing their way. The dead man, it appeared, had been unable to find his way out of the cave. The thought of getting lost is a concern of most cavers and Gurnee admits that it has worried him at times. But he feels that the tingle of fear is part of the fun. People go to horror movies for the same reason, he says. Getting lost is, nevertheless, a major problem in spelunking, and the NSS advises its members never to cave alone and always to notify someone aboveground of their expected time of return.

The "dead man's cave," though a forceful warning against getting lost, did not interest Gurnee archeologically. The dead man was not prehistoric, and the cave was small. So they trekked on, "always," as Gurnee says, "looking for that other cave." Fanatic cavers could, of course, cave all night—the caves are dark anyway. But after a long day in the hills, the Gurnee group returned to their little hut, usually around nine o'clock, and spread their sleeping bags on the floor or on wooden bed frames. When they had cleaned their caving gear, they went to sleep. Not counting the student, Norm Olson, the average age of these cavers was around 35. It is not surprising that they did not have any energy left for a game of bridge.

Settling into his sleeping bag in that bare hut, Gurnee could remember when he had slept in a bare cave. Eight years before, in 1953, Gurnee had lived inside a cave for seven days. On that occasion, classed as an "explorer," Gurnee participated with 63 others in America's biggest cave expedition, an assault on the endless mazes of Crystal Cave, Kentucky.

The Crystal Cave expedition of 1953 proved that caving can be a very complex and, in contrast to Gurnee's relaxed style, a very formal enterprise. The Crystal Cave expedition was as large and painstakingly organized as an Antarctic expedition. The goal was to concentrate as much exploration as possible into a seven-day period, and at the end of this time, those who participated were quite exhausted.

Unlike La Cueva de Las Conches, Crystal Cave measures up to what a tourist might expect in a cave. It is El Silvino, multiplied by 50 and then twisted all around in an endless pretzel.

The cave has given up its secrets only with a struggle. For one thing, an explorer has to crawl 1,300 feet just to get in. In 1925, Floyd Collins, the discoverer, explored it alone. (Collins was trapped in a nearby cave when a rock fell on his leg, pinning him down, and he died of exposure before rescuers could get to him.) Cavers who followed him found that in exploring the vast cave system they reached their "endurance limit" after several days, with large areas of the cave still unseen. What was needed was a large-scale exploration of the cave, with base camps inside the cave.

The NSS, whose motto is "The Last Frontier of the Pioneer," decided to organize just such an expedition. They had to gather together, besides explorers who would do the actual caving, a sizable group of "support" people: doctor, surveyor, stenographer, cartographer, cook, wireman, storekeeper and so on. The 15 men and three women who participated as frontline cavers or "explorers" had varied backgrounds. There was a scenario writer, a farmer, a dance instructor, a college student, a bacteriologist and a postal inspector. Their ages ranged from 19 to 57.

The expedition started out by building a "tent city" over the cave and stringing telephone wires to the underground camps. While the "explorers" worked below, men in the tents above analyzed and mapped the discoveries. Inside Crystal Cave, the cavers set up a base camp. Their equipment was slight: "hard hat," carbide lamp; gloves (to keep hands clean for making notes and using cameras, among other reasons); knee pads (banged-up knees and shins are the caver's nemesis); canteen; flashlight, candle and matches (good cavers always take three sources of light, for safety); and canned rations. Some wore water-resistant pants, others overalls or jeans. Nobody had to spend much money (for this reason, caving is sometimes called "churchmouse exploration"). From the base camp, the leader instructed the explorers to split off and set up secondary camps in the various sectors. While the explorers advanced, other cavers brought supplies up to them—food, dry clothing, sleeping bags and air mattresses.

Sleeping in caves is not a normal procedure in spelunking. "There's no particular advantage to it," Gurnee says, "because you have to carry in everything you use. It's poor logistics to bring everything in a cave and lug it out again. But if the cave is as big as Crystal Cave, we had no choice." As for the breed who sleeps in caves when there's no reason to, Gurnee calls them "flagpole sitters. One guy does it for 30 days so somebody else has to do it for 40. It's like a fad unless a definite scientific study is being conducted."

The Crystal Cave explorers spent their days and nights— though they soon lost track of which was which—walking, crawling and sliding through the bewildering labyrinths. Climbers often joke that caving is only "mountain climbing upside down in the dark." Actually cavers don't often use the climber's piton, hammer and ropes. In the Crystal Cave expedition, only three men were officially designated "rock climbers." These men used their mountain skills to secure ropes and ladders for the others. The average caver spends his time like the very adventurous hiker. He may scramble on all fours up stony slopes. He may "chimney" his way up between parallel walls. He may edge inch by inch along a narrow ledge. But a caver does not have to be an expert mountain climber. Gurnee finds that his 500 feet of rope ladder handles most situations, and he points out that most people can climb a ladder. Climbing with ropes, on the contrary, is quite complex. The other great danger is drowning: cavers sometimes use scuba gear to get from one flooded passage to another. Diving is not essential, however; Gurnee has been in water up to his neck many times, but he does not use an aqualung. Cavers who thrive on danger will often seek out those caves which require ropes or diving. But for every adventurer there are hundreds of cavers like Gurnee who are not at all interested in the riskier aspects of the sport.

After a week underground, the Crystal Cave explorers had mapped a convoluted cave several miles in length. Although there were still question marks—passages whose end had not been reached—the expedition was considered a great success. No one had been hurt, and only one of the 64 people—a reporter, not an NSS member—indicated that he had no desire to go caving again.

The Crystal Cave expedition and the activities of men like Gurnee reflect a growing American interest in caving. Spelunking is essentially a modern hobby. The first speleological society was formed in 1895 in France, a country where caving is especially popular. The National Speleological Society of the United States, which now has 3,000 active members, was not organized until 1939. The first International Congress was held in 1953, the year of the Crystal Cave expedition. The present period of intense exploration can be called the Golden Age of Speleology and the coming decade could well be the peak years of discovery and exploration. Twenty or thirty years from now, Gurnee feels, the major activity of spelunkers will be the protection and preservation of caves that have already been discovered.

For the most part, cavers are amateurs who simply like going into caves. "You may get a biologist or a geologist to go into a cave once or twice to look for specimens," Gurnee says. "But he won't become a dedicated caver, unless he's really interested in caves themselves. Some people have work that's as exciting or as dangerous as caving. But it's their job, they're doing it because they're paid to. Cavers aren't in it for money."

Gurnee enjoyed his week underground in Floyd Collins's Crystal Cave. He left Kentucky with pleasant memories of the fellowship of the cavers, the excitement of exploring numerous unknown tunnels and the beauty of one of the country's largest caves.

After four fruitless days of looking for caves near Santa Eulalia, Gurnee at last concluded that there weren't any extensive caverns in the neighborhood. But the spelunkers didn't mind too much. They still hoped to make discoveries in the last four days of the expedition when they reached the Cuchumatanes, 13,000 feet above sea level, where they hoped to find the highest cave in the Western Hemisphere. (Colorado then had the highest known cave at an altitude of 12,700 feet.) Their map showed a broad zone of the Cuchumatanes higher than that. They were very optimistic, and imagined that they would quickly locate a record-breaking cave. They had no idea that their maps were inaccurate.

Driving up to the Cuchumatanes, they saw scenery—open fields, pine trees and snow-covered peaks—that reminded them of the European Alps. At the top, they immediately met an American engineer who was in the area looking for manganese. His outpost, at an elevation of 11,500 feet, commanded a magnificent view of the lower mountains 5,000 feet below. The engineer helped them bring in their equipment and then found a house for them. But he didn't know anything about caves in the area so they had to explore on their own. Another problem was that at night the temperature dropped below freezing and the cavers had to keep a fire burning. Since the house had no chimney, they had to endure the smoky rooms.

Early the first morning, the cavers began to reconnoiter the beautiful countryside. They quickly found caves. In fact, during the next three days they found a large number of caves and sinkholes (that is, caves whose roof has fallen in). But according to the altimeter, none of these was above 11,400 feet. Puzzled, the cavers checked the height of scores of caves each day.

During this search they found two caves which were not contenders for the record but were of good size and interest. These basins, called the Sumidro de Chemal, were shaped like huge funnels leading down into the earth. Located on level plains, each one drained away all the rain which fell in an area of several square miles. The water rushed down into these funnels over a series of falls. The natives believed that the water descended 5,000 feet through the caves and then reappeared in a spring on one side of the mountain. The cavers tried but failed to confirm this theory with fluorescin, a powdered dye that hydrologists use to trace water routes underground. It turns water a vivid, sparkling green and can be detected in water 20 miles from the point where it is thrown in.

Gurnee descended several hundred feet into one of these funnels and discovered pottery and ladders left by the Indians. But the farther he went the more unnerving the cave became. "It was like being in a shower," he recalls, "with no way to turn off the water." For a full survey, a caver would have to descend much farther down into the jagged, twisting cone. In his official report to the NSS, Gurnee set down his belief that nobody would try it.

Meanwhile, the cavers still couldn't find the high cave they sought. As the days wore on, they became increasingly suspicious of their maps. By a bench mark at the mine and with their own surveying gear, they checked some of the readings and discovered that the map was, in fact, wrong. Prepared by the United States Air Force, the map added an extra 1,000 feet to every peak to keep pilots at a safe distance. Consequently, none of these beautiful limestone mountains reached above 12,000 feet. They had, obviously, no chance of finding the highest cave in the Western Hemisphere.

They did, however, find the second highest one. On a level plateau at an elevation of 11,400 feet, they discovered a vertical pit, a dead end only 70 feet deep. Not an impressive find, it was still a true cave. Indian shepherds had built a fence around it to keep their sheep out, and they used the cave as a trash can for dead trees and animals. Gurnee secured his rope ladder and, with little enthusiasm, climbed down into the pit. Actually, he felt that finding the highest cave was comparable to finding "the tallest midget or the shortest giant." Still, Kinne did need a story and the second highest cave was better than no cave at all.

The problem was: how could a photographer dramatize the discovery of the second highest cave when it was just a hole in the ground? Kinne had hoped they would find a large, tunnel-like entrance. But his luck had been poor all along. Then Kinne got an idea. In San Juan Ixchoy they had bought some skyrockets used by the natives for rituals in front of their caves. Why not send one of these up out of the pit? The rocket, the sparks and the smoke, all pregnant with meaning to the Indians of the Cuchumatanes, would dramatize the photograph. The cavers thought it was a fine idea. Gurnee was still down in the cave, and they shouted down to him, telling him Kinne's idea.

"I was down in the bottom of the pit," Gurnee says. "They passed a rope down with a couple of skyrockets. It didn't seem illogical. The cave was 70 feet deep—rather like a launching pad for a missile. I thought Kinne's plan was sensible enough. But maybe the altitude had gotten to us. Anyway, I set the rocket up on the bottom of the cave in the pile of debris. In order to light it I had to lean over, still on the ladder. The ladder was hanging free, like a pendulum. I took my carbide lamp and I lit the rocket. Then I swung over to the side and grabbed hold of the wall. The rocket was sputtering away in the center of the pit. Suddenly the stone I was holding broke away from the wall and I started to swing, and I swung right across the pit over the top of the skyrocket. Fortunately, I had passed the center when the rocket went off. So I thought that was great. I had swung past it and I was out of danger. The rocket started up, like the rockets at Cape Kennedy. Unfortunately, it didn't have enough force. It didn't make the top. It hit the wall about 10 feet from the top and started to come back, ricocheting around the inside of the hole. So there I was on the ladder, with the rocket shooting around. Then it came toward me and I remembered that we had asked the fellow to make it with a bomb timed to explode after a certain number of seconds. Just then the bomb went off. Only, by the grace of God, it didn't find me."

Mrs. Gurnee, standing with the others around the edge, remembers, "All we could hear was 'zoom, zoom, zoom, zoom!' I was waiting for that 'boom' at the end! And then smoke floated out of the hole and we went over and looked down. We had no pictures. And until the smoke cleared, no Russell."

"It's always difficult," Gurnee says candidly, "for an explorer to admit the odd situations he has been involved in. They seem reasonable at the time. Here we were doing serious work—mapping, collecting, photographing. We were doing the normal things to be expected on an expedition. But when that rocket started buzzing around, I realized it was one of those thoughtless things you do that you can't stop. You've gotten yourself into a situation and you can only sit it out. I thought about this story because it's a good warning to others."

Russell Gurnee can admit his mistakes because he has made very few. A veteran of 800 caves, he has been hurt just once—and then in a minor accident. Helping someone photograph a West Virginia cave in 1957, he got a third-degree burn from the flash powder. Like most cavers, Gurnee is highly conscious of safety.

Two days later the group was back in Guatemala City. They had not broken any records nor had they made any earth-shaking discoveries. But they had enjoyed themselves. They had traveled in good company, met interesting people and seen unusual ways of life. And they had done their job—the mapping of Guatemala's caves.

Only Kinne, who knew he didn't have a story, wondered if it had all been worth the trouble. Today Kinne says he enjoyed crawling into passages which he knew were virgin because the floor had never been disturbed. "That was the exciting part." But he also remembers that it was "cold and wet" in the caves. And, true to Gurnee's prediction about the man who is not "really interested" in spelunking, Kinne has not been in a cave since he left Guatemala. He prefers flying, skydiving, sailing and other things spelunkers would never give up caving for.

Soon after his Guatemalan trip, Gurnee went off to study the caves of Puerto Rico, a project he is still engaged in. Gurnee is always looking for "that other cave." His appetite for new caves is insatiable. But he does not forget the old ones. Part of Gurnee's pleasure is that he has become "a connoisseur of caves." "A filthy hole" on the Rio Dulce, Doña Maria with its living carpet of insects, the smoke-filled shrine cave of Santa Eulalia, the second highest cave—these were some of the steps along the way—and doubtless there will be many others.

Gurnee has to keep going so long as there are unknown, unexplored caves somewhere. As he says, "I have a thorn in my thumb and I have to get it out."

seven

The Water Barrier

M AN, the biologists tell us, came from the sea. Now, in increasing numbers, he is going back. In the last 20 years, spurred by a variety of motives, man has launched a new era in the exploration of the sea. Three times as extensive as the land, a mile deeper than the highest mountain, the earth's oceans, man's primordial birthplace, are a vast new frontier waiting to be explored.

Mendel L. Peterson, a curator of the Smithsonian Institution, goes underwater to find what others have lost. He spends his summers looking for shipwrecks off the coast of Bermuda and other islands of the Caribbean Sea. One of America's foremost marine archeologists, he is interested in the discovery, salvage and preservation of articles surrendered to the sea centuries ago. This goal takes him down into the bright waters of the Atlantic, where once-mighty French men-of-war and Spanish galleons lie rotting in the white sand. Swimming over these fragile, sand-covered wrecks, Peterson maps them, excavates them, retrieves them from oblivion. He calls these lost ships "accidental time capsules": each one provides a fresh, powerful glimpse of life as it was lived in times past.

At 60 feet the clear water off Bermuda, or some more southerly island, is as brightly lit as an office. The sandy bottom is level, clean and white. A few gaudily colored fish nose about, turning abruptly. They are curious but seldom hostile. Peterson loves to dive into this shining water. A heavy-set man with a small potbelly who somehow looks as if he should have a cigar clamped between his teeth, Peterson usually wears a white T-shirt, dark trunks, a heavy diving belt, a face mask and foot flippers. Air is pumped down into his face mask through a long, winding black hose. This is perhaps the simplest underwater breathing gear a diver can use. A dense stream of bubbles foams away from the mask as he swims. Far above he can see the black hull of his ship. The sunlight streams down in a comforting glare, reminding the underwater man of the sunlit world above. Peterson can work happily for hours in this time-less, crystal area. The white sand, the shimmering light, the exotic fish, the physical labor—Peterson likes every aspect of his undersea explorations. But most of all he loves the history buried in the sand.

The long-lost shipwrecks that Mendel Peterson finds are often barely detectable. Little except a few timbers and metal parts survives the worms, the tides and the years. But Peterson can imagine these frigates and galleons sailing majestically before the wind, he can picture sea battles, storms and terrified seamen riding sinking ships to the bottom. Peterson loves the lore of the sea with the zest of a small boy. But he regards marine archeology as serious work. There are more shipwrecks than he will ever have time to see. He makes sure that his reveries don't interfere with business.

Finding shipwrecks is only part of Peterson's job with the Smithsonian. During most of the year, as chairman of the Institution's Armed Forces History Department, with his staff of 30 assistants he is responsible for the famous museum's displays of old sailing ships, cavalry swords, uniforms and guns. Like every department chief at the Smithsonian, Peterson has, in addition to his desk job, a personal project. His is shipwrecks and he has pursued this activity with distinction. Since he began his underwater archeology in 1951, Peterson has developed many of the standard techniques for shipwreck hunters, and his book, *History Under the Sea,* is a comprehensive guide to marine archeology. "I was the first museum man to get started in this country," Peterson points out. "I suppose that makes me a pioneer."

The wrecks Peterson hunts for litter the ocean bottom by the thousands. Fortunately for marine archeologists, the majority of them lie along the well-known trade routes. Peterson knows, for example, the precise path followed by virtually all Spanish ships trading in the New World: from Spain, south to the Canary Islands; then straight across to the island of Trinidad near South America; then through the Caribbean to Panama to pick up gold; northwest to Havana, Cuba, where they met other galleons bearing Central American treasure, as well as riches from the Philippines carried by ship across the Pacific to Acapulco and by mule to Vera Cruz; then eastward to the Bahamas and, in the summer months, northeast to Bermuda before returning to Spain.

As Peterson noted in his book, the voyage could be a dangerous one:

While the Spanish could do much to save themselves from the other nations, they could do little to save themselves from the severe tropical storms which sometimes lash the western end of the treasure route from the Caribbean to Bermuda. As a result, hundreds of shipwrecks dot the length of this route from Colombia to Bermuda. Frequently, enemy ships sailing the same route met the fate of their intended victims and their bones joined those of the Spanish vessels.*

Peterson estimates that one out of every ten people crossing the Atlantic in this period either drowned in a shipwreck or died of disease or was killed by pirates. When the sailors left Spain, they kissed their friends farewell and "more or less gave up."

Although a thorough knowledge of the trade routes is a good head start for the hunter, pinpointing wrecks is still a difficult task. The search often starts right at the Smithsonian, in old handwritten ledgers. Countries kept records of all their lost ships, and Peterson often finds his clues in these ancient registers. The general location of the sinking may be indicated, along with the size, the number of cannons and the cargo on board. On the other hand, Peterson may find the wreck first and then return to his records to pin down exactly which ship he has found; in this way he can date precisely all the artifacts. Whichever way the chase unfolds, Peterson manages to mix history and research in an exciting pursuit.

Peterson's first plunge into marine archeology illustrates how the clues can fall into place. In 1951 some friends invited him to accompany them to the Florida Straits, where they had discovered a shipwreck. Diving over Looe Reef in 35 feet of water, Peterson helped to locate and identify numerous coins, buttons and ship's fittings. Simply by examining the coins, Peterson knew that the ship was English and that she had sunk

* Mendel H. Peterson, *History Under the Sea* (Washington: Smithsonian Press, 1965).

between 1714 and 1750. A certain kind of iron ballast proved that she was a warship. And the fact that her cannons were not prepared for firing showed that a storm, not a battle, had destroyed the ship. Back in Washington, Peterson combed through the British records of warships sunk in America, discovering this notation: "February 5, 1744, Looe, 44 guns, Captain Utting, Commanding, lost in America."

"The conclusion was obvious," Peterson wrote. The name of the British frigate had been bestowed on the reef which had sunk it. Later, in London, Peterson found a detailed report of the *Looe's* last voyage. Sailing to America, Captain Utting had captured a mysterious ship, apparently in the service of Spain. He lost both ships on a reef in the middle of the night, though the two crews were saved. Utting was eventually court-martialed and acquitted in England.

The sea has intrigued Peterson for many years. Although he grew up in the mountains of Idaho, he dreamed of ships and oceans and faraway places. This childhood enthusiasm, he says, was odd, unless you believe he inherited his love for the sea from his two Danish grandparents. In any event, when he saw the Gulf of Mexico at the age of 10, he found the sight of so much water "absolutely intriguing. I was awed by it. I just wanted to go and see ports and look at ships and dream about exotic places. I collected stamps and coins and dreamed about the places where they came from." He received B.S. and M.A. degrees in history before World War II, when he joined the Navy as an ensign. He asked for sea duty and served in the Pacific (he was mustered out as a lieutenant). He returned to graduate school for two years' study in engineering. In 1948, at the age of 30, Peterson became curator of naval history for the Smithsonian Institution. Three years later, he went to study his first shipwreck and, as Peterson says, "It was such an interesting thing, and I thought it had such potentialities, I just stayed in it."

Peterson confines his shipwreck hunting to the summer months, when the Caribbean weather, though blazingly hot, is not stormy. Peterson is in no hurry to finish up any particular wreck and he may return to a rich site season after season. He has been working on one 200-foot, 60-gun French frigate for five years and thinks he will be going back for ten more. One reason there is no particular rush is that, in Bermuda, at least, where he works with Teddy Tucker, the great Bermudian diver, the discoverer of a wreck can file a claim on it just as prospectors do on mineral deposits, and this claim gives him the exclusive right to explore the wreck.

More than anything else, the weather controls where the work starts each morning. Quiet seas are ideal. If the wind is blowing from the north, the hunters go around to the south side of the island where the water will be calmer. On the few completely windless days, Peterson suspends his excavation of known wrecks and concentrates on searching for new ones.

There are many ways to discover wrecks. The basic approach is to peer into the water from the side of a slowly moving boat. Peterson usually operates from a 56-foot boat that looks from a distance like a handsome white yacht. A closer inspection reveals that the decks are covered by ropes, compressors, diving gear, storage vats, coils of tubing and winches. For a better view than he gets from the deck of this boat, Peterson sometimes floats around in a glass-bottom boat, the size of a rowboat. And he often sends a few strong swimmers into the water to check sightings. Peterson has also used a magnetometer, an electrical gadget which detects metal in water, beer cans, unfortunately, as well as coins and cannons. On rare occasions, Peterson rents a light plane from which he can survey the azure waters, and he is considering using a hot-air balloon.

Peterson welcomes whatever help he can find because wrecks are normally buried and well camouflaged. When there are no ripples, a man can easily see down to 70 feet in the Caribbean. But the bottom is very deceptive, white and dark by turns. The dark areas, coral reefs or plants which may live just below the surface, are shallower than the white sand. Boating or swimming over this bottom, Peterson looks for unusual shapes which may betray the presence of a shipwreck. The primary rule he keeps in mind is that a straight line on the bottom is probably not nature's doing, but a cannon or a timber.

The wrecks Peterson finds are not picturesque ghost ships, lying on one side, eerily intact, algae streaming from the masts. The fact is that sunken ships are quickly destroyed by the sea. Wooden parts survive only when they are covered over by sand. The metal parts are coated with coral, sand crust and barnacles. And whatever does remain, in whatever form, blends in with the sea bottom, so that the faint clue of barnacle-encrusted metal is very difficult to spot. In addition, as Peterson says, seeing well under water is a skill that must be learned. A man out spearfishing might swim right over a shipwreck without even knowing it.

Diving down to the site, using the air hose-face mask arrangement that gives him a steady supply of fresh air, Peterson is able to put in several hours of hard work at 60 feet. He insists that aqualungs (which use a compressed air tank attached to the diver's back) are not as good for long periods under water, no matter how well trained the diver is. For one thing, a diver's jaw gets tired when he has to clamp his teeth on the air hose mouth-piece for a long time.

The need for a diving apparatus—Peterson's air mask, an aqualung or a diving suit—points up a basic condition of the sea: It is an alien environment to man. Moving up the evolutionary ladder, man lost the ability to remain naturally in the water. The doors of the sea closed behind him. Now the surface of the water is at once a barrier to men and the ceiling of an entirely different world. We live with seasons and we take support, the ground or the floor, for granted. Fish know little of either. To return to the sea, man needs the help of technology, for without breathing equipment even the best divers can descend only 100 feet, and then only for a few moments.

The technological conquest of the sea started, slowly, long ago. The Greeks, who used divers in operations against the Persian Navy, knew about trapping air in containers and the trick of obtaining air through a tube held above water by a float. Much later, in the 19th century, various inventors perfected the diving suit, with its metal helmet and spaceman-like costume. Suited divers can go down to 300 feet, but the suits are cumbersome and inhibit a diver's movement because he works at the end of an air hose which leads to the surface. Self-contained gear, enabling a diver to carry his own air supply, wasn't developed until World War II. Then the French perfected the first efficient self-contained apparatus, called "scuba" gear (self-contained underwater breathing apparatus). But the practical limit for scuba divers is 150 feet. Beyond that depth, the water pressure is too high for the scuba diver to operate safely. The pressure mounts to 44.5 pounds per square inch at 100 feet, and 223 pounds per square inch at 500 feet (compared to 15 pounds of atmospheric pressure at sea level), and this mounting pressure restricts breathing and circulation, distorts vision, and finally produces unconsciousness. Ultimately, at great depths, an unprotected man is literally crushed to death.

From 40 to 400 feet, man is most vulnerable to pressures in another, rather unexpected way. At these depths the nitrogen, which is 79 percent of air, is forced into his blood stream, along with the oxygen—something which never happens at normal atmospheric pressure. If a diver rises to the surface too quickly, the nitrogen comes out of the blood, sometimes harmlessly, but often in tiny bubbles which can cause strokes and death. This disease, called the "bends," can be prevented only by surfacing slowly, so that no bubbles form, a process called "decompression."

Divers have to pay strict attention to decompression tables, which prescribe how long they can safely stay at each depth and how slowly they must surface to guard against the bends. At depths of less than 45 feet, the bends rarely occur. But if a diver works for an hour at 60 feet, he should wait ten minutes at 20 feet before going all the way up. Each person responds to underwater pressure differently. Peterson has known men who followed the tables to the second and still got the bends. He himself has noticed a headache even after working at shallow depths, and he suspects it is related to the bends.

Obviously, the sea presents relentless and formidable obstacles to its explorers. Every foot of depth increases both the pressure and the diver's distance from the sanctuary above the surface. Peterson knows that some divers have ventured below 200 feet with just the air hose-face mask gear. But if the compressor fails, cutting off the diver's air, he either drowns or gets the bends. Peterson believes in treating the dangers of the sea with great respect. He has already decided on several precautions when he extends his group's work to depths beyond 80 feet. He will be using the best compressors, he will devise precise signals for help and he will scatter reserve tanks of compressed air around the site so that he can save himself if the compressor stops. With these precautions and using artificial light, Peterson believes they will be able to excavate down to 200 feet. But he can never go much beyond that depth with present equipment. The sea is an alien world and visitors must adapt to it. "You can never assume anything," Peterson declares. "I've noticed that the best divers always take great care in checking their equipment."

Once down on the site, Peterson uses mapping techniques that he has helped devise. First he puts a "bearing circle," which looks like a steering wheel with a chain hooked to the center, in the middle of the site. Mapping and measuring are done from this "datum point." The chain is stretched to any object he finds. On a sheet of white plastic the distance is marked from the object to the center point and the bearing, in degrees (north is zero degrees, east is 90 degrees, south 180 degrees and so on). The sheet might read: "timber, 260°, 25 feet; spike, 75°, 38 feet; chest, 110°, 18 feet." Since each site's "datum point" remains fixed from year to year, these two figures—degrees and feet—give the exact location of any object.

After Peterson's group discovers and maps a site, the next step is to excavate it. Unlike the land archeologist, they do not dig deep trenches—the sand is too soft to hold a trench. Instead, Peterson usually uncovers a shipwreck square by square. He uses an airlift to remove the sand which usually lies over a ship's remains. The lift consists of a long metal pipe into which air is pumped. The air bubbles rise through the pipe, expanding and creating a lifting action. Positioned near the bottom, this odd vacuum cleaner sucks up the sand the way soda is sucked up through a straw. The sand churns upward to the surface and then drifts off.

Fish are especially fond of the airlifts because a lot of worms come up with the sand. They dart in and snap at the food. The fish, Peterson reports, are "very friendly, very pretty." He says he has noticed that they are a lot like people. "The small ones are the aggressive ones and the big ones are easygoing." Peterson is himself a large man. "The small ones come around and nip you, the big ones usually just come and take a look." Peterson says that he has even gotten to know individual fish. One fish, called "Sam" by Peterson and his co-workers, has turned up on a site in Bermuda for six years. "He has a mark on his jaw," Peterson says. "He's been injured with a hook, so we know it's the same one." As for sharks, they don't cause much trouble. "They actually have a schedule they keep," Peterson says. "They leave the shallow water in Bermuda by ten when we get there. And they come in at five. You can almost set your watch by it. The little ones appear first. As soon as you see the little ones, you know mama and papa are right behind."

While Peterson is mapping and excavating a site, he enjoys the sensation of slipping back into history. If he finds a bit of dinner plate, he knows he is swimming where the officers used to dine. Cannon balls and hemp rope evoke an image of the supply room. Buttons and insignia call to mind a gang of tough laughing sailors. With little effort Peterson can turn the clock back 300 years, and "set the ship afloat" once again.

There is also, of course, the exciting possibility of finding something rare or valuable. "You don't know what you'll find. There's always an element of discovery," Peterson says. His parties have retrieved from the sea just about everything that men used in those days: a horn-handled razor, shoe soles, teeth, rosaries, swords, navigation instruments, gold bullion, bottles and glassware, gold rings, bells, anchors, nails, forks, "pieces of eight" and more.

To Peterson all these finds are valuable. Unlike the treasure hunter, he is not trying to make himself rich, he is trying to reconstruct history. He wants to know how men lived two, three and four centuries ago. Shipwrecks contribute innumerable facts and artifacts to this goal. A ship's cargo, for example, tells what was being traded at the time; records of this were seldom preserved. Peterson might find some items the captain was smuggling on the side—never recorded, of course. To Peterson, there is a special pleasure, too, in determining just how a ship was constructed. Seventeenth-century shipbuilders did not use blueprints. Instead they chalked their plans on the floor, built a ship and started over again with another design. By studying the wreck's timbers, Peterson can bring permanently back to life a plan that existed before only briefly on a shipwright's floor. Another dividend is the store of plain, everyday objects—forks, belt buckles, shoes, buttons—used by the crew and passengers. Shipwrecks preserve many ordinary articles not often saved on land.

The advantage Peterson has over the land archeologist is that once he knows the ship's name, he can date precisely every artifact. He can tell other scholars that a certain technique, invention or product was in use in the New World by a certain year, solving in this way the minor mysteries that arise because of the historian's scant records.

Watching Mendel Peterson working at a shipwreck site, an observer might think, "Oh, just another treasure hunter." But they had better not say so. With vigor and pride, Peterson says, "I'm a museum man." He disavows any connection with people who go rummaging through wrecks for gold coins only. In fact, he strongly condemns this activity. He feels that treasure hunters are irresponsible. They go into a wreck, tear it apart in a frantic search for valuables and then move on to another wreck. After they have gone, Peterson's work is doubly difficult. "They think every ship is loaded with loot," Peterson says. He points out that a lot of ships carried nothing more valuable than tobacco, and that the Spanish didn't abandon their treasure just because the ship went under. If the Spanish found a wreck in less than 60 feet of water, they sent down native divers to bring up the treasure. On the other hand, responsible treasure hunters can help by calling on professionals like Peterson to work with them.

Peterson's own attitude toward underwater treasure is, of course, that of the historian, rather than the man out for profit. "If we find treasure," he says casually, "we pick it up." The treasure Peterson picks up ordinarily finds its way to the Smithsonian or some other museum, and this takes a good bit of the excitement away from a gold find. On one expedition, Teddy Tucker found a 40-ounce gold bar worth about $40,000. Peterson looked it over casually and said, "Well, it looks like I'll write a magazine article about this." The crew was as casual as Peterson about the gold bar, except for one "rookie," who owned a TV station. He thought the bar was an earthshaking discovery. But since the others remained so calm, he decided that they must be playing a joke on him, that the bar wasn't actually gold. He could not be persuaded otherwise, and he never did report the find on his TV station. "We get jaded," Peterson admits.

The coins, swords and other finds from a shipwreck must, of course, be taken on board the boat, and sometimes this presents problems. For tiny, fragile pieces of wood and pottery, the only thing delicate enough to touch them is the human hand. Bells, spikes, plates and similar items are lifted up by the boat's winch. And some of the 10,000-pound cannons can be brought aboard only by a floating crane.

Once salvaged, many finds are difficult to preserve, particularly those composed of organic material. In these, the water has generally broken down the cell structure. If allowed to dry, a piece of wood or leather would quickly shrink to an unrecognizable and worthless hulk. Peterson has had to devise wet packs—often sawdust in wine barrels—to keep the artifacts from drying out. Back in the laboratory, his assistant, Alan Albright, can replace the water with such chemicals as polyethylene dissolved in alcohol, a solution that hardens inside the organic matter, giving the museum an artifact that would have been ruined if brought into the air by unprepared or unskilled divers. Peterson and Albright have also worked out techniques for dealing with various other kinds of material —hair, weed, fiber, pottery, glass, lead or iron. The metals, for example, have to be carefully cleaned with special chemicals or by electrolysis. Peterson has to double as a chemist for this exacting work.

Peterson has worked on more than 100 wrecks in the last 16 years. This, he feels, is just the beginning. There may be another 15 years of work around the island of Bermuda alone. He estimates that there are around 400 pre-1800 shipwrecks in the Florida Straits, and there are thousands more along the rest of the treasure route. This being the case, Peterson is quite sure that his summers are mapped out for a number of years to come.

Unlike Mendel Peterson, Dr. Jacques Piccard is not particularly interested in man's past involvement with the sea. For one thing, he operates at the deepest levels of the ocean world, where man has left scant traces. More important, Piccard thinks of the sea as a challenging barrier to man's mastery of his environment. The undersea world is a hostile place which men can enter if only they are clever and determined enough. In Piccard's view, the exploration of the oceans is a scientific problem and he is the engineer who will help to solve it, through the design and construction of ships in which men can travel to the bottom of the sea. He worked on the first ship designed to explore the farthest depths of the oceans, the bathyscaphe, and he has worked on and piloted more of these "deep-ships" than any other man. Indeed, Piccard's career is the story of modern deep-sea penetration.

Curiously, Jacques Piccard set out not to conquer the sea but to become an authority in economics, politics and history. A Swiss citizen, born in Brussels, where his father was a visiting professor at the university, he earned two degrees in economics from the University of Geneva (in 1946 and 1947), after having served during World War II in the French First Army. While completing his studies, he taught history as a graduate assistant at the university, and a few years later, intent on a professional life, he went to the free city of Trieste to begin a dissertation on its economic future.

His academic career did not last long. An inventive, almost compulsive scientific genius runs through the Piccard family. Both Jacques' father, Auguste, and his uncle, Jean, were famed scientists and explorers. Jean's son, Donald Piccard, is the foremost balloonist in the United States. Jacques' father, Auguste, had distinguished himself through pioneering efforts in many scientific fields. He discovered Uranium 235, devised a highly sensitive balance and seismograph, made the first space cabin, and built and flew his own balloons to an altitude of 10 miles in order to study cosmic rays.

Just before World War II, Auguste Piccard began work on a

deep-ship. Deterred by the war, he returned to the venture in 1946, and he is credited with the design and construction of the first bathyscaphe, which he named the F.N.R.S. 2. (F.N.R.S. is the abbreviation for Fonds National du Recherche Scientifique du Belgique, the Belgian scientific foundation which financed Piccard's invention. The F.N.R.S. 1 was the name of one of Auguste Piccard's balloons, a project the foundation financed before World War II.) The bathyscaphe descended to 4,500 feet in 1948, some 2,600 feet deeper than any submarine could then venture. But this success was qualified. Nobody was aboard, and Auguste Piccard wanted to put men deep down into the sea, not just a machine.

Jacques Piccard assisted his father in building the bathyscaphe and accompanied him on its testing trips. Unlike the many skeptics, he believed in the future of the deep-ship. Though a history teacher, the younger Piccard was spending more and more time in his father's laboratory. It is interesting that he learned nearly all his physics from his father, not at the university, where he took nothing more advanced than experimental physics. At this point, however, Jacques Piccard was still a teacher, not a scientist or an explorer.

After the 1948 dive, Auguste Piccard began lengthy negotiations with the French Navy, which finally agreed to improve the bathyscaphe, now officially named the F.N.R.S. 3, at the Toulon navy yard. Despite Piccard's impatience, however, the Navy moved slowly: not until 1954 did they send the F.N.R.S. 3, with two men aboard, down to 13,000 feet.

Long before that, Auguste Piccard had lost his enthusiasm for working with the bureaucratic, tradition-bound Navy. He wanted to build an entirely new bathyscaphe, and he wanted to supervise its construction personally. In the winter of 1951–

1952, Jacques Piccard came to help his father accomplish this goal—and he never left.

Jacques set out to obtain financial backing from private sources in Trieste, and the two Piccards began work on a new bathyscaphe in an Italian shipyard. Auguste Piccard named the new deep-ship the *Trieste* in gratitude to his supporters. Having put his books aside and turned his energies completely to the deep-ship, Jacques Piccard at the age of 30, in 1952, became a full-time scientist and explorer, which has been his vocation ever since.

A lean, very tall man, Jacques Piccard is the kind of precise-minded individual who is likely to take out his pocket slide rule to check figures used in conversation. He sometimes has a preoccupied air which suggests that his mind is playing with a new idea. But he is not, for that, the less gracious. Highly literate and deeply intelligent, fluent in French, English, German and Italian, Piccard is polite, perhaps a little distant, not in the least vain or flamboyant. His work, he says, is his life, and because his work is so important to him, he is reluctant to talk about it in an offhand, conversational way.

In August, 1953, five years after the dive of the F.N.R.S. 2, the *Trieste* was ready. Out of the water the bathyscaphe looked like a bloated, white blimp, 80 feet long, with a tiny spherical cabin tucked directly underneath. In the water, with only the top of the float (the blimp) and the conning tower showing, it looked like a submarine. What seemed to be the body of the sub, the float, was actually a huge tank of gasoline. The bathyscaphe's two passengers stayed in the small cabin, which hung underneath.

The *Trieste* was actually very much like a blimp. Essentially, Auguste Piccard had used the principles of ballooning in the design of the deep-sea craft. Like his manned balloons, the

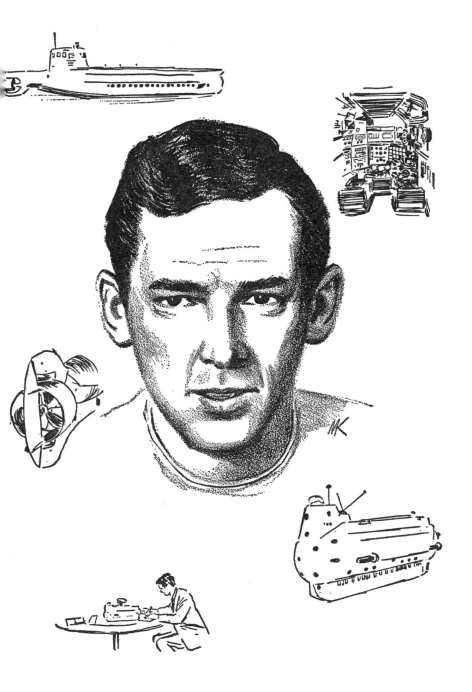

bathyscaphe consisted of two parts—the float and the cabin. A balloon was filled with helium or some other gas lighter than air, while the bathyscaphe's float was filled with gasoline or some other liquid lighter than water. This 58-foot tank of gasoline naturally floated on top of the water just the way a balloon rose to the top of the atmosphere. Since the bathyscaphe was designed to float, it could be made to sink only by adding tons of lead weights as ballast. The *Trieste* was thus theoretically quite safe. Should anything go wrong deep in the ocean, the pilot had many ways to jettison the weights and bring the ship back to the surface.

The bathyscaphe's seven-foot spherical cabin, made from three specially formed metal parts—a ring and two capping pieces—was attached beneath the float like a blimp's cabin. Filled with air, the cabin had to withstand the tons of water pressure encountered far down in the ocean. (The pressure on the thin metal float, on the other hand, was not a problem: unlike air, gasoline is non-compressible.) The cabin of the *Trieste* was crowded with instruments, leaving barely enough room for two men. In fact, Jacques and Auguste Piccard, both about six feet six, could just straighten up to their full height. From the cabin's two windows, the passengers could study the world beneath the sea. (Submarines, of course, do not have windows.) The Piccards faced a difficult problem in designing windows which could withstand pressures up to eight tons per square inch. Auguste Piccard came up with the solution: large truncated cones of Plexiglas that fit precisely into the seven-inch-thick wall of the sphere. The greater the water pressure against the windows, the more watertight they became.

On August 11, 1953, the two Piccards made the *Trieste's* baptismal dive, taking the ship down to a depth of 26 feet. Observers were surprised by the agility of the 80-ton craft.

With the addition of a few pounds of ballast, it sank rapidly. Lightened by a few pounds, it rose with ease. The *Trieste* was designed so that its weight in air would be almost exactly offset by the buoyancy in water of the 25,000 gallons of gasoline. On a scale underwater, the *Trieste* would weigh only a few pounds —a state of equilibrium called "neutral buoyancy," which made the ship extremely sensitive to small changes in ballast.

After this test dive, the Piccards were ready to head for deep water. A tugboat towed the bathyscaphe down to Capri, where the Italian government had dispatched a small warship to keep curious boats out of the area. The two Piccards took the *Trieste* down to 3,540 feet. Going down they saw a phosphorescent fish and streams of small white particles called "sea snow." The ocean bottom came into sight so suddenly that the two men had no time to jettison ballast. Both grabbed for support, expecting a rude shock. But the sea floor turned out to be a soft, white ooze. The cabin sank down four and a half feet. Hoping to see strange, unknown sights, the aquanauts could see only the mud against their windows. The father and son glanced nervously at each other. But the *Trieste* responded immediately when Auguste Piccard pushed the button releasing several hundred pounds of ballast. As the iron BB pellets shot down into the mud, the *Trieste* lifted away from the treacherous bottom.

In September they dove seven more times. Dive number six, a record-breaking descent, reached 10,300 feet. The Piccards touched down gently on the soft bottom in 63 minutes. Since sunlight does not penetrate past 2,000 feet, the Piccards could see only what their powerful searchlights revealed. "The sea floor," Piccard later wrote, "was a featureless and lifeless light-colored plain fading in the distance to blackness."

While Jacques Piccard searched in vain for some movement

on the drab landscape and duly recorded the emptiness, his father tended the instruments. Auguste Piccard was officially the pilot. He had to worry about the strength of the batteries, watch the pressure gauges, keep track of the oxygen supply and of scores of dials that indicated just how shipshape they were. Both men, characteristically intense, chatted little and joked less. Neither did they move about much. The interior of the *Trieste* resembled a small closet whose every wall was covered by shiny, somehow ominous gauges. The air became chilly and damp. But neither man minded the discomfort. They had descended two miles, deeper than any man before them. After Auguste Piccard had dropped the ballast and the *Trieste* had begun its ascent, each explorer allowed himself a tight smile of satisfaction.

Back on the surface, the father and son received the Italian boatswain's whistled blasts which are usually reserved for admirals. The commander of the Italian ship assigned to protect the *Trieste* called the Piccards "Admirals of the Abyss." But this record dive was Auguste Piccard's last: he was now in his seventies. For the next seven years Jacques Piccard would pilot the *Trieste* himself, while other men would take the place of the brilliant elder scientist.

During 1954, Jacques Piccard made another series of dives in the harbor near Naples without setting any records, since the Mediterranean isn't very deep at this point. Piccard concentrated on studying the sea life in the first 500 feet below the surface. He also tried to interest scientists in the possibilities of the bathyscaphe. The *Trieste* was receiving some publicity, and scientists were becoming convinced that it was more than just a daredevil device to break records. But newspapers dramatized Piccard's work, so that he worried about losing the support of serious men. "The *Trieste* was built to serve science," Piccard wrote. "Oceanographers were standing by waiting their chance to go quietly to work. The press seldom helped to establish the proper atmosphere during this period. The *Trieste* was depicted as some sort of crackpot machine designed solely for death-brushing adventures." This experience instilled in Piccard a permanent suspicion of journalists. "They don't understand," he says unhappily.

What Piccard wanted the public to notice was that the *Trieste* was an entirely new kind of craft, a boon to science. It was not a submarine and was not a diving bell. Submarines were essentially windowless underwater military weapons, not observation platforms for scientists. They rose and fell by pumping water in and out of ballast compartments. World War II submarines were "red-lined" at 400 feet while the *Trieste* easily descended below 10,000 feet.

Reporters would have been more discerning if they had compared the *Trieste* to deep-diving bells (or bathyspheres). In 1934 William Beebe the famous American explorer, biologist and author had descended in a deep-diving bell to 3,028 feet—a record for a number of years. But, as Piccard points out, a diving bell or sphere is not a free submersible. It is a cage on the end of a chain. A bathysphere rises and falls as the waves toss the mother ship. And a bathysphere cannot rest on the bottom, for then its lifeline would go slack and possibly become snarled. If that happened, the diving sphere might never be brought up.

Piccard tried to make the world see that the *Trieste* was a new breed of diving vessel. But this recognition came slowly. During 1955, the *Trieste* stayed in drydock because Piccard had no money. Funding his projects, in fact, has always been Piccard's greatest obstacle. Taking the *Trieste* down 5,000 feet cost $1,000, more than half of which went for the ballast of iron pellets jettisoned on each dive. Piccard estimates that he spends a year raising money for every year he actually builds or tests his inventions. This is unfortunate: Jacques Piccard's work is not likely to make him rich, but there is little doubt that mankind will profit immeasurably from it.

In 1956, the situation improved. The Italian Olympics Committee helped finance that year's dives, the committee apparently agreeing with Auguste Piccard that "exploration is the sport of scientists." Piccard and a geologist from the University of Milan made six more dives in the Mediterranean, one to 12,110 feet.

In the autumn of 1956, Piccard achieved the recognition he had sought. The United States Office of Naval Research began to take an interest in the *Trieste*. Piccard spent several months in the United States and found American scientists enthusiastic about his work. Early in 1957, he signed a contract with the ONR for a summer of test dives in the Mediterranean. These would enable American oceanographers to evaluate the bathyscaphe's potential. Piccard made some 25 dives that summer, showing the American specialists just how the bathyscaphe could be of value to them. While Piccard looked after the depth, rate of descent, ballasting, gasoline temperature and speed, the passengers studied light penetration, sound transmission, flora and fauna, bottom formations and other mysteries of the deep.

When the *Trieste* sank a few feet below the buffeting waves of the surface, it entered a world of perfect calm, sinking with an almost imperceptible motion. The water appeared bright and empty, but billions of tiny one-celled diatoms and other microscopic creatures actually filled it the way dust fills the air. All marine life in the ocean ultimately depends on these tiny organisms—they are the beginning of the "food chain" in which the smaller sea life serves as food for the larger. At 500 feet, the *Trieste* entered the dim "twilight zone" which is barely illumined by surface light. Piccard switched on the floodlights. The sea snow, which appeared to stream upward, increased with the depth. Many of these particles were living plankton; others were merely the dead husks of past life. At 1,100 feet, with the lights off, the divers saw flashes of bio-luminescence (light given off by certain organisms, both marine and terrestial). A bizarre procession of bluish-green creatures and glowing fish passed before the windows. Most of the fish that live as deep as the twilight zone have luminescent organs. Scientists do not always know why. To light their path? To attract food? To attract the opposite sex? Finding an explanation is complicated by the fact that many of the fish are blind and cannot see their own or another fish's light. As the *Trieste* descended, the sea snow reached blizzard proportions. (Scientists suspect that the heavy concentration of these or similar organisms at this depth disrupts radio signals.) Approaching 2,000 feet, the light faded to a dark gray. A few hundred feet farther down, the sea was totally black. The marine life that lives below 2,000 feet must depend on nourishment settling from above, because nothing grows at this depth. Legends hold that sea monsters inhabit these depths, but though deepsea fish are often grotesque looking, scientists have found no evidence of genuine monsters. On the graphs of an echo-sounder, a sea monster would appear as a tight dark smudge, called a "black angel." But thus far only "gray angels," which are probably schools of fish, have been recorded. At 3,000 feet, Piccard has seen, to his great surprise, many kinds of small fish which are just as colorful as the tropical ones that live closer to the surface.

Now the bottom came into sight, fuzzily at first, like a

picture out of focus. The light-brown silt was studded with mounds six inches high and two feet wide. These were the homes of blind, burrowing fish. Occasionally a fish resembling a catfish swam by. The clouds of dust left by the fish as they nosed about showed that the bottom was not hard-packed soil but a loose, powder-like sediment. Many scientists think that these particles, which resemble quicksand, move in currents, just as water does.

Ready to return to the surface, Piccard pushed the button that released the iron-pellet ballast from the bottom of the *Trieste*. The bathyscaphe rose several feet a second, and took about 40 minutes to reach the surface. The arrival was marked by a gentle bump as the ship again breasted the waves.

The summer's 25 dives proved so successful that the United States Navy bought the *Trieste* outright in 1958 and took it, with Piccard as pilot, to the Naval Electronics Laboratory at San Diego, California. The *Trieste*, then the only deep-ship in the country, attracted great publicity. Piccard was especially pleased by the impact his bathyscaphe continued to have on scientists. "It opened the eyes of many people who then decided to go underwater," he says. The new era in oceanography had officially dawned. Now, less than 10 years later, there are dozens of deep-ships in the United States.

The *Trieste* made 10 dives near San Diego from December, 1958 to September, 1959. The most serious work centered around the 4,000-foot San Diego Trough. But most of this period was really a period of adjustment during which the Navy specialists and the American scientists learned how to handle and exploit the new property.

Meanwhile, technicians in Germany were forging a new cabin so that the *Trieste* could be taken down to still greater depths. Everyone at the NEL knew that the *Trieste* would eventually be taken to the island of Guam, where it would attempt a descent to the ocean's deepest point. Code-named Project Nekton, this risky venture had little official status at first because it appeared so likely to fail. But the Navy had presumably bought the *Trieste* to secure this "first"—if only the red tape and official objections could be cleared away. Piccard and his supporters in the Naval Electronics Laboratory naturally worked hard to make the Navy adopt this goal, and in the summer of 1959, the project was approved by Washington. The public, however, was told only that the *Trieste* would try for 20,000 feet in the course of research in the Pacific. In early October, Piccard and the scores of people attached to the project boarded the SS *Santa Maria* for the trip to Guam—200 miles from the Challenger Deep, the sea's deepest canyon.

The Challenger Deep, discovered only a few years before, was 35,800 feet or seven miles deep, and Piccard's decision to take the *Trieste* this far down must be considered in the light of the difficulty presented, only a few years before, in going beyond the first 500 or 1,000 feet. But Piccard felt a supreme confidence in the ship which he and his father had created. Piccard maintains that if you "build with sufficient care, it's not dangerous. It is less dangerous to go under water than to cross the street or take a taxi or fly a plane. You just have to be sure it is less dangerous than the other things you are doing every day."

After two test dives early in November, Piccard took the *Trieste* down to a record 18,150 feet or about three and a half miles. The two-hour-and-fifteen-minute dive (of which all but 10 minutes was spent rising or falling) passed routinely until the last minute. On the return, 15 yards below the surface, two violent explosions occurred, alarming Piccard and his passenger. They later found that the cabin's central ring had shifted in relation to the two capping end pieces. Piccard considered this a trivial accident, since the water pressure would hold the three pieces together even if the epoxy resin used to bind them no longer held. Still the *Trieste* had to be drydocked for two weeks. When two test dives proved that the repairs had been successful, the *Trieste* was again ready for deeper dives.

The next dive took place on January 8, 1960, a cloudy, blustery day. Swells and whitecaps washed over the *Trieste* as it was towed 70 miles to the Mariana Trench off Guam. Once again Piccard managed a smooth dive, this time to 23,000 feet, a record achievement that made headlines all over the world. Below 20,000 feet the *Trieste* could still hear the mother ship via radio but Piccard could not talk to the men topside. The bathyscaphe descended and ascended at three feet per second— about the speed of a freight elevator—too fast to study the sea life. The only excitement came when two outside pipes collapsed with a bang under the tremendous pressure; there was no particular danger.

The grandest dive was yet to come, as, by this time, the press knew. Even though the official press release had not mentioned the Challenger Deep, word had leaked out that Piccard would soon try to take the *Trieste* down to the deepest part of the ocean. He had been working toward this goal for years. Piccard wrote that he "felt destined for this culminating plunge." Regrettably, the Navy tried to take this final victory away from Piccard at the last minute. A few days before the ultimate dive, the Navy announced that two submarine officers, neither as experienced as Piccard, would pilot the *Trieste*. Knowing that the dive would make history, the Navy wanted two Americans to do the honors. But Piccard won back his place. He produced his contract, which gave him the right to make any dives that "present special problems." The Navy agreed that the clause should be applied to the first 35,000-foot dive.

On a stormy Saturday, January 23, 1960, Piccard was ready for the Challenger Deep. The 200-mile tow trip from Guam had lasted through the night. The scientists aboard the *Trieste's* destroyer escort spent the early morning looking for the deepest part of the canyon. They dropped hundreds of mines into the rough ocean and then counted the seconds until the echo returned from the bottom. Just a few hours before the dive they found a slot, four miles long, a mile wide, a full seven miles down. Piccard and Lieutenant Don Walsh, USN, sank below the surface at 8:10 A.M., nearly the last possible minute if they were to complete the 14-mile round-trip journey before dark.

Piccard dropped the *Trieste* as swiftly as possible. In the back of his mind, he had the worrying thought that a deep current might push them into the side of the one-mile wide trench. The two men ate chocolate bars for food—nothing else. As usual, the cabin became cold and damp. Condensed water vapor glistened on the shiny metal instrument panels. Plunging through the metal-dark waters, they reached the old mark of 23,000 feet at 11 o'clock. Less than one percent of the ocean bottom is that deep. They sent back the two-tone signal, which meant, "All's well." There was also a signal for distress—five tones. But it would have been useful only to historians, for the *Trieste* was quite beyond anyone's help.

Piccard slowed down the descent to two feet per second. They were now as deep as Mount Everest is high. The searchlight showed the water to be clear and empty. Shortly after noon, the echo sounder picked up the bottom. A frightening thought seized Piccard. Suppose the bottom was a deep soup of fine silt. The *Trieste* might sink right out of sight before Piccard could drop enough ballast to stop the descent. At 32,400 feet, an explosion shook the cabin. Piccard couldn't figure out what had happened, but the two men agreed to continue down. They touched bottom at 35,800 feet—seven miles down.

Almost immediately, Piccard saw a foot-long fish which he recognized as a genuine vertebrate fish. The sight of that fish put to a stop centuries of speculation over whether life existed at such depths. Most scientists had concluded that the pressure ruled out life entirely—or at least everything but primitive one-celled organisms. The vertebrate fish also indicated that the seemingly stagnant water must circulate, otherwise no oxygen would reach that abyss.

Miraculously, Lieutenant Walsh made radio contact with the surface. The radio operator above, barely audible, wanted only to know the depth reached. Once he had that information, he signed off, obviously very excited. The unexpected contact pointed up one of the sea's mysterious qualities: sometimes radio waves are transmitted straight and strong through the ocean, other times they are bent or bounced back.

While making his scientific observations, Walsh discovered the cause of the mysterious explosion. One of the windows had cracked because the sea pressure had changed the shape of the metal holding it. Because of the break, Piccard kept the *Trieste* on the bottom only 20 minutes. Just before 1:30 P.M. he released 800 pounds of iron pellets and the bathyscaphe started back to the surface.

The *Trieste* broke the surface late in the afternoon, and the support ships steamed in to pick up the men. Photographers aboard a small rubber raft pulled alongside to take their pictures. Within the week, President Eisenhower decorated Piccard and Walsh for their epic achievement.

After 65 dives spanning seven years, Piccard turned over the *Trieste* to the United States Navy. But he had few regrets. He had shown what his father's invention could do. He had brought it triumphantly through the final test. Now he was ready to move on to different sorts of underwater ships.

Piccard is not the sort of man who wishes only to plant a flag on a mountain or the ocean bottom and then sit back and write his memoirs. Most of his enjoyment had come from designing and building the *Trieste*. The 65 dives were tests to show what the *Trieste* could do. Once he had proved the soundness of the concepts that guided the *Trieste's* design—which the Challenger dive certainly did—Piccard was eager to test still other concepts. He realized that the *Trieste* was not the perfect deepship for all sorts of work at all depths. Different ships would serve other purposes better. Years before the sixty-fifth dive, Piccard had already thought of a number of new projects. Piccard's engineering instinct dominates his thinking, and building ships which break through the barriers of the sea is his pleasure. "I enjoy building them," he says, "and testing them. But when they are going well, then I like to make another one."

Piccard's next project was a deep-ship called a mesoscaphe (or middle-depth ship). This was a "super submarine," designed to take oceanographers down to 3,000 feet. Piccard conceived it as a long cylinder crammed with scientific equipment. But for two years he could find no one to finance the mesoscaphe solely as a research ship. Previous searches for money had taught Piccard the value of being flexible. So he redesigned his mesoscaphe as a tourist submarine, and the Swiss National Exhibition at Lausanne put up the money to build it. Launched in February, 1964, the world's first mesoscaphe took visitors to the Geneva Fair on journeys to the depths of Lake Geneva.

The 94-foot mesoscaphe, called the PX-8 and officially

named the *Auguste Piccard,* looked much like an airplane inside, with a line of 20 swivel chairs on each side of a wide center aisle, enabling each passenger to see the deep through his own porthole. The PX-8 had 61 incandescent floodlights which lit up the watery shadows. It could move at almost seven miles an hour on an 80-horsepower electric motor, and its air system allowed it to stay down at least 48 hours, although the sight-seeing dives lasted only an hour. The "collapse depth" was calculated to be 5,000 feet, and to observe the usual safety factor of two, the *Auguste Piccard* was never intended for operation below 2,500 feet. During the course of the Swiss fair, Piccard's ship made some 700 dives, carrying 20,000 people down into Lake Geneva for a look at the underwater world. Eventually it completed 1,100 dives with some 30,000 passengers.

Unlike the bathyscaphe, the mesoscaphe did not have a huge buoyancy tank. In most respects, in fact, it looked and functioned like an ordinary submarine. As in a sub, water flowing into two ballast tanks was the basic means of descent. However, the pilot usually kept the ship slightly lighter than the water (by retaining air in the tanks) and took the ship down by using the forward thrust of the screw and the downward push of the diving planes. This method operated as a safety device: if the motors should stop, the mesoscaphe would rise to the surface. Piccard had installed another fail-safe device: five tons of iron shot or "security ballast," which was held electromagnetically and could be released by breaking the current.

Piccard had wanted a mesoscaphe for scientists. But the *Auguste Piccard* had the advantage of showing a wider public just what deep-ships could do. The *Auguste Piccard,* in fact, symbolized the arrival of a new age in ocean exploration, though it was an invention which many scientists still did not endorse. Piccard was demonstrating that deep-ships—whether bathyscaphes or mesoscaphes—could be used for all kinds of work and research. And the message hit home. Even as tourists peered at strange fish, more and more scientists awoke to ways that they could use deep-ships. Without having gotten the scientific mesoscaphe he wanted, Piccard had succeeded in making converts to the cause of ocean exploration.

Once the PX-8 was running smoothly, Piccard was eager to move on to the development of new ideas. One was a very fast submarine, specially designed for underwater exploration. Another was a small, light, cheap diving ship for work in shallow waters. Piccard knew that he could not afford to become attached to a single idea. He had to have several projects to interest prospective backers or he would miss a lot of opportunities. "The problem is the financial side," Piccard says. "You need somebody who can support large ventures." Raising money is the only part of his work Piccard dislikes. "I lose so much time."

As could be expected, Piccard lost another two years looking for his present financial partner, the Grumman Aircraft Engineering Corporation, who, ironically, found him instead. Piccard signed a five-year contract with Grumman to serve as consultant and designer in the fall of 1966. Like other large corporations, Grumman is aware that the underwater world will be a significant element in man's future. The contract, Grumman declared, marked the company's "entry into the field of 'inner space' vehicles, a rapidly expanding market for scientific exploration, military operations and commercial exploitation of the world's oceans." Grumman envisions the use of underwater ships for salvage, farming, construction, prospecting, mining, military missions beyond what submarines now can handle, and even underwater "houses" in which men would work and study. Like other giant corporations such as Lockheed, General Electric and Westinghouse, Grumman wants to be ready with the equipment to make these new operations possible. As soon as the company decided to establish an Oceans Systems program, they sought out Piccard.

After looking over Piccard's varied suggestions, Grumman decided to finance a second, more scientifically oriented mesoscaphe. Named the PX-15, Piccard's second mesoscaphe is 49 feet long, with 29 portholes and four 25-horsepower motors that can be rotated for propulsion in any direction to achieve speeds up to five miles an hour. Since its collapse depth is 4,000 feet, the PX-15 will operate to a depth of only 2,000 feet. Like its predecessor, the PX-15 will have a central corridor. But there will be no room for tourists. The interior will be divided into laboratories and bunk space for six. Piccard has designed the ship so that it will hover at any depth even without the motors going. No mechanical vibration or electrical interference from the motors will disturb delicate measurements, making the PX-15 an ideal undersea laboratory.

The PX-15 has been built by the same company in Monthey, Switzerland, that constructed the PX-8. The ship was thus close to Piccard's laboratory in Lausanne. The new mesoscaphe, which will cost about one and a half million dollars, is scheduled to be launched in 1968.

A few months later, in early 1969, the Grumman-Piccard PX-15 will be put to work on the Gulf Stream Drift Mission. Piccard, two of his own PX-8 crew and three American scientists (a marine biologist, an acoustics expert and an oceanographer) will spend four to six weeks drifting in the Gulf Stream from Miami to Nova Scotia. The mesoscaphe's depth will fluctuate from 300 to 2,000 feet as the scientists make measurements and observations.

When that mission is over, the PX-15 will be modified for various sorts of underwater experimental work. Among the additions Grumman is considering are a diver lock-out so that divers can enter and leave the mesoscaphe, a manipulator for heavy lifting, and a powerful drill for taking samples from the ocean bottom.

Predictably, Piccard is already working on plans for new ships. He foresees the day when half of man's food will come from the sea, when most oil will be brought from ocean wells, when underwater mining will be as extensive as land mining is now. Each of these efforts will require a special craft. Piccard hopes he will be able to make "that next ship."

Meanwhile, Piccard leads a quiet but intense life. He lives in Lausanne, Switzerland, with his wife and three children. When pressed, Piccard will admit some enthusiasm for photography, manned ballooning, reading history and mountain climbing. But his standard response to a question about hobbies is: "Nothing. Oceanography is my hobby."

Piccard's work will inevitably lead to great harvests of knowledge about the sea. But Piccard himself has never been chiefly concerned with gathering new facts. He is pleased to help, of course, and is as curious as the next man. But Piccard is not in the main a research scientist. He is a designer who helps scientists to do their work. One of the most eminent of the men who devote themselves to the actual scientific study of the ocean's unpredictable secrets is Dr. Eugene C. LaFond. Dr. LaFond was investigating the sea long before Piccard built his bathyscaphe. Now, like many other ocean scientists, LaFond makes use of Piccard's inventions to seek new knowledge of the sea.

Dr. LaFond is the senior scientist and head of the Marine

Environment Division at the United States Naval Electronic Laboratory in San Diego, California. In this capacity, he supervises most of the Laboratory's ocean research. He and his staff of 40 explore and chart many aspects of the ocean which could conceivably be of use to the Navy. Taxpayers' money supports the Naval Electronics Laboratory (NEL), so the research is supposed to be practical. But the Navy has learned that militarily useful facts tend to hide in strange places, and LaFond and his colleagues work on a staggering variety of projects.

"The more you know about the ocean," LaFond says, "the more effective you can be at operating and detecting ships. How exactly does a submarine go through the water, for example? If you put a sub down there, what's going to grow on it? Anything that's useful to the Navy, we try to cover."

LaFond's group studies currents and tides, the characteristics of the sea bottom, sea animals (especially if they seem to get in the way of sound waves), and the water's physical structure (for example, its temperature and chemical properties). A Deep Submergence Program, which so far has used two bathyscaphes and two mesoscaphes, is an integral part of this research. The NEL also uses surface ships (one of which is among the Navy's last sailing ships), self-operating buoys, many scuba divers and an oceanographic tower.

Dr. LaFond, a short, bald, soft-spoken man, came to the Naval Electronics Laboratory in 1947. He was put in charge of the newly created Marine Environment Division. Starting as a one-man unit, the Division has grown over the past 20 years to include 40 other scientists. From his desk in San Diego and on many expeditions, LaFond has emerged as both a leader and a pioneer in contemporary ocean research.

Educated as a chemist and physicist, LaFond is concerned with the physical aspects of the oceans. Although he supervises

work in many other fields of oceanography, LaFond himself is most fascinated with the ocean's temperature changes, chemical content and movements such as tides and currents. Like the swimmer, LaFond wants to know: How's the water? Often LaFond's research and expeditions try to answer questions just that basic: How cold is the water? How clear? How salty? What's the undertow like?

LaFond, who calls himself a "physical oceanographer," gained wide attention for his studies of the Indian Ocean in the mid-1950s. A prolific writer, LaFond described his Indian findings in more than 50 reports with such titles as: "Beach Erosion Cycles near Waltair on the Bay of Bengal," "The Profile of the Continental Shelf off Visakhapatnam Coast," and "On Upwelling and Sinking off the East Coast of India."

In 1958, LaFond directed the oceanographic research team on the USS *Skate* which made the second submarine cruise under the Arctic Ocean ice pack. This was the first cruise to surface through the ice at the North Pole and at eight other places in the Arctic pack to study ice. While the sub traversed the Arctic, acoustic signals measured the ice thickness overhead and the depth of the water below. This was LaFond's fifth expedition to the Arctic; previous ones were on ice breakers and oceanographic vessels.

The following year LaFond conceived the idea of building a tower one mile off the California shore, the first such oceanographic research tower ever built. Finished in June, 1959, the 85-foot tower, 25 feet of which cleared the water, looks like a boys' fun house, only larger. Sitting above the water on four metal legs is a squat shack, decorated with a confusion of pipes, wires, lines, antennas, a flagpole, signs, pulleys, life preservers, stairways, railings and landings. Vertical railroad tracks on three sides allow instrument carts to be positioned at any depth. The tower is connected by underwater electric cable to the shore and is permanently manned by two or three scientists. Instruments constantly record sea swells, temperatures, plankton samples (drawn in through a submersible tube), chemicals, light transmitted through the sea, sound transmission and weather information. These interrelated facts about the ocean help scientists to understand what is taking place in the water.

In 1960, LaFond journeyed to the Gulf of Thailand and the South China Sea to investigate ways to increase marine food for nearby countries. Two years later, in 1962–1963, he made a similar biological study of the Indian Ocean. At this time he and his wife, Katherine, who works with him, headed the first cruise of the Research Vessel *Anton Bruun* as part of the United States effort in the International Indian Ocean Expedition. The object was for 29 nations to make a concentrated study of the Indian Ocean. The expedition explored the geology, physics, meteorology, chemistry and biology of the entire ocean. One thing that LaFond discovered, for example, was that the greatest number of fish would be found where the offshore winds were most persistent and strong. These winds blow away the surface water, bringing up the nutrient-rich water from deeper depths, where dead plant and animal life have settled and decomposed.

In 1960, LaFond also took his first dive in a bathyscaphe. After Piccard made his record dive into the Challenger Deep, the Navy handed the *Trieste* over to the NEL. There, LaFond and the other scientists immediately put it to use. With the bathyscaphe, LaFond points out, he can do research which would be impossible from a surface ship. He can go down and watch fish in their own habitat, studying such things as how they swim and how they burrow. "You could never study these fish in this way using a dredge haul. You couldn't even catch the fast fish. With a bathyscaphe, we can get down to the bottom and take a sample of it. You couldn't do that from the surface without stirring up the bottom and destroying the purity of the sample."

The NEL has also used two other deep-ships—a diving saucer called the *Soucoupe,* designed by Jacques Yves Cousteau, another underwater pioneer, and the *Deepstar 4000,* a mesoscaphe built by Westinghouse. Both are intermediate-range vehicles. The *Deepstar 4000* is a yellow smooth-surfaced, teardrop-shaped vessel that accommodates three people—two scientists and a pilot. It can hover in the water and also rest on the bottom. One scientist lies down and observes the sea through forward, underside portholes, more or less at a 45-degree angle. The other scientist sits upright to tend the inside recorders. Their instruments are mounted externally on the overhanging prow. Weighing seven tons in the air, the 15-foot *Deepstar* is almost neutrally buoyant in water. An additional 200 pounds of ballast puts it into a dive. Using various probes and a claw, a scientist in the *Deepstar* can examine anything he encounters in the ocean, to a depth of 4,000 feet.

In 1963, LaFond took a year off from underwater exploration to serve as deputy director of the Office of Oceanography for UNESCO. Here again his work focused on making the sea produce more food for developing countries by providing training and equipment to foster these goals.

Back at NEL, LaFond returned to "sea duty." He made dives in both the *Soucoupe,* to depths of up to 1,000 feet, and the *Deepstar,* usually to around 4,000 feet, to study temperature and nutrients at the bottom. Late in 1966, he coordinated the Japan Sea Expedition, which was essentially a slow cruise across the Pacific from San Diego to Yokohama. Using a new device called a *thermistor chain,* LaFond and other scientists from the NEL obtained thorough measurements of the ocean's temperatures at all points along the route to a depth of 750 feet.

The temperature of the ocean varies, of course, both from place to place and from top to bottom. The vertical changes are the most interesting to LaFond. (When the ocean's temperature structure is depicted on paper, oceanographers use isotherms—or lines of equal temperature—to indicate these layers, just as weathermen draw isobars through all the points where the pressure is equal.) LaFond often found that these isotherms were wavy, rather than level. For example, a 65-degree isotherm might stay roughly at a depth of 300 feet for a few miles, then drop like a roller coaster to 600 feet and then climb back to 200 feet a few miles farther on. LaFond is now trying to find out why these layers form, how they are maintained, why they oscillate vertically, and what effects they have on weather, sound transmission and marine life.

To obtain the sea's temperature profile, the NEL's laboratory developed the thermistor chain, which is actually a 900-foot-long string of thermometers. Held nearly vertical in the water by a 2,300-pound "fish" or streamlined weight, the chain's temperature sensors register the temperatures at many depths and relay the information by wires to a recording device on the ship. There is one thermometer every 25 feet along the chain. The signals from the sensors are scanned electronically every twelve seconds, and the isotherms are printed on a 19-inch-wide tape. With the ship moving at six miles an hour, LaFond can record a complete picture of the sea's vertical thermal structure every 120 feet.

When they had finished probing the Sea of Japan, LaFond

and his fellow scientists knew what temperature the water was at each depth, all the way across the Pacific Ocean. The thermistor chain was also towed in crisscross patterns near Japan, Hawaii and Central America. Overlapping runs allowed the oceanographers to see how the isotherms change with time, curve around themselves in turbulent areas and circle each other in huge eddies.

LaFond's fascination with the water began when his family moved to the West Coast from inland Washington, when he was eight years old. The family then went to San Francisco, where his father piloted a ferryboat, before moving to San Diego, where LaFond lives today with his wife. LaFond always had his own sailboat; today he has a 19-foot *Lightning*. In school, he took courses that pointed toward his eventual career —mathematics and chemistry in college, physics, chemistry and biology in graduate school at Berkeley. He carried on further graduate work at the Scripps Oceanographic Institute, one of the world's foremost oceanographic research centers. When LaFond joined Scripps, it had 25 members; today there are 1,000. He received a Doctor of Science degree from Andhra University in India for extensive work on the temperature and related properties of the Bay of Bengal.

With the advent of World War II, most of the scientists at Scripps, LaFond included, went to work for the Navy's Division of War Research. After the war, LaFond spent a year back at Scripps, then returned to the Naval Electronics Laboratory as chief of the newly created Marine Environment Division.

Currently the marine biologists at NEL are spending much of their time investigating animals that disrupt sound in the ocean. LaFond's staff has played a major role in pinpointing the organisms which compose the Deep Scattering Layer (DSL), a blanket of marine organisms that deflects sound in the ocean. The DSL tends to hide whatever is beneath it from sonar because the sometimes impenetrable layer bounces back, or scatters, sonar waves. Electronic sonar devices have also mistaken the DSL for the bottom itself.

As LaFond's scientists have discovered, some of the organisms that make up the DSL are small and gelatinous animals with gas floats. There are other marine organisms in the DSL, such as fish, which have gas bladders. These organisms tend to concentrate in layers, which migrate down during the day and up at night. The gas in their floats and bladders is what scatters sound, making detection of submarines difficult.

The biologists at NEL are constantly finding new forms of undersea life. One curious specimen is now referred to as "mucous balls" for lack of a more scientific name. Often seen in photographs, mucous balls have yet to be captured in nets, since they are so fragile. The organism itself appears to live in a small "house" about one inch across. But this "house" is always engulfed in a 16-inch ball of wavering, speckled jelly or "mucous." Mucous balls point up an important fact: in an age when many people think that scientists have identified all species of life on earth, new life forms continue to be discovered.

The geologists at NEL, of course, pursue a different course from that of the biologists. They want to learn how the bottom is shaped, what it is made of and how it changes. Using various sonic devices, they can draw profiles of the bottom without ever leaving a surface ship. But the geologists also find deep-ships useful because in them they can actually see what the bottom looks like. Among the sea's more fascinating phenomena are its spectacular and diverse submarine canyons. A few miles off Baja California, for example, there are several sand-falls, 200-foot-long cascades of sand that run silently and mysteriously off a cliff deep under the surface. Other motion along the bottom is less obvious. The scientists have learned, however, that the sediment in the sea's canyons and gullies is always moving. They have put markers on an apparently solid bottom; in a few days the markers have changed their location and position. They speculate that this restless sediment has carved out the ocean's canyons, many of which are so huge that they dwarf the Grand Canyon.

LaFond's own findings are perhaps less colorful than mucous balls and sand-falls. But his discoveries have far more significance to the average land dweller. The tides and temperatures of the seas—which cover nearly three-fourths of the earth's surface—drastically affect our weather. And the chemicals in the sea decide what fish can live where, and in what numbers.

LaFond's most recent accomplishment was to pin down the "temperature structure," as the physical oceanographers call it, of the ocean, especially near the bottom. To do this research, LaFond made nine dives off the California coast in the *Deepstar 4000* in 1966 and another four in 1965, usually going down to about 4,000 feet.

LaFond made his precise temperature measurements at various shallow probes into the bottom ground itself, and at intervals from the bottom up to a distance of 200 feet above the bottom. Cold water settles, of course, so that generally the deepest water is the coldest. But LaFond suspected that he would find some revealing divergencies from this rule at the very bottom of the ocean—what oceanographers call the seafloor interface.

Since the *Deepstar's* pilot could make the mesoscaphe hover at any depth, LaFond had no trouble obtaining readings at precise intervals in the 200 feet of water closest to the bottom.

To measure the temperature of the bottom itself, LaFond took advantage of the *Deepstar's* more sophisticated abilities. Before making a dive, he attached his sensitive thermometer —calibrated to 0.001 degrees centigrade—to the remote-controlled hinged arm which extends from the front of the *Deepstar*. When the craft had settled on the bottom, this arm was dropped down against the sediment. To push the thermometer down into the sediment, LaFond did not move the arm. Instead, he moved the *Deepstar*. The pilot shifted the mercury ballast to the front and the *Deepstar* rolled forward on its curving belly, pushing the arm down into the bottom. After several minutes, when a constant reading had been obtained, the pilot shifted the ballast again and the thermometer went deeper for another measurement.

LaFond discovered that beneath the cold water of the ocean floor there is a thin layer of slightly warmer water directly above the bottom ground. This warmer layer of water is the same temperature as the bottom itself. Moreover, the temperature of the bottom varies with the depth, the temperature rising the deeper one goes.

This temperature variation is caused by the constant flow of heat from the earth's center. We often forget that we live on a planet filled with fire. Heat from this burning center spreads up slowly through the earth. In deep oceans, whose lower depths are not affected by surface weather, this outflow of heat is detectable, although the effect is only a fraction of one degree. LaFond proved that the earth's center actually heats the oceans and that there is a slightly warm layer at the bottom of thousands of feet of cold water. LaFond's next questions are: do these strata of temperature affect sound transmission? Does the heat flow from the earth's center have an effect on our climate?

To answer these questions LaFond will be going down to the bottom of the ocean again. LaFond is the kind of scientist who enjoys seeing for himself, and deep-ships have made it possible for LaFond to practice his firsthand approach to oceanography, for he and other scientists can now peer into the darkest, most mysterious corners of the ocean's depths.

Eugene LaFond, Mendel Peterson and Jacques Piccard are three of the resourceful, pioneering men who are now exploring the oceans. Their activities reflect the sea's vastness and variety. Their achievements mark the new age in man's attempt to conquer the seas. Long an ill-suited, imperiled visitor, man will soon make the sea a second home.

eight

The High-Energy Sky

O N MARCH 18, 1965, the Soviet Union took a dramatic forward step in man's effort to conquer space. Lieutenant Colonel Aleksei Leonov, tethered to a thin lifeline, drifted out from the door of the spaceship *Voskhod II*. Looking like a silver snowman, he floated several feet away from the capsule. Through the window of his space helmet, the astronaut could see the gaily-colored earth—the blue oceans and the green forests, here and there obscured by puffy clouds. In the other direction, black space stretched away through bright stars. Though weightless and unconscious of any motion, Leonov was circling the earth at 16,000 miles an hour. After a few minutes, he climbed back inside. Leonov and his co-pilot, Colonel Pavel Belyayev, landed safely after 17 orbits and 26 hours in space.

Four days later, the United States showed that it too had advanced its skills. Major Virgil Grissom and Lieutenant Commander John Young maneuvered their 700-pound capsule Gemini III through space—forward, backward, right side up and upside down, shifting easily from one orbit to another.

Grissom, a quiet man who recorded 100 combat missions in the Korean War (and, tragically, died in the 1967 Apollo fire) and Young, his scholarly partner, demonstrated that astronauts could control and steer their own capsules in space. They splashed down in the Atlantic Ocean after three orbits and four and a half hours in space.

One day later, the unmanned American rocket Ranger 9 crashed on the moon. The final stage, 10 feet long, weighed 800 pounds. Just before impact, the rocket's cameras sent back clear pictures of the moon's surface.

These history-making achievements reflect man's dream of reaching worlds beyond our own. The earth sweeps through endless space, cut off by great voids from her nearest neighbors. We do not have much contact with the rest of the universe. Starlight, which we see with our eyes and huge telescopes, shows us where other celestial objects are. Meteors tell us that the materials existing on earth occur elsewhere in the galaxy. And cosmic rays bombard us constantly, perhaps bearing more secrets about the universe than we are able to understand. These intimations raise more questions than can be answered. We still do not know how our planet, our solar system, our galaxy evolved as they did.

And, so far, our attempts to solve the mysteries of space have been baby steps. Space capsules have barely soared beyond 200 miles. The moon, whose presence has always fascinated man, hangs silent and mysterious, 256,000 miles away. Even when man reaches the moon, he will still be at the beginning. One has only to look at night into the starry heavens to realize that we have probed just fractions of inches into a space that extends forever. Our own solar system, which measures seven billion miles, is miniscule in the scheme of the universe and infinite space shall always dwarf our most prodigious exploits. But still, the great unknown calls to man, and he responds. The Japanese have an appropriate proverb: "Remember that a journey of a thousand miles begins with but a single step."

The vastness of space is reflected in the size of the effort to conquer it. Every astronaut whizzing through space is supported by perhaps 100,000 scientists on the ground, experts in metals, fuels, computers, orbital guidance and many other scientific disciplines. The astronauts have little in common with the enterprising adventurers of preceding centuries who, sometimes singlehandedly, explored the earth's unknown corners. A space probe must work like a huge, intricate machine, with every gear turning according to plan. The astronauts themselves are cogs in this machine and they must follow precise plans.

But more independent explorers of space operate on the fringe of the manned space program. They are scientists who are only indirectly concerned with the task of putting a man on the moon or other planets by a certain date. They explore where they please, engaged in work that may have no immediate, practical application to an astronaut's journey through space, but that may unlock the darkest secrets of our universe.

One such scientist is Dr. Serge A. Korff, professor of physics at New York University, who studies cosmic rays, specifically, fast neutrons—one of the twenty different kinds of secondary cosmic rays that are formed when primary cosmic rays speed in from outer space and collide with atoms and molecules in the atmosphere.

Korff is a tall, slender man who, appropriately enough, looks and acts like a college professor. His manner is polite but formal. He came to this country from Finland at the age of 10 and still speaks with a slight accent. To his assistants he is accessible and helpful, but he is also the boss and he maintains a certain distance. Technically a baron (his father was the last Russian lieutenant-governor of Finland), Korff knows and mingles with the nobility of several continents, and he manages to mix worldliness with scientific ardor. He has served as president and director of the Explorers Club in New York for many years, and for relaxation he likes to go mountain climbing.

Seeking data on fast neutrons, he has traveled to various parts of the globe, including Puerto Rico, Panama, Mexico, Peru, Canada, Greenland, Alaska and the Galápagos Islands. He has launched balloons into the atmosphere, climbed mountains to man observation stations and even shot off rockets—all to record the incidence of cosmic rays in space. The author of several books and many articles, Korff has been awarded a number of prizes for his work, including the Pregel Prize in 1955 and the Curie Medal in 1957.

While Russian and American astronauts were circling the earth in March, 1965, Dr. Serge Korff was busy interpreting information he had just brought back from Hyderabad, India, where, since the middle of February, 1965, Korff and his assistants had operated as one of 13 teams composing the Equatorial Expedition (EQEX), an international effort to gather information about cosmic rays. Each team studied a different type of cosmic ray, and the participating scientists came from many universities and laboratories in the United States, England, Australia, Ireland and India.

Korff and his four associates were a typically diverse group. Like Korff, Mrs. Rosalind Mendell, a cordial, attractive woman, was a professor of physics at New York University and an authority on cosmic radiation. Steve Holt and William Sandie, both graduate students at New York University, were doing their doctoral work on cosmic rays. In fact, Holt used the data from the Hyderabad trip in his Ph.D. dissertation. Yuval Zeria, the team's electronics expert and a citizen of Israel, had the responsibility of keeping all the complex equipment in working order.

The five researchers did not travel to Hyderabad together. Korff and Sandie arrived first, checking into the elegant Ritz Hotel, where most of the other scientists were staying. Steve Holt and Mrs. Mendell flew in the next day, followed by Yuval Zeria, a short, dark, heavyset young man who worked intensely but never lost his sense of humor. Since the five scientists work together all year long, there was nothing very dramatic about their rendezvous. But as scientists from all over the world streamed into the Ritz, there was a tension, a pre-hunt excitement in the air.

The cosmic rays that had brought these 50 scientists to Hyderabad are invisible radiation from outer space. Although not what most families talk about at the dinner table, cosmic rays are an important phenomenon of our world. The term cosmic rays is used to describe all the fantastically high-speed particles and radiation that reach the earth or its atmosphere from space. Cosmic rays are more than 99 percent atomic particles: 85 percent protons and 14 percent alpha particles. The less than one percent remaining is radiation, such as visible light and radio waves, which come from the sun, the stars or other celestial sources. The particles first smash into our atmosphere, which starts 30 miles up, as primary cosmic rays. Primary cosmic rays create showers of so-called secondary cosmic rays when they collide with other matter in our atmosphere. Slowed down by these collisions, virtually none of the primary rays reaches the ground, but the secondaries, of which there are 20 kinds, rain down on us by the billions. Like Korff, the scientists in the 12 other groups had come to Hyderabad to study their own particular cosmic ray specialty.

Why go to Hyderabad, India, to find cosmic rays? To begin with, the scientists were particularly interested in measuring the incidence of cosmic rays at the Equator, and India is the country having the best access to the air above the Equator. Hyderabad, in the center of India, is well located for launching balloons near the Equator and recovering them on land. The scientists couldn't go too far south because a balloon launched at the narrow tip of the country might fall into the sea instead of the land. The reason the scientists were so interested in measuring cosmic rays at the Equator has to do with the earth's magnetic field, whose lines of force curve through space from one magnetic pole to the other. (The magnetic poles are very close to the geographical ones.) If you have seen iron filings line up over a magnet, you know what the earth's magnetic field looks like. The lines of force rise straight out of one pole, then go into a slow curve which can swing tens of thousands of miles out in space and they eventually return in a nearly vertical line to the other pole. These lines of force, stretching out from one pole to the other, cover the 360 degrees of the earth's circumference. A diagram of the phenomenon would show the earth as a sphere inside a doughnut-shaped magnetic field of force. Because this magnetic field is weakest at the poles and strongest at the Equator, only the very high-speed primary cosmic rays can penetrate the magnetic umbrella over the Equator. At the poles, these high-speed rays come in, but so, too, do a lot of weaker rays, which Korff calls "low-energy garbage." Korff and the other scientists had come to Hyderabad because they wanted to deal only with the fastest primary cosmic rays. Korff hoped to find out what effect these primary rays had on the production of the secondary fast neutrons. Would there, he wondered, be more fast neutrons at the Equator than over Canada?

The expedition soon found that Hyderabad possessed other assets besides its strategic location. The Ritz, a great stucco palace, was built atop one of the city's highest points, giving its occupants an excellent view of the entire city. Beneath the spring sun, Hyderabad's low white buildings were outlined against the green background of trees in a lovely panorama. The trees and houses, of the same height and all mixed together, appeared to share the land equally. The grandest edifices, which rose to perhaps four or five stories, were, like the Ritz, genuine palaces built by the ancient rulers. In these less royal times, the palaces had become hotel, city hall, hospital and botanical gardens.

In this pleasant setting the scientists quickly settled down to a routine. After breakfast at the hotel, Korff and his associates taxied to their laboratory at Osmania University in one of the numerous cars provided by the hotel. During the 15-minute ride, the scientists could do a little sight-seeing. The native driver told them, in halting English, about the glories of his town. Around their cab, swarms of bicycles and pedicabs competed with the automobiles for room on the avenues. The city was remarkably clean and attractive—except for a foul-smelling stream filled with water buffalo which they had to pass on their taxi ride.

Korff's group moved their equipment into the assigned laboratory at the famous Indian university. They had brought two identical detecting and recording devices, one for each of his two scheduled balloon launchings. In a few days these instruments would be carried high above Hyderabad to measure cosmic rays. Highly delicate, the instruments needed constant checking and calibration. Immediately, however, the scientists ran into an unexpected problem. They found that their electric plugs did not fit the wall outlets. They had anticipated different voltages and had brought transformers. But the antiquated sockets came as a surprise and there was nothing to do but improvise. Zeria had to wire the machines directly and rather crudely into the oddly spaced holes in the wall.

Another problem turned out to have a surprising solution. The scientists couldn't seem to find any trash cans. They questioned one of the local scientists and he blandly told them there were none in Hyderabad. Throw everything out the window, he said. This solution didn't appeal to the Americans, but the Hyderabadian assured them that his city did not mind. The citizens are so poor, he explained, that they will pick up and find a use for anything. A wizened old Indian woman might sit for hours trying to undo a balled-up piece of tape. Still feeling guilty, the Americans followed the local custom: everything out the window. Hyderabad, however, remained as immaculate as ever.

Each day Korff and his associates ran "systems checks" on the 100 pounds of equipment he had designed to count fast neutrons. If they discovered that the electronic gadgets had "drifted" and become inaccurate, the scientists recalibrated, adjusted, modified or replaced a part. From the moment the balloon left the ground, all the way to 140,000 feet, this complex rig would be on its own. It had to be built so that it worked by itself. "You can't push the buttons," Korff says, "you won't be there." If a component failed, the balloon and months of preparation would be wasted. The date of the first flight was unposted, so they had to be constantly ready.

The equipment had six main parts, together with numerous lesser devices. The smallest but most important item was called a scintillator. Whenever neutrons in the energy range being

studied by Korff struck this two-inch-by-two-inch detector, it emitted tiny flashes of light. The higher the energy of the particle, the larger the flash. (Neutrons are atomic particles without any electrical charge. Particles with an electrical charge, such as electrons, can be detected in a photographic emulsion or a cloud chamber, while neutrons can only be detected by a scintillator.) A photomultiplier magnified these flashes of light so they could be distinguished and counted, and a "pulse height analyzer" calculated which energy range the particle was in and recorded it as such. A camera took pictures of the counters, while a four-track tape recorder listened to the count, expressed as "beeps," which would later be translated into a numerical count by a computer. Finally there was a high-voltage power supply which kept all these parts working.

Unfortunately, this complex setup, which weighed about 50 pounds, could not be bought at the local TV shop. Korff and the others had to design and build the equipment themselves in the laboratory at New York Universtity. First they constructed a metal rack about four feet tall and one foot square. All of the components were installed in this rack, with the detecting equipment on top. The electronic circuits were completely transistorized and designed to function in a wide range of temperatures. After completion, the design was tested extensively, and the entire process took a year.

On the balloon flights, the equipment was encased in a bright yellow gondola. This metal shell, with a polyurethane lining, protected the "payload" from the cold and from damage in landing. Ready to go, the scientific package looked like a fat five-foot bomb.

For Korff, the preparation in Hyderabad was a serious but hardly dramatic affair. He made the equipment work as well as he could. That was all he could do. Korff knew that "everything could go wrong." But in Korff's exploration a malfunction does not mean explosions or death. A failure means only that he won't take home "good measurements."

That is bad enough, of course, since good measurements of cosmic rays were what Korff had come for, and what he cared about. Korff, who has spent most of his life trying to measure cosmic rays, found his scientific calling at an early age. As a teen-ager in Washington, D.C., interested in science, he built a radio and earned his "ham operator" license. He also took up photography, which he still pursues as a hobby. He studied physics and astronomy at Princeton University, taking three degrees, including a Ph.D. in 1931, from that school. Almost immediatcly he moved into cosmic ray research, at the same time teaching physics and astronomy to both graduate and undergraduate students at New York University.

Thirty years before the expedition to Hyderabad, Korff led a cosmic ray expedition to Mexico and Peru. When neutrons were discovered in 1936, Korff decided to concentrate on them. "Here was a field," he recalls, "that nobody else was working in and it looked like it was an interesting scientific problem." He sent up his first balloons at Swarthmore College in Pennsylvania. And in the years that followed, he roamed the globe to make his measurements at all possible latitudes, from Panama to the Galápagos Islands, and, of course, Hyderabad, which Korff calls the "most exotic place" he has visited. On most of his expeditions he has launched balloons. For the use of balloons, the first requirement is a region with few air lanes. Sometimes Korff recorded data at a high-altitude "observing station" atop a snow-covered mountain. (There are about 70 such cosmic ray posts in the world.) On each expedition Korff has investigated neutrons with a particular energy range at a specific latitude on the earth's surface. Sometimes he has tried to pinpoint their intensity at a particular altitude and sometimes at all altitudes at that latitude. All his expeditions, however, are really part of the same effort: to obtain accurate measurements of the neutron influx at all points on the earth.

Of what possible use could even the best measurements be? Korff can easily point to three. First, these neutrons produce radioactive carbon 14, which eventually ends up in trees, leather, bones, paper and everything else which contains carbon. (Carbon 14 is created when a neutron strikes a nitrogen atom, becomes attached to it and knocks off a proton.) Carbon 14's radioactivity, which can be readily measured, diminishes steadily with time. Therefore, the age of an Egyptian mummy or a skull can be calculated by measuring its carbon 14 content. Korff's early measurements laid the foundation for the discovery of the carbon 14 dating technique.

Second, cosmic rays, like any other radiation, are possibly dangerous to human tissue. We must have accurate measurements of their strengths before we send a man into space. Closer to home, there will soon be supersonic airplanes flying at 70,000 feet in the sky. At such altitudes the cosmic-ray intensity will be much greater than near the ground. How much greater? Will the rays be dangerous? Korff is working on these questions. Furthermore, in 1968–1969, the sun will "flare up" again, as it does every 11 years. During this flare-up, when the sun shoots out flames and gases, its output of primary cosmic rays is greatly increased. Thus far, the astronauts have not been exposed to the huge bursts of cosmic rays that are produced during a flare-up. Whether they (or supersonic air passengers) will be endangered by the increased intensity of cosmic rays is something scientists don't know. Without this knowledge, designers of planes and space suits are working somewhat in the dark.

Third, cosmic rays come from outer space, perhaps even from other galaxies. Scientists do not know yet where they originate or all that they indicate about the universe. Korff's data help reveal the speed and mass of the primary particles, and that information contributes to our knowledge of the size and structure of the universe.

Having given these "uses" for the measurements of cosmic rays, Korff says: "But these are not the main thing. We are gathering new knowledge. We are all ultimately studying the basic facts of how the world we live in operates. We don't know most of the facts, that's why we do the research." What Korff is emphasizing is that he seeks knowledge for its own sake. He assumes that "eventually it will be useful to mankind." But for the moment, that's not his concern. Like scientists everywhere, he just wants to know how things work.

At Hyderabad, Korff's search for knowledge did not move ahead very quickly. The National Committee for Atmospheric Research (NCAR), the United States governmental agency which administered the American scientific groups, got tangled up in Indian customs regulations. NCAR tried to ship the large equipment—trucks, hoists and gas cylinders used jointly by all the American scientists—through Bombay. But the Indian customs laid down an unexpected requirement. They wanted assurance that none of this equipment would remain in the country. NCAR finally had to send back to the United States for a large sum of money which they deposited with the customs officials.

Meanwhile, waiting for the heavy equipment, Korff and his associates had all of his instruments ready to go. While the NCAR-customs negotiations went on, his group still had to check their systems every day. But the pressure was off. So for three or four days they spent much of the time being tourists.

Hyderabad, an ancient strategic city, use to be walled, and even today four gates or archways remain, reminding its present citizens of their warlike past. An echo of this past intruded into the present in 1948, when the native ruler, the Nizam, revolted but did not succeed in establishing Hyderabad as a state apart from the Republic of India. Korff, a man often more concerned with his research than with his surroundings, took an unusual interest in Hyderabad's diversity, both past and present. Many of the city's beautiful buildings and palaces have a Moorish flavor, since the Muslims ruled the city for centuries. The later British colonial rule left as its legacy two-story buses and left-hand drive for automobiles.

The scientists did have one unpleasant experience. Hyderabad is not one of India's beaten paths, and the residents see few foreigners. The beggars and fakirs who prey on tourists in Calcutta and New Delhi are not present in Hyderabad. But the citizens of the city had heard that Americans are wealthy. On one excursion, a gang of children crowded around Mrs. Mendell until she handed over six rupees ($1.20).

Riding to the ruins of Golkonda, a huge fortress-city, the scientists saw other evidence of India's poverty. On the banks of the Musee River the people had created a grand open-air laundromat. Women washed clothes on rocks in the stream. They spread them to dry in a nearby field. From the road the rectangular saris looked like hundreds of flags, most white, but some red and blue.

The scientists were amused, on the other hand, by soft drinks available in every hue—red, green, purple or blue. Korff dubbed the startling beverages "coca-cholera," which may explain why none of the Americans ventured to try any.

The scientists also enjoyed some social life. The Nizam's grandson, Mukkaram Jah, who knew Korff, invited the American group to dinner, and they also attended an Indian wedding, in which the bridegroom was decked with jasmine flowers. More official entertainment included dancers and concerts and plays. As Mrs. Mendell happily acknowledges, these sights and shows are the fringe benefits of worldwide cosmic ray research.

The Americans spent some time talking to a reporter from the *Dekan News*, a regional newspaper. Like most of his countrymen, the newspaperman was pleased to see visitors in Hyderabad. He spent time at Osmania University and at the Ritz, interviewing various scientists. Korff told him that people sometimes mistake his research balloons for UFO's, or Unidentified Flying Objects. Asked if he believed in UFO's himself, Korff maintained his scientific neutrality: "I have never seen one. So I have no reason to think about it one way or the other."

Shortly after this, Korff's first balloon flight was scheduled, for March 7. On that morning Korff got up at 3 A.M. and had a quick breakfast in the hotel's huge dining room. Outside the curtained windows the first faint light of dawn had appeared. The giant research balloons had to be launched early in the day because the air was stillest then. Moving sleepily to the ever-waiting taxis, Korff and his team rode to one of the polo fields belonging to Osmania University.

They found the balloon crew, employees of the manufacturer, the Raven Balloon Company of Sioux Falls, South Dakota, already at work. Korff zipped up his windbreaker against the early morning chill, and headed straight for the instruments, which had been trucked to the field from the laboratory. A few scientists from other research groups had come out to watch the proceedings.

The balloon crew had already laid out the 300-foot balloon

on a long white mat, and they were pumping helium from large cylinders through a plastic sleeve into the top end of the balloon. Soon the "bubble"—as the top is called when filled— stood up in the air like a charmed snake. After an hour of filling, the "bubble" reached the height of a five-story building, still only a seventh of the balloon's full size. A rope tied across the uninflated portion of the balloon still on the mat prevented the bubble from rising any farther. Made of a thin, whitish plastic, the balloon seemed to glow against the crimson Indian sunrise.

Several hundred feet away from the bubble, on the back of a truck, Korff and the others made last-minute checks on their instruments. The workers had already connected the balloon's bottom end to the canopy of an extended, unwrapped parachute whose shroud lines were, in turn, attached to the case of instruments. Near the truck a meteorologist sent up a small orange weather balloon to compute the wind's speed and direction. One by one, Mrs. Mendell activated the various circuits which would measure and record the fast neutrons. In the rosy half-light, Korff felt a sense of relief that the long months of preparation would soon be translated into tangible results.

A little after six o'clock the bubble—but not the balloon itself—was released. It shot up and spread out. For a few seconds, due to the wind resistance, the bubble assumed a mushroom shape. Then the bubble stretched the balloon to its full 300-foot height. A guy line attached to the balloon's base went taut. Now the balloon stood like a long, slender, upside-down teardrop, hanging straight in the brightening light. From the base of the balloon another line ran downwind to the parachute, still laid out on the mat, and then to the gondola on the truck. Korff made his final adjustments. The workers shouted to everyone to stand clear.

At 6:34 A.M. an explosive charge went off, snapping the restraining cable. The balloon was now free, and its top momentarily flattened against the air. As the balloon rose, peeling the parachute off the ground, it drifted over the truck. The driver put the motor into gear and edged forward. The balloon had to lift the gondola straight up, otherwise the delicate instruments would be dragged across the ground. The truck moved forward slowly, trying to stay directly beneath the balloon. Finally the yellow gondola lifted gently into the air. Now Korff had to sit and wait. His equipment would be doing the work.

The balloon was eerily beautiful. Shaped like an exclamation point, it reminded Korff of a huge jellyfish. The balloon would retain its graceful shape for many miles of its upward flight. Soon the scientists could see only a small white dot, which was the bubble, not the entire balloon. Catching the sun's rays, it looked like a small, shining star.

As the balloon floated high, trackers stationed on the university's rooftops monitored the signals sent out by the small transmitter suspended beneath the gondola, and a mobile radar truck also followed the course of the valuable wanderer. Korff's balloons had to be carefully tracked. Since his apparatus did not transmit data to the ground, he had to recover the gondola to obtain his measurements. (Korff is now experimenting with telemetry, which enables data to be radioed to the ground, making recovery unessential.) Tracking the big balloons is sometimes difficult. In Canada, for example, some balloons have traveled over 400 miles, and one was lost in a thunderstorm. The Indian flight, however, offered few problems. With clear skies and slight winds, the balloon remained in view throughout the day.

The instruments in the gondola ran constantly as the balloon climbed, diligently counting fast neutrons, analyzing the energy pulses and tallying up separate scores for the various particles. The tape recorder's reels turned, listening to the clicks that meant two neutrons in one energy range, three in the next. Every 75 seconds, the camera snapped, recording the time, pressure, temperature and numbers on the counters.

After two hours the balloon reached the top of the earth's atmosphere—140,000 feet, or 28 miles. At this point, because the air pressure was near zero, the balloon expanded to its full size, becoming a giant 300-foot sphere. The balloon's bottom third would just fill up a football stadium. This fragile helium-filled ball bobbed on the top of the air just the way an air-filled balloon floats on top of the ocean. Since 99.5 percent of the atmosphere was below it, the balloon was essentially in outer space. And there it stayed for most of the day.

Quite beyond man's vision, billions of cosmic particles were shooting in all directions around the balloon. The primary rays come in at about the speed of light, or 186,000 miles each second. The enormity of distances, speeds and sizes in outer space is difficult to comprehend. It is bewildering to discover that 186,000 miles per second equals 670 million miles each hour—about 300,000 times the speed of a rifle bullet. In any event, these tiny particles—25 million lined up side by side equal one inch—travel fast, and because of their speed, they possess great energy, which gives them the capacity to do a lot of work, or a lot of damage if they hit something. The energy of house current is normally 110 volts. Cosmic ray scientists don't start counting until they get to a million electron volts, or 1 MeV, which means that the particle has been accelerated across a potential difference of one million volts. Primary rays have energies in the billions of electron volts, or BeV's. When these high-speed particles slam into the atoms and molecules in our atmosphere, the primary rays use up their energy in the collisions and consequently few primaries reach the ground. But the collisions create a hail of secondary cosmic rays, 20 kinds in all. These shower down on the earth in great numbers. Passing through this shower, Korff's equipment counted only the fast neutrons.

Primary cosmic rays tell us some interesting facts about the universe. Most obviously, their high energies indicate that out in space somewhere there are great magnetic fields capable of bringing these particles almost to the speed of light. Scientists think that huge clouds of gas or nebulas might be the accelerators. What scientists call "high energy events," such as exploding stars, might also be a source. We know for sure only that the starting point of the primary cosmic rays must be distant. They cannot possibly come from the nearest stars, for they arrive from all directions and travel in an endless variety of complicated paths. The trajectories of many of them look like battered corkscrews. Affected by all the overlapping magnetic fields in space, they spiral and twist into the atmosphere with utter randomness. Scientists speculate that they may have been speeding through space for millions of years, some perhaps circling from one end of the galaxy to the other (taking, at their rate of speed, about 400 years for the round trip). Scientists even speculate that some of the largest, fastest cosmic particles must come from beyond our galaxy because they could not be accelerated to such fantastic speeds within the comparatively small confines of a single galaxy, and if they could be so accelerated, the galaxy's gravitational field would not be strong enough to contain them and they would move into another galaxy.

Secondary cosmic rays have much less energy. They zip off in all directions. Some go back into outer space. Most strike a nearby particle and release a different kind of secondary ray.

This cascade, or chain reaction, continues down into the denser air of the lower atmosphere. Many secondary rays lose their energy and, instead of shattering what they hit, merely become attached to it. In this way the chain reaction starts to slow down. The number of secondary rays in the atmosphere drops steadily as the earth is approached. But, still, a billion billion cosmic rays strike the earth every second. If you are lying down, about 7,000 secondary rays pass through your body every minute, and a few of these may end their journey in one of your cells. Some scientists believe that these cosmic rays may cause cancer or, more possibly, genetic changes. (Cosmic rays may well have given evolution a push forward every now and then. There is some evidence for this idea in the fact that new species seem to develop in the mountains more often than in the lowlands.) In any event, cosmic rays, like any uncontrolled radiation, are more likely to do harm than good.

The amount of primary rays is constant beyond an altitude of 30 miles, at the top of the atmosphere, where Korff's balloon was floating. At lower altitudes, where primary rays create secondary rays, the combined count rises, mounting sharply in the zone between 18 and 14 miles above the earth until the peak is reached at around 13 miles. Here the total count is twice what the primaries alone numbered at 30 miles. From 13 miles to sea level, the count falls steadily as the primary rays diminish in energy and are absorbed and many of the secondary rays also diminish in energy.

Korff's instruments had climbed through these changing intensities and now the huge balloon moved westward, remaining at an altitude of about 28 miles for nearly five hours. The equipment whirred and clicked diligently. The counting machine was indifferent to all particles except fast neutrons, those with velocities of one to ten million electron volts. One counter kept a "total particle count," while seven others registered the neutrons at various speeds, from one to ten million electron volts.

Korff terminated his first balloon's flight in the afternoon. The balloon carried an explosive charge at its base and, at a radio command, it exploded, separating the balloon from the parachute and gondola. The immense, shiny balloon—its material as thin as the cellophane on a cigarette pack—soon became a dot to those on the ground as it rose through the clear air. Climbing into the nearly perfect vacuum above 30 miles, it exploded into many small pieces and the ragged bits drifted off on the wind.

Meanwhile, the parachute opened and, supporting the gondola, dropped quickly for several miles, until it reached the lower, denser air and fell more slowly. Korff had been waiting below in a small one-engine plane and even before the explosion released the parachute, he and his pilot had taken off from the airport at Hyderabad. Now he squinted up at the tiny prize, glistening in the blue sky. Speaking into a walkie-talkie, he guided a jeep to the probable landing spot. The plane climbed up to meet the swinging chute and then banked around so that Korff could get a close look at his package. There was nothing wrong as far as he could see.

The parachute took almost an hour to reach the ground. Finally the yellow gondola jolted to a stop on a green hill 50 miles southwest of Hyderabad. The pilot flew down close. Korff saw that the ground party had reached the gondola, waved to them and then signaled the pilot to circle around and head back toward Hyderabad. Everything had gone according to schedule. This is what Korff, of course, hoped for. "One of the things that often happens," Korff says, "is that newspapers ask us, 'What adventures did you have?' Well, most of the time we don't have any adventures. The people who have adventures are usually the people who are incompetent, who don't know what they are doing and go off and get themselves into trouble in one way or another. We try to plan what we're doing ahead of time. We try to anticipate the troubles so that we won't have them. Usually a person who does a job competently doesn't run into many adventures."

It is revealing that Korff's balloon had been sent up to measure just one of the 20 secondary cosmic rays, and this ray only in a particular range of speed. Each of the 12 other groups at Hyderabad had also singled out one particle to study. One group was measuring neutrons also, but only those in a lower energy range. Scientists, of course, specialize in this way when the area of study is large and complicated. As Korff says, "You can't hope to do more than one part. Too complicated. You know what the other people are doing by reading the scientific journals. But you are lucky to master your own part." Korff's specialization indicates just how vast and complex space exploration is. A single man can explore a continent. But only large groups of men, working on hundreds of different problems, can hope to conquer space.

The money for this exploration comes from a variety of sources, many of them government agencies. The National Science Foundation paid for Korff's trip to Hyderabad. The NSF's recompense will come when Korff publishes his findings in scientific publications, for the enlightenment of all. At other times the National Aeronautics and Space Administration (NASA) has financed Korff's research on a more direct basis. In these cases he must do specific research and report the results to them. And, of course, Korff is just one of thousands of scientists engaged in cosmic-ray studies, for which millions of dollars are paid each year.

That evening Korff and the others relaxed at their hotel. Their "package" was safe in the laboratory at Osmania University. They didn't know exactly what the measurements were, but a quick look had revealed that all "systems" had functioned perfectly. Now they could sit back and talk shop. Although "a very serious group," the scientists enjoyed nothing more than long discussions about what the other groups were up to. Since cosmic rays have no known military use, there is no need for secrecy. "The cooperation with other countries," Korff notes, "is very good." Every two years the cosmic ray specialists hold an international convention, which is attended by some 250 scientists from all over the world. Since there were scientists from various countries and universities at Hyderabad, their evening get-togethers quickly became unofficial conventions.

Unfortunately, when scientists talk to one another, the rest of the world is likely to be shut out. The exploration of space and cosmic rays sounds simple enough. But the details quickly become very technical, and almost from the start there is a communication gap. The scientists, sharing common training and knowledge, widen this gap by conversing in their own special dialect. In reporting on his cosmic ray research in the *Journal of Geophysical Research* ("Fast Neutron Latitude Variation in the Atmosphere at Solar Minimum," November, 1966), Korff started his concluding remarks as follows:

Using the best-fit power-law spectrums, the 1-10-MeV fluxes have been evaluated everywhere in the atmosphere at the four latitudes. The results are presented in Figure 6, with the calculated 1-10-MeV solar-minimum fluxes of Lingenfelter [1963a] (personal communication, 1965) drawn in for purposes of comparison. The calculation is a multigroup diffusion approximation to the Boltzmann transport equation for neutrons, utilizing experimentally measured slow-neutrons attenuation lengths and the star-production of Lord [1951] for the altitude dependence of the source spectrum and a nuclear temperature of about 1 MeV for the contribution from evaporation neutrons. The calculated fluxes are normalized with the results from previous slow-neutron detector experiments.

If that paragraph does not leave a reader breathless, he is probably a scientist.

The Equatorial Expedition's one mishap occurred early the next morning. The scientists were not at fault. A member of the balloon crew set a timed-explosive incorrectly, and the charge went off 30 minutes too soon. Korff, the other scientists and the workers jerked around. Before their startled eyes, the balloon shot up against the sky. Fortunately, the gondola had not been attached and the balloon sailed swiftly and pointlessly to its demise in the upper atmosphere.

During these two weeks when balloons were constantly sailing above Hyderabad, many local residents probably remarked, "You couldn't get me up in one of those things for a million rupees." Unless an observer was close to the balloon, it was reasonable for him to think that the gondola held a man. The early experimenters did, in fact, go up with their balloons, mainly because they lacked the sophisticated recording equipment and recovery techniques used today. In fact, Victor Hess officially discovered cosmic rays in 1905 by making a series of 10 balloon flights. But after World War I, scientists stopped going along with their balloons.

Korff has never found it necessary to go up with his balloons, and it is unlikely that he has ever yearned to do so. To Korff, balloons have certain capabilities, they solve certain problems.

They take his equipment up to 28 miles and they hold it there. They hold no romantic excitement for him in themselves; they are one means to an end. If he had been interested in obtaining measurements at 10,000 feet, he might have used a mountain. Had there not been a mountain at the proper latitude, he would have turned to a balloon again. If he had been interested in measurements at 80 miles above the earth, he would have used a rocket, since a balloon, of course, can go no higher than the atmosphere. "It all depends on the problem," Korff notes. He has launched three rockets so far. About a year before Hyderabad, Korff and his group took their instruments to Wallops Island, Virginia, and put them into a pencil-shaped Aerobee, a 16-foot-long rocket. The Aerobee shot 150 miles above the Atlantic. For a few short minutes the transmitter sent back valuable data about the cosmic rays up there. Then the rocket arched over and plunged into the ocean. Since recovery would have been very complicated, NASA, the sponsoring agency, did not attempt it. The rockets, like the balloons, are wondrous things to behold. But the scientists were concerned, naturally, with how well the device would provide data. Rockets are, in fact, not particularly useful in Korff's research, since most of the fast neutrons are in the earth's atmosphere. The balloon remains Korff's best tool, and he uses it as he might use a slide rule.

On March 8, Korff watched his second payload leave the ground at 6:55 A.M. The flight seemed to go as smoothly as the first. But for some mysterious reason the instruments failed five miles up. Weeks later the scientists would discover that the instruments had not functioned during most of the ascent. At the top of the flight the instruments mysteriously began to work again. So they obtained measurements near the ground and "at altitude" but not in between. Such a frustrating breakdown in equipment on which the scientists had worked for months was terribly disheartening. There was, however, a brighter side. Korff discovered later that the measurements he did retrieve from this flight were identical to those of the first, which is the sort of confirmation guaranteed to make a research scientist happy.

The wind was so still on the second balloon flight that the parachute came down only 15 miles from the university. Mrs. Mendell, who flew in the search plane this time, was disappointed that she did not have to fly out into the wilderness. She had even worn her heavy snake boots to be ready for a forced landing. It was, she felt, rather undramatic of the parachute to land in the suburbs of Hyderabad. But the natives seemed to find the event exciting. In line with their clean street policy, they quickly took the parachute. The scientists did not mind, for they considered a used parachute a risky item anyway. When Mrs. Mendell reached the scene, she found the yellow gondola surrounded by a huge mob of Indians. The natives were happy to carry the bright yellow gondola back to the university, as though the package of instruments were a very important person.

The recovery of the second gondola marked the end of Korff's scientific program in Hyderabad. For the next three days, he and his group had only to pack their bags, box their equipment and generally get ready for the trip home. The scientists made their final tour of Hyderabad's many shops. Now that the expedition had passed with no major mishap, they felt better about splurging a little on such things as the excellent glass and silk cloth made by the local craftsmen.

When they had returned to the United States, Korff and his team spent many months analyzing the data they had collected. In scientific terms, the data from Hyderabad state that fast neutrons occur near the Equator at the maximum rate of .17$\pm^{0.02}$cm^{-2}sec^{-1}; that is, at about 64 per minute per square inch at an altitude of 14 miles. This conclusion, together with the results of Korff's many other expeditions, indicates that only one-tenth the number of fast neutrons are present at the Equator as near the poles—as might be expected, since fewer primary rays get through the stronger magnetic field at the Equator.

What is the significance of Korff's data? Where will it lead science—and man? "My inclination," Korff responds, "is to answer the question strictly from the scientific point of view. Basically, we are interested in obtaining new knowledge. Now where the new knowledge will lead, you can never really tell, because, after all, if you knew where it was leading, then it wouldn't be new knowledge. Basically, new knowledge has its own completely unpredictable surprises.

"Let me give you an example. Suppose someone had asked you to find a better way to help surgeons set bones. Probably it would not occur to you that the right thing to do was to study the passage of electricity through a rather poor vacuum. And yet it was by doing just that that X rays were discovered. And X rays are certainly the best way to help surgeons set bones.

"If someone were to ask you what would be the best way to determine the date of a piece of wood which you had found in an Egyptian tomb, you would probably start thinking about, well, how does wood age and how can you analyze it chemically? It would probably not occur to you that the best way was to study the neutrons produced by cosmic rays in the upper atmosphere. And yet it was by our research into the neutrons in the upper atmosphere that we laid the foundation on which Willard Libby was able to develop the carbon 14 technique that can be used to determine the age of the piece of wood in the Egyptian tomb.

"My point is simply this: that you have no way of telling ahead of time where a bit of research will lead. All you know is that you are gathering new knowledge. Nobody has ever been wise enough to say where that new knowledge will come in handy. It has been man's experience that the new knowledge has always come in handy in some totally unexpected place or totally unanticipated way, of which I've just given you two illustrations. Now, therefore, when somebody asks me, well, where will this lead? I have no idea, I can't possibly tell him."

Does Korff care where the knowledge will lead? "Frankly, no, because this isn't my business. Where it will lead will ultimately be obvious. A fact is a fact. You can't make it disappear. If you don't find it, somebody else will. Sometimes scientists worry about the uses made of their research, but they can never, ever control it. A lot of condemnation of scientists for irresponsibility comes from people who don't know how science works. In due course, people will find out where the facts will lead. And it has always been mankind's history that the facts have led to something useful in some totally unexpected field. Sooner or later. This is true of all basic scientific research."

Korff's answers may leave so-called practical people a little unsatisfied. But practical people have a way of being satisfied with what was good enough for their fathers. The kind of passionate, all-embracing curiosity that Korff exhibits has been responsible for many of our technological wonders, as he has indicated. The same approach demands that we venture into space, just so that we can learn more. This conviction, that knowing our world is worthwhile in itself, lies behind all exploration.

During the weeks after his return to the United States, Korff kept busy studying the data from Hyderabad. While he pondered his esoteric facts, the astronauts of both his country and the Soviet Union captured the world's attention by scoring spectacular breakthroughs in outer space. Their achievements and Korff's, different as they might seem, are, in fact, related, and part of a common goal—the conquest of space. While the astronauts make headlines today, the research scientists pave the way for the headlines of next year and 10 or even 100 years after that. Hyderabad, then, was one step to the moon and beyond.

About the Author

Bruce Price was born in 1941 in Norfolk, Virginia, and grew up in that state. He graduated with Honors in English Literature from Princeton University in 1963 and served in the Army for two years, where he was a photojournalist. Since then, he has been engaged in a number of writing projects, working as a ghost writer, editor and feature writer.

Currently Mr. Price, who lives in New York City, is completing a novel. *Into the Unknown* is his first published book.

Suggested Readings

Riding the Wind

Your Future as a Pilot by Captain Kimball J. Scribner. New York: Richards Rosen Press, Inc., 1968.

Fighter Aces by Col. Raymond F. Toliver and Trevor J. Constable. New York: The Macmillan Company, 1965.

Cross-Country Flying by Martin Caidin. New York: E. P. Dutton & Co., Inc., 1961.

The Man Who Rode the Thunder by Lt. Col. W. H. Rankin. New York: Prentice-Hall, Inc., 1960.

Wind, Sand and Stars by Antoine Saint-Exupéry, tr. by L. Galantiere. New York: Harcourt, Brace & World, Inc., 1949.

Fastest Man Alive: A Test Pilot Tells His Story by Lt. Col. Frank K. Everest, Jr., as told to John Guenther. New York: E. P. Dutton & Co., Inc., 1958.

The following handbooks and others may be obtained for one dollar from the Soaring Society of America, Box 66071, Los Angeles, California 90066:

"History of American Soaring"
"Training"
"Ground Launch"
"Airplane Tow"
"Meteorology"
"Cross Country & Wave Soaring"

Coordinates of Ice

Antarctic Conquest by Capt. Finn Ronne. New York: G. P. Putnam's Sons, 1949.

Antarctic Command by Capt. Finn Ronne. Indianapolis: The Bobbs-Merrill Co., Inc., 1961.

The Voyage of the Huron and the Huntress: The American Sealers and Their Discovery of the Continent of Antarctica by Eduoard

Stackpole. Mystic, Conn.: Marine History Association, Inc., 1955.

Quest for a Continent by Walter Sullivan. New York: McGraw-Hill Book Co., 1957.

"Antarctic, One Continent" by Capt. Finn Ronne. *Explorers Journal,* Sept.–Dec., 1948.

"Antarctic Mapping and Aerial Photography" by Capt. Finn Ronne. *Scientific Monthly,* Nov., 1950.

"The Ronne Expedition" by Capt. Finn Ronne. *The Geographical Review,* July, 1948.

The Manners of Monkeys

Social Communication Among Primates, ed. by Stuart A. Altmann. Chicago: University of Chicago Press, 1967.

Territorial Imperative by Robert Ardrey. New York: Atheneum Publishers, 1966.

The Naturalistic Behavior of Nonhuman Primates by Clarence Ray Carpenter. State College, Pa.: Pennsylvania State University Press, 1965.

Primate Behavior: Field Studies of Monkeys and Apes, ed. by Irven DeVore. New York: Holt, Rinehart & Winston, Inc., 1965.

Lemur Behavior: A Madagascar Field Study by A. Jolly. Chicago: University of Chicago Press, 1966.

On Aggression by Konrad Lorenz. New York: Harcourt, Brace & World, Inc., 1966.

The Year of the Gorilla by George B. Schaller. Chicago: University of Chicago Press, 1964.

The Evidence of Yesterday

Gods, Graves and Scholars by C. W. Ceram. New York: Alfred A. Knopf, Inc., 1967.

Where the Sun Stood Still by James G. Pritchard. Princeton, N.J.: Princeton University Press, 1962.

Archeology in the Holy Land by Kathleen Kenyon. New York: Frederick A. Praeger, Inc., 1960.

The Archeology of Palestine by William F. Allbright. Baltimore: Penguin Books, Inc., 1960.

Portals to the Past by Katherine B. Shippen. New York: The Viking Press, Inc., 1963.

"Ancient Hebron, the City of David" by P. C. Hammond. *Natural History Magazine,* May, 1966.

"The American Expedition to Hebron" by P. C. Hammond. *Explorers Journal,* Dec., 1967.

The Past Tense of Man

In Search of the Primitive by Lewis Cotlow. Boston: Little, Brown & Co., 1966.
Ecuador: Andean Mosaic, ed. by Rolf Blomberg. Hugo Gebers Förlang, 1952.
Man, God and Magic by Ivar Lissner. New York: G. P. Putnam's Sons, 1961.
Patterns of Culture by Ruth Benedict. Boston: Houghton Mifflin Company, 1934.
Primitive Man and His Ways by Kaj Kirket-Smith. New York: The New American Library, Inc., 1963.

Pockets in the Earth

Visiting American Caves by Russell H. Gurnee and Howard N. Sloane. New York: Crown Publishers, Inc., 1966.
Cave Life by Russell H. Gurnee and Charles E. Mohr. New York: Doubleday & Company, Inc., 1965.
The Life of the Cave by Charles E. Mohr and Thomas L. Poulson. New York: McGraw-Hill Book Co., 1967.
World of Caves by Anton Lubke. New York: Coward-McCann, Inc., 1959.

The Water Barrier

The Sea Around Us by Rachel Carson. New York: Oxford University Press, Inc., 1951.
Frontiers of the Sea by Robert C. Cowen. New York: Doubleday & Company, Inc., 1960.
The Secrets of the Sea by William J. Cromie. New York: Prentice-Hall, Inc., 1962.
The Waters of the Sea by Pier Groen. Princeton, N.J.: D. Van Nostrand Co., Inc., 1967.
Seven Miles Down by Jacques Piccard and R. S. Dietz. New York: G. P. Putnam's Sons, 1961.

The High Energy Sky

The Story of Cosmic Rays by Germaine and Arthur Beiser. New York: E. P. Dutton & Co., Inc., 1962.
Cosmic Rays by Bruno Rossi. New York: McGraw-Hill Book Co., 1964.
What Is Science? ed. by James R. Newman. New York: Simon & Schuster, Inc., 1955.

A *Comprehensible World* by Jeremy Bernstein. New York: Random House, Inc., 1967.

Of Stars and Men by Harlow Shapley. Boston: Beacon Press, 1958.

From Earth to Heaven by Isaac Asimov. New York: Doubleday & Company, 1966.